IN THE
PUBLIC
INTEREST

The League's first Board of Directors, Victory Convention, Chicago, February 1920. *Standing left to right*, Katharine Ludington (regional director); Marie Stuart Edwards (treasurer); Della Dortch (regional director); Edna Gellhorn (vice-chair and regional director); Mabeth Paige (regional director); Mrs. C. B. Simmons (regional director); and Pattie Ruffner Jacobs (secretary). *Seated, left to right*, Maud Wood Park (chair); Grace Trout (president of the Illinois Suffrage Association); and Carrie Chapman Catt (honorary chair). (Chambers Studio, Chicago)

IN THE
PUBLIC
INTEREST

The League of Women
Voters,
1920–1970

LOUISE M. YOUNG

With the assistance of
RALPH A. YOUNG, Jr.
Foreword by
PERCY MAXIM LEE

CONTRIBUTIONS IN AMERICAN STUDIES, NUMBER 96
Robert H. Walker, *Series Editor*

GREENWOOD PRESS
New York • Westport, Connecticut • London

Library of Congress Cataloging-in-Publication Data

Young, Louise M.
   In the Public Interest : the League of Women Voters,
  1920–1970 / Louise M. Young.
     p. cm.—(Contributions in American studies, ISSN 0084–9227;
  no. 96)
   Bibliography: p.
   Includes Index.
   ISBN 0–313–25302–1 (lib. bdg. : alk. paper)
   1. League of Women Voters (U.S.)—History. I. Title.
  II. Series.
  JK1881.Y68   1989
  324′.3′0973—dc20   89–7476

British Library Cataloguing in Publication Data is available.

Library of Congress Catalog Card Number: 89–7476
ISBN: 0–313–25302–1
ISSN: 0084–9227

First published in 1989

Greenwood Press, Inc.
88 Post Road West, Westport, Connecticut 06881

Printed in the United States of America

∞

The paper used in this book complies with the
Permanent Paper Standard issued by the National
Information Standards Organization (Z39.48–1984).

10 9 8 7 6 5 4 3 2 1

OCLC# 1955 41 96

Contents

Illustrations

The photograph of Carrie Chapman Catt was provided by the Arthur and Elizabeth Schlesinger Library on the History of Women in America, Radcliffe

College; while that of Jane Addams was made available by the Jane Addams Memorial Collection, University Library, University of Illinois, in Chicago. All other photographs were provided by the League of Women Voters of the United States. The author wishes to record her thanks.

Foreword

Dr. Louise Young has written a comprehensive account of an important piece of American history. It covers not only the political activities of women, but it reflects the state of the nation during those years. It is sad to reflect that succeeding generations know less and less about the struggle for woman suffrage and the people who worked so tirelessly and unselfishly to achieve it. Dr. Young's work fills a critical need and she succeeds admirably in blending issues and people.

When I was president of the League of Women Voters I was acutely aware of how little members knew about their past. They were too busy building the future to examine the lessons of earlier times. I knew then of one person uniquely qualified to bring this history to life, and that was Dr. Young. The problem was how to induce her in her busy professional life to undertake such a monumental task. In the early 1960s Dr. Young was persuaded to use her influence in the Library of Congress to have appropriate League documents accepted as an historical collection. She succeeded and thus became more than ever entangled in League history, for she took on the task of cataloging the material.

It was apparent that members of the League thirsted for knowledge of the past, but never had time to seek it out. Every time Dr. Young addressed League meetings she had her audience in thrall. We could never get enough of her experience, her insights, and her judgments. Since she was not directly involved with a leadership function, she could be completely objective. This makes her views in evaluating League activities exceedingly valuable.

As one who was thoroughly involved in the restructuring of the League in 1944 and 1946, I would like to emphasize the fundamental change that occurred in 1946, not without pain. These years marked a watershed between the inherited suffrage organization and the modern League. It was at this time that the League changed from a federation of states to an association of members. Under Anna Strauss's leadership we traveled the country meeting with League groups and examining the purpose and character of the organization. The membership itself determined what the League would be. I believe this tremendous effort by volunteers saved the League from dissolution, and caused a more cohesive, more effective, and more durable organization to be built.

The hope is that this book will be widely read and will supply some valuable perspective on the times it covers. It is a remarkable review of the major political issues that mark the first half of the twentieth century. It is also testimony to the dedication and effectiveness of the political women. In 1983 Dr. Young wrote me about her research and made a comment that echoes my most profound belief. She wrote: "In all its history the League has never failed to come to the rescue of the Constitution; to fend off attacks when the going is roughest, the League does bring all its emotional weight to bear at the community level." May it always be thus.

Percy Maxim Lee
Mystic, Connecticut

Preface

When the League of Women Voters was approaching its fiftieth birthday, its president, Julia D. Stuart, expressed a desire that I take a backward look at the road the organization had traveled since its foundation in 1920. The project appeared a detachable part of a political history of American women on which I was already engaged, and I agreed to embark on it. A society constructed under such novel conditions, and by a mixture of peoples from such varied cultural backgrounds, was bound to fashion a pattern for the political participation of women that resembled no other; the book on the League of Women Voters offered an opportunity to cover a limited and definable part of what I wanted to say about how the political role of American women was shaped.

In responding to the challenge to assess the organization's experience, however, it soon became clear that the scope of the task would not permit early completion. The League's fiftieth birthday in 1970 came and went, and I had barely begun my review of the building of a unique political institution. When the manuscript was finished in 1973, it was too late to meet the requirements of the original publisher, and the draft was set aside while efforts resumed on my larger project. I was subsequently persuaded to return to the manuscript by Percy M. Lee, who had served as the League's president from 1950 to 1958, and by Professor Robert H. Walker, then director of the American Studies Program at George Washington University; for their warm and constant encouragement I am deeply grateful.

My indebtedness to the national board and staff of the League of Women Voters, both present and past, is also gratefully acknowledged. Their interest has always been helpful, their cooperation generous, their respect for my independence of judgment complete. Placing the organization's history in the context of surrounding events involved touching on many controversial areas.

I am aware that many members and officers remembered things otherwise than they appear in the record, or felt an impact from their experience that I have failed to reflect. For this I am hopeful of receiving their indulgence. I have made my own interpretations and none have tried to influence my views. Such mistakes as have resulted are strictly my own.

Particular acknowledgment is due Anna Lord Strauss, who read and made helpful suggestions on those parts of the manuscript concerning her years as president (1944–50). I am also happy to record my indebtedness to former presidents Percy Lee, Ruth S. Phillips, Julia Stuart, and Lucy W. Benson for discussions of League policy during their administrations. Friendly associations with many board members over the years have also been helpful in gaining an understanding of the inner workings of the League. Present and former staff members have provided most able and willing support; I am especially indebted in this regard to Martha T. Mills, recently retired as the League's deputy executive director, Monica C. Sullivan, its current director of publications, who each gave careful reading to the final draft, and, before all, to Mary Ann Guyol, a former director of public relations for the League who has been an invaluable source of advice and assistance at different stages of the manuscript's progress, and who is now serving as editor for a companion volume in this series of documents relating to the League's development over its first five decades.

Other debts must be acknowledged: First of all to the Library of Congress, whose fine staff and study facilities I was privileged to enjoy; and particularly to the director and staff of the Library's Manuscript Division, where the papers of the League of Women Voters are housed. I am also greatly indebted to the director and staff of the Arthur and Elizabeth Schlesinger Library on the History of Women in America, Radcliffe College, with its incomparable Women's Archives; and to the Radcliffe Institute for Independent Study for the privilege of spending a semester within its hospitable walls.

A listing of all those who have shared my interest in the feminine tradition and have influenced my views is impossible, but special mention is due to the late Dr. Jeannette P. Nichols, long a professor of history at the University of Pennsylvania, and Dr. Anne Firor Scott, professor of history at Duke University. Many rewarding conversations with scholars of the neofeminist generation left an imprint on my views that is reflected in these pages, particularly those with my daughter, Dr. Alexandra Pierce, professor of music at the University of Redlands.

I have also been privileged to have the advice and encouragement of my two sons—Crawford Young of the Department of Political Science, University of Wisconsin-Madison, and Ralph A. Young, Jr., of the Department of Government, University of Manchester (England)—and of Crawford's wife Rebecca, who found the League an excellent stepping-stone to public office. They each read the manuscript with immense care and offered many suggestions.

Particular gratitude goes to Ralph Young, Jr., who at a critical moment stepped in to assume responsibility for final revision of the manuscript. An eye operation

I underwent made this editorial assistance indispensable. Ralph set aside his own research for many months to undertake this task; with meticulous care he accomplished the compression required by Greenwood Press, while verifying and strengthening the footnoted documentation.

Finally, let me record my special debt to my late husband, Dr. Ralph A. Young. Despite a rigorous schedule of his own, he always found time to read, to constructively criticize, and above all to tirelessly encourage these pages toward a conclusion.

One editorial postscript is required here. In a small number of cases, the archives have left me no choice but to record the actions of women under their husband's names. As specialists in women's history will be aware, the practice of listing women in formal records under the name of their spouse was frequent in an earlier age; it persisted to a diminishing extent throughout the period covered by this book. Every effort has been made through consultation of standard biographical sources and knowledgeable individuals to restore to every woman her own full identity. In some instances, to my regret, this has not been possible.

Abbreviations

AASS	American Anti-Slavery Society
AWSA	American Woman Suffrage Association
DAR	Daughters of the American Revolution
ERA	Equal Rights Amendment
FDA	Food and Drug Administration
GFWC	General Federation of Women's Clubs
LC	Manuscript Division, Library of Congress, Washington, D.C.
LWV	League of Women Voters
NATO	North Atlantic Treaty Organization
NAWSA	National American Woman Suffrage Association
NCESL	National College Equal Suffrage Association
NCL	National Consumers' League
NCPW	National Council for the Prevention of War
NELA	National Electric Light Association
NIRA	National Industrial Recovery Act
NWP	National Woman's Party
NWSA	National Woman Suffrage Association
NWTUL	National Women's Trade Union League
TVA	Tennessee Valley Authority
UN	United Nations
WCTU	Woman's Christian Temperance Union
WJCC	Women's Joint Congressional Committee

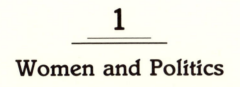

1

Women and Politics

When the Nineteenth Amendment brought women the constitutional guarantee of full voting rights in 1920, the event was widely regarded by news media and politicians alike as creating a potentially revolutionary situation. No group of comparable size had ever won the vote more wholly by its own efforts, nor appeared more deeply preoccupied with transforming its political assets into the hard cash of political power. Some thought that the very foundations of society had been shaken, that half the population was on the move. But events soon revealed that while some of the tents had been struck, many others still stood pegged. The organized feminists had been unified in rejecting their subordinate political status, but split on other political goals, and the whole sex was criss-crossed with wide bands of recessive elements. The levers of power did not change hands.

It is important to distinguish between what some hoped—and others feared—would happen, and what transpired. Changes in American political society soon became apparent, but they were different, less conspicuous, and far less pervasive than had been expected. Because changes on the anticipated scale had not occurred, it was possible to assume that nothing had altered. Thereafter, and until the last two decades, the political emergence of women received the barest nod from political and social historians, who turned to more rewarding subjects.

This book seeks to illumine key aspects of that political emergence of American women by tracing the life experience of the League of Women Voters, among the longest enduring offspring of the suffrage movement, over the first half century of its existence.[1] The League's records reveal what actually happened to those women who, having sought so long the right to share in shaping the common destiny, then faced a prolonged struggle to give full measure to their hard-won political status. The League emerged in 1919 as an auxiliary of the

National American Woman Suffrage Association; its independent existence was affirmed a year later at NAWSA's Victory Convention (held six months before the Nineteenth Amendment's final ratification). Its leaders were seeking to hold intact the immense suffrage army of two million women activists—a vain hope, of course. But those who chose to reenlist for new campaigns included the most active, ambitious, and politicized of the younger generation of suffrage workers.

The history of the League of Women Voters dismantles the myth that the Nineteenth Amendment "did not take." Yet it also reveals the complexity of the psychocultural process required to make political participation a meaningful engagement for so severely subordinated a class. If the struggle for the ballot had been highly educational for those most actively involved, the lessons learned had to be adapted to a new situation. Once stitched into the Constitution, the franchise became merely a political instrumentality, one whose implications had to be explored by those enfranchised. The League's creators had expected the path to be hedged with painful external obstacles thrown up by a resisting political system. But they also met with stubborn subjective barriers. A profound reorientation of attitudes could not be accomplished overnight because of the deep deposits of historical experience that lived on in the feelings, habits, and expectations of both sexes. Women did not cease to be "the governed"; as Jane Addams had predicted, the development of a "new consciousness" was required.

Viewing themselves as representative of organized women, League leaders sought to transform the enthusiasm for a common goal into collective commitment to more limited but specific goals. Internal differences arose which, if hastening the development of procedures for reconciling conflicts, exacted an emotional toll. More difficult to absorb was the vexation of the older suffrage leaders whose millennial hopes were not immediately realized.

With such circumstances furnishing the context, the infant organization was forced to assess its objectives. One clearly was to promote the political education of newly enfranchised women citizens. Another was the establishment of some modus vivendi with the political parties that would yield access to opportunities for women to take part in the governing. Again, the League quickly committed itself to an ambitious agenda of liberal legislative reforms (including many of the yet unrealized demands of the Progressive platform of 1912), though problems remained in fashioning means of developing a coherent program commanding majority consent, and an organizational structure sufficiently coordinated to apply pressure on federal and state legislators.

All agreed that the prime necessity was to educate those whom their agitation had enfranchised—initially by a crash program in the mechanics of voting and the institutions of governance. It soon became clear, however, that few women would be motivated to function in a new role by lessons in civics; the ballot was merely the entry ticket to full citizenship, and the impulse to participate would have to be galvanized. The first crude attempts to compensate for the flaws in women's education—their "inherited political disinterest"—gave way to more subtle techniques of conveying learning by actual experience with the political system. League leaders perceived the possibility of fusing aims and methods by making the means they used to reach their legislative objectives serve also as tools for political socialization. Women had been trained for centuries to yield primary allegiance to their families; they now had to be shown where their old habits and loyalties fitted into their new civic responsibilities. Thus the League sought to initiate new lines of involvement along the fringes of the political system. Beginning with the narrowly specified activities related to the electoral process, the League improvised ways of linking other activities making up women's lives to the points where these touched the political sphere— improvizations that acquired the character of a coherent and intelligible way of thinking about the political process in terms, for example, of women's relationships to schools, community services, law enforcement, or public health.

Learning to conceptualize the political life of the community as the way in which people manage their common affairs and translate their social needs into public policy gave shape and meaning to a political role congruent with women's other roles in the family and the community. With this, for those who were League members, went an attitude toward the acquisition of political knowledge as a form of involvement preparatory to action. Study before action became axiomatic. A legacy from the settlement house movement that had sprung up in the 1890s, and a feature that was to provide a keystone to the process of fashioning consensus within the League, it was also the case that, initially, collective awareness of their political inexperience heightened the motivation to acquire knowledge. Both program and procedures contributed to an understanding that the policies chosen for study were not only desirable in themselves but also the means of sharpening capacities for political action.

The proceedings of the early conventions mark the growth of the League's concept of its role-determining function. From 1920 to 1926, the annual conventions both made and recorded the organization's history. Knowledge gained the preceding year was analyzed; assignments for the coming year were laid out. Consciousness-raising sessions of shared testimony were interspersed with problem-solving workshops and seminars in practical politics. A system of internal communications and the rudiments of an hierarchical structure were developed. Guidelines were etched; and most important of all, program-making methods were explored. Out of this cumulative experience was to evolve the organization's purpose as stated in the Bylaws today: "To promote political responsibility through informed and active participation of citizens in government," and to "take action on governmental measures and policies in the public interest." League evolution encapsulates women's emergence from political subjection to a measure of freedom as politically relevant citizens.

In 1969, the League of Women Voters numbered 156,780 members—an historic high. These were organized in nearly thirteen hundred local leagues in fifty states, the District of Columbia, Puerto Rico, and the Virgin Islands.[2] Local leagues are organized in state leagues; state leagues combine in the national organization. Membership is open to all women and (since 1974) men citizens aged eighteen and over. From the membership are drawn the nonsalaried officers at local, state, and national levels. The bulk of the League's work at the local level is undertaken by members on a voluntary basis. The individual member, working through a local league, has a voice at each tier of government on the issues that have been adopted as the organization's program.

Within the political order, the League shares a position with other interest groups, the news media, and the political parties on the input side of the political process. With the parties it shares the task of informing and galvanizing the electorate, but differs from them in operating continuously on a nonpartisan basis. As an interest group, it interacts with other groups and with legislative and executive agencies at all levels of government. The greater part of the League's activity is overtly political, and most of it is symbolic of its historic purpose.

Following the League's intellectual itinerary reveals a system of sustaining beliefs traceable to the era of Progressive reform and Wilsonian idealism, and bridging the period between the two Roosevelts. The organization's persisting preferences would include dedication to the principle of international cooperation in both economic policy and diplomacy, unflagging support for the ideal of effective representative government, and commitment to the general welfare and due process clauses of the Constitution, and to the notions of governmental responsibility for the conservation and development of both human and natural resources. Laissez-faire doctrines, from a feminist perspective, have served too well the bastions of male privilege, offering discouragement to the feminists' desire to aid the disadvantaged, including themselves. The League would repudiate the concept of a passive, noninterventionist government, standing aside while competition guaranteed the survival of the strongest. Within the League's ideology, the proper role of government is to govern, to referee the conflicts generated by the self-chosen activities of the citizens, to keep order, and preserve the peace. Where the state might promote the general welfare by positive action, it has the responsibility to do so, but it is the responsibility of the people to decide where such action is needed.

The revolution that brought the League of Women Voters into existence politicized women's relationship with the community. Today, it is open to women to play a relevant political role, to "live within the polity." Over the past two decades, resurgent feminism has sought to take a further step by politicizing certain aspects of the individual woman's relations with the state—a development for which there is a clear historical logic, given the cumulative impact of social and economic forces acting to transform the premises underlying the institutions of marriage and the family. The experience of their predecessors holds instructive lessons for this new feminist generation, though the transmittal of a revolutionary experience is always difficult. Today's feminists were caught in the emotional backwash of disappointment when the expectations of their mothers were not fulfilled. Each generation is part of an ongoing cycle that carries forward a measurable deposit of social change as mutations find expression in action. Richard S. Titmuss was surely correct when he wrote a generation ago that "the development of the personal, legal and political liberties of half the population of the country within a span of eighty years stands as one of the supreme examples of consciously directed social change."[3]

NOTES

1. This shortened title will normally be employed in both the text and footnotes. Its official title is the League of Women Voters of the United States, a designation adopted in 1946. Between 1920 and 1946, its formal title was the National League of Women Voters.

2. Since then, membership has experienced a gradual though significant decline.

3. Richard M. Titmuss, *Essays on "the Welfare State"* (New Haven: Yale University Press, 1959), 88.

2

The Politics of Woman Suffrage

The League of Women Voters is the politically most distinctive descendant of the woman suffrage movement. Its organizational biography may be opened in 1890, but the influences that shaped its origin lie deep in the nineteenth century, and in the varied processes of change that were gradually working to transform the status and role of women within American society.

Several European observers earlier in the century—Frances Wright after 1818, Alexis de Tocqueville in 1831–32, Harriet Martineau in the mid-1830s—provided perceptive record that such changes were in motion, that already the context of the lives of American women had no parallel elsewhere.[1] While these commentators were not in accord over the import of these changes, nor the extent of their diffusion across a novel social landscape, they were agreed that the "general equality of condition" that was helping to mould the political institutions of the young republic was also modifying all aspects of social life, including relations between the sexes.

Within the political sphere, women were establishing a discernible presence by the 1830s under the impact of developments that were shifting the center of political gravity to the new states west of the Alleghenies as well as encouraging a deepening penetration of the practices of democratic government.[2] With two exceptions, American women had nowhere enjoyed electoral privileges before the end of that decade.[3] Yet they were achieving access, individually and collectively, in many areas of political activity, contributing to the public dialogue on current issues. With the Jacksonian era, mass political campaigns emerged, which indeed took on the character of folk festivals, especially in the socially undernourished frontier states; whole families, women as well as men, were involved in the sociopolitical events that accompanied the unplanned steps

Suffrage parade, New York City, shortly before the November 1917 elections, when the suffrage campaigners carried New York State. Carrie Chapman Catt, center, leads the marchers, with Dr. Anna Howard Shaw on her right. Behind the public display here was a sophisticated grass-roots organization that Catt had partly copied from Tammany Hall.

toward the development of an electorate possessing a sense of popular power and competence.

Women had also started to seek out direct opportunities to influence the determination of public policy, both by participating in debates over current political questions (often in the face of public disapproval) and by exercising a politics of pressure upon state legislatures and Congress. Both Emma Willard and Frances Wright lobbied for publicly supported education for women. And in 1828 Wright became the first woman in the United States to ascend a public platform and make a political speech; she soon became well known as a champion of a variety of causes that were to be a focus of public attention over the rest of the century—among them, the abolition of slavery, reforms in marriage and divorce laws, birth control, and universal public education.

The rise of antislavery agitation in the 1820s provided women with the initial issue on which they were to have significant political impact, while stimulating the emergence of the formative generation of feminist political leaders. In December 1833, various antislavery groups from the New England and Mid-Atlantic states came together in Philadelphia to form the American Anti-Slavery Society; women activists, though allowed to speak at the meeting, were not offered membership but instead encouraged to form their own auxiliary societies.[4] Lucretia Mott, "imbued with women's rights," as she later wrote, since her Nantucket childhood, swiftly assembled twenty women, mostly fellow Quakers, to form the Philadelphia Female Anti-Slavery Society.[5] In 1837, with a network of similar groups in being, she helped form the Anti-Slavery Convention of American Women.[6]

Mott was also instrumental in the inspiration she provided other women abolitionists. Through the Philadelphia Female Anti-Slavery Society, she helped launch the careers of the Grimké sisters, whose experience campaigning for the antislavery cause was to supply a bridge linking the slavery issue and woman's rights.[7] At the World Anti-Slavery Convention in London in 1840, she befriended Elizabeth Cady Stanton, young bride of the New York abolitionist Henry Stanton; a pledge made then was to be redeemed eight years later in their decision to organize, with three other women, the first convention "to discuss the social, civil and religious condition and rights of women."[8]

The outcome of the assembly of some three hundred women and men who met at Seneca Falls, New York, in July 1848 was a vigorous feminist manifesto that marked the commencement of a sustained, arduous, and often bitter campaign to enhance and protect the status of women in American society that has continued since. Entitled a Declaration of Sentiments, the manifesto drew on the American Declaration of Independence in phrasing eighteen grievances against men's "repeated injuries and usurptions," and eleven resolutions for redress. Several of these latter engendered sharp debate—none more so than the ninth, which demanded woman suffrage and only passed by a narrow margin.[9] The Seneca Falls meeting occasioned others, and a number of woman's rights groups sprang up, modeled upon the female antislavery societies; national wom-

Left, Jane Addams at her desk in 1910. Spiritual godmother to the League, Addams played a pivotal role in the suffrage movement, and in events leading to the creation of the League. A number of the first generation of League leaders drew their inspiration from their association with Addams at Hull-House and in the suffrage campaign. (Jane Addams Memorial Collection, The University Library, University of Illinois at Chicago) *Right,* Carrie Chapman Catt, on her arrival in New York City, August 28, 1920, following the ratification of the Nineteenth Amendment.

an's rights conventions were held annually, save for one year, between 1850 and 1860. Though the fledgling women's movement suffered problems of finance, organization, and leadership, a growing number of woman's rights partisans emerged, among them Susan B. Anthony and Lucy Stone. The feminist cause, borne aloft on the wings of the abolition movement, seemed to its eager adherents "fairly to the doors of Congress."

Then came civil war over the slavery issue, and the promised triumph was snatched away. With the war's close, woman's rights became hopelessly enmeshed in the politics of the Fourteenth and Fifteenth amendments. Protests by Susan Anthony and Elizabeth Cady Stanton over the insertion of the term "male" into the former—a clear betrayal by their abolitionist allies—initiated a rift in the women's movement; New England feminists clustered around Lucy Stone were willing to delay their demands for the ballot until the freed slaves had secured full citizenship, while others, led by Stanton and Anthony, rejected any compromise. As often with radical movements, disagreement over strategy deepened into conflict over aims and ideology, and in 1869 the feminists split into rival groups: a Boston-based American Woman Suffrage Association with a membership of men and women drawn mainly from the abolition movement; and a militant New York–based group gathered around Anthony and Stanton, with a membership limited to women, that called itself the National Woman Suffrage Association.[10]

Deeply divided, the feminists remained a small and marginal group during the 1870s and 1880s. The AWSA, treading a path of moderation, concentrated its energies on the suffrage question, and studiously avoided the controversial issues that engaged the NWSA leadership. The initiative during these years came primarily from the Stanton-Anthony partnership, dating from 1851 and remarkable for its union of complementary talents, personalities and circumstances.[11]

The postwar "Republican betrayal" was to channel feminist grievances into a core demand for the ballot. The architects of Reconstruction policy, in forcibly enfranchising the freed men, spurred the indignant feminists to view the denial of the right to vote as a symbol of all wrongs requiring redress; the longer the struggle lasted, the more millennial their faith in the ballot became. At the same time, the opponents of woman suffrage knew that they had now surrendered any rational grounds for not enfranchising women on the basis of qualifications. They were driven back on narrow interpretations of common law, or forced to cleave emotionally to "God's ordinance" regarding the proper spheres of the sexes, or to theorize that politics was "modified warfare" and hence unsuitable for women, whose "high and holy mission" was "to make the characters of coming men." The preoccupations on both sides of the controversy over the "oligarchy of sex" became a focus of bitter and unyielding hostility.

The reform impulse, if ebbing in the eastern states, retained some vitality in those beyond the Mississippi. In 1869, the Wyoming territorial legislature succumbed to the persuasions of Esther Morris, an Anthony convert, and made

Wyoming women the first in Western civilization to be fully enfranchised.[12] The following year women also gained the vote in Utah Territory as a result of a misconceived congressional attempt to suppress plural marriage among the Mormons.[13] Given their limited populations, the victories in these territories were peripheral, but foretold that the suffrage tide would move from the West eastward.[14] Many of the activists were educated Eastern women who had gone west after the Civil War with their families, or to teach school; some had caught the virus of revolt through speaking tours by Stanton and Anthony. In the more settled prairie states, women with feminist convictions were increasingly visible in the dissident third parties, which drew readily on their moral energies.

While suffrage support grew slowly during the 1870s and 1880s, the women's temperance movement was enlisting many thousands of activists in a process broadening political as well as social awareness. The Woman's Christian Temperance Union was formed in November 1874, in the wake of a vigorous grassroots women's antisaloon crusade. In 1879 the magnetic and resourceful Frances Willard assumed its leadership, and forged it into a highly effective organization with a peak membership of 200,000 in 15,000 local unions. Under her guidance, the WCTU's aims were redefined to embrace a variety of social and political problems to which the struggle against alcoholism could be linked. By 1889, the WCTU at the national level had become divided into thirty-nine departments, the second largest of these dealing with the suffrage question.[15] Willard's capacity to generate momentum for social reform while working within the parameters of public acceptability underpinned a stature unique among early women reformers. She fashioned the WCTU into an instrument through which feminist activism could be professionalized and techniques of public persuasion refined; she also helped create a national constituency for both political and social reform, and thus prepared the way for Carrie Chapman Catt and Jane Addams, the key women of the next generation.[16]

Various factors were reshaping the position of American women in this period, not least their dramatic influx into industrial employment after 1860. Susan Anthony had involved herself in helping organize women workers between 1868 and 1872, and Willard had allied the WCTU with Terence Powderly and the Knights of Labor in 1886. A handful of women labor activists had been alerted to the ballot question. But not until after the turn of the century did Stanton's daughter, Harriet Stanton Blatch, organize suffrage support among working women in New York City, and the National Women's Trade Union League unite middle-class women with working women to carry forward the efforts of Willard and Powderly.[17]

The large-scale entry of women into higher education was to prove more significant at this stage, however, in shaping patterns of political behavior. The struggles for political rights and for higher education were closely linked, and both fostered the growing solidarity among women. Neither would have sufficed without the other. Education heightened aspirations and motivated the search for use of trained talents. Interaction in organizations was a response both to the heightened aspirations and to the increasing numbers who possessed organizational skills.

Moreover, the quickening concerns of intellectually awakened young women seeking to establish their identity found a formula for a broadened interpretation of equality and democracy in terms of social justice. The rebellious ones rejected the prevailing laissez-faire individualism and its materialist ethos as well as the settled domesticity of the urban, middle-class family pattern. Industrialization, if sharpening the gap between rich and poor, had also widened it between husband and wife, as the latter's functions were curtailed and her status proportionately downgraded. If the competitive struggle in the marketplace was visibly unfair to women and children, the economic dependence of the middle-class housewife was equally unsatisfactory.

With Oberlin College formally opening its doors to women in 1837, the movement for coeducation advanced rapidly west of the Alleghenies, spurred by public policies and by the rivalry among Protestant churches to establish sectarian colleges. By the end of the century, a third of the students in degree-granting institutions were women. Yet the long-established Eastern universities not only refused to admit women but provoked a public debate on the advisability of educating women, providing in turn an incentive for the establishment of several women's colleges with exacting criteria for admission, to serve, in effect, as proving grounds for women's educability. Exclusion from graduate and professional schools remained entrenched, however, and drove some of the most able and ambitious women to round out their education in more sophisticated centers abroad.[18]

Among the first generation of women to enjoy access to college education in significant numbers were four who were to markedly broaden the intellectual dimensions of the suffrage movement: Jane Addams, Julia Lathrop, Florence Kelley, and Carey Thomas. A composite portrait reveals interesting similarities. All four were born between 1857 and 1860—the dawn of Darwin's century. Three were daughters of legislators, three from families with Quaker connections. The fathers of Addams and Lathrop had helped found the reformist Republic Party in Illinois. Kelley and Thomas came from the Philadelphia-Baltimore intellectual center of Quakerism. Lathrop's mother was a pioneer feminist; Kelley's congressman father was a friend and supporter of Susan Anthony. All enjoyed environmental influences tinged with reform. None married except Florence Kelley, her marriage ending in divorce. All four underwent a painful search for vocations—leading three to sojourns in Europe—that would utilize their moral and intellectual energies in a period when the position of educated young women was in extreme confusion. Thomas became a noted educator and, in 1894, president of the recently founded Bryn Mawr women's college; during her regime, Bryn Mawr was a center of feminism, furnishing a liberating education to a dozen future League of Women Voters' leaders. Addams helped found Hull-House, one of the pioneer settlement houses, in the Chicago slums in 1889; she was joined in 1891 by Lathrop and Kelley to form the nucleus of an extraordinary group of women whose "vitality and compassion reshaped American liberalism . . . [and] educated a whole generation in social responsibility."[19]

It was at a national convention in February 1890 that the great suffragist schism of 1869 was finally healed through the merger of the American Woman Suffrage Association and the militant suffragists led by Susan Anthony and Elizabeth Stanton. With the formation of the National American Woman Suffrage Association, the "pauseless campaign" for women's political rights entered a new phase. This was to consume a further three decades in a struggle lasting more than seven, and saw the transformation of a fragmented and weakly institutionalized grouping into a broadly based movement which had developed formidable organizational sinews.

Among those present at the 1890 convention was Carrie Lane Chapman, a thirty-one-year-old Iowa delegate making her first appearance at a national meeting. With her handsome presence, fine, resonant voice, and forceful ideas, she found herself recruited before the convention closed as an organizer for a forthcoming suffrage referendum campaign in South Dakota. As Carrie Chapman Catt, she rose quickly to prominence, providing a moulding influence over the suffrage movement down through the ultimate achievement of the Nineteenth Amendment in 1920, and guiding its resurrection as the League of Women Voters.[20]

The years from 1890 to 1895 were to furnish Catt with a demanding education in the politics of woman suffrage, and drought-stricken South Dakota proved a good place to begin. Since prohibition had been adopted in 1889 after a vigorous campaign spearheaded by the WCTU, the brewers and distillers were mobilized to defeat the suffrage referendum—not the first sheaf of evidence that they would prove implacable foes. The suffragist cause received scant partisan backing. The populist Independent Party, committed in principle but responsive to expediency, refused endorsement lest their party suffer the wrath of the liquor lobby. The Democrats and Republicans contemptuously ignored the referendum while battling for the votes of the new Russian immigrants and recently enfranchised Sioux Indians. Bribery was commonplace. In the space of a few weeks, Catt witnessed in microcosm most of the forces that would be arrayed against suffrage in the next thirty years.[21]

The referendum was a disaster, but Catt learned lessons that never had to be repeated, and absorbed others as Susan Anthony prepared her, step by step, for larger opportunities. In 1891 she was asked to testify at the annual suffrage hearings before a congressional committee—an already ritualized occasion, with the representatives bored and inattentive; the result was negative as well as demeaning. The fires of indignation were building up against the presumptions of those who denied her status as a citizen; but she was also gaining an exasperated realization of the flaws in their own efforts. The year 1893 brought the first state-level referendum success in Colorado, enhancing Catt's reputation as a campaigner. Then came Kansas, and a losing referendum battle that Catt always recalled as the most heartbreaking of the suffrage struggle. It provided an ominous warning that the suffrage issue was a political shuttlecock; neither major party would accede until both were compelled to.[22] Further, surrendering independence to become party loyalists would not necessarily be rewarded with access to a share of the power.[23]

At NAWSA's Atlanta Convention in 1895, Susan Anthony asked Catt to draft a "plan of work" for the coming year. The plan unveiled two days later underlined the suffrage movement's shortcomings and called for a revolution in organizational structure and methods of work. Anthony promptly named Catt chair of a new Committee on Organization; she in turn chose a committee of four, all suffrage activists from the Midwest.

Reform was vital. NAWSA was a bundle of seven hundred nearly autonomous auxiliaries, with perhaps thirteen thousand members; ten states lacked any visible organization. The national board was lax about records, informal in its procedures. Catt was determined to focus energies upon concerted political action, and also to organize the many potential advocates she felt existed in other women's groups, and not least the civic-minded women brought under the umbrella of the General Federation of Women's Clubs in 1890.[24]

For five years Catt served as director of operations, and energetically applied herself to organizational strengthening. She made dozens of speeches herself, wrote thousands of letters, and raised money to finance NAWSA activities. Her annual reports were a blend of facts, admonitions, and exhortations. Despite internal resistance, she succeeded in turning NAWSA in a new direction, and a smoothly functioning administration replaced rule by improvisation. Idaho, strongly Populist, was placed in the suffrage column, but an arduous and carefully planned referendum campaign in California failed.

In 1900 Susan Anthony, now in her eightieth year, surrendered the NAWSA presidency to Catt, her chosen successor. The moment was ripe for vigorous leadership to apply the momentum gained in the previous five years.[25] In her first presidential address Catt asserted that a tightened organizational structure and training in political techniques were the key to success. She proposed that auxiliaries organize from the electoral precinct upward, to parallel the parties; and that every state auxiliary undertake a political project: school suffrage, municipal suffrage, the removal of a discriminatory law. Her conviction that the suffrage crusade would not in itself be productive of an effective political role for women rested on her intuitive understanding that the civic arts required both the acquisition of knowledge about political institutions and direct political experience.[26]

During her four-year presidency, Catt encouraged political involvement by inviting convention speakers whose message was calculated to awaken interest in political reforms. Her views on the flaws in contemporary society focused less on social inequities than on the oligarchic usurpation of power by political bosses and machines and the debasement of the political process by corruption. Combatting these abuses, for Catt, could construct the framework for alleviating feminist grievances.[27]

The convention of 1906 marked the entry of Jane Addams as a galvanic force in the suffrage movement, typifying the upsurge of reform activism in the Midwest.[28] Her convention speech, "The Modern City and the Municipal Franchise for Women," conceptualized a political role for women that gave new political and ethical dimensions to the strategy earlier mapped out by Frances Willard. It was in the municipal sphere, she told delegates, that politics was most corrupt, government most shoddy, and the social costs of industrialization most evident in the manifold problems of human welfare that were rightfully women's concerns. Seeing the suffrage movement as marking a point in the evolution of self-rule when "new human interests have become the object of governmental action," she urged delegates to concentrate their efforts on securing the municipal franchise and seizing responsibility for running municipal government.

NAWSA's 1907 convention was held in Chicago for the first time, with a program designed to force delegates "to drink at the wells of human experience." A symposium on municipal housekeeping heard Hull-House residents discuss the workings of the new juvenile court—an innovation the Hull-House group had pioneered—the extent of infant mortality, and working conditions in the sweatshops.[29]

The forward surge of the feminist movement in this period created powerful counterpressures. The increase in young women with industrial jobs was loosening family ties. Even more threatening to the established order was the swelling army of those with college degrees, capable of supporting themselves, delaying marriage, or even not marrying at all. The swelling tide of opposition from the pulpit, the conservative press, and male politicians drove a regiment of women intellectuals and professionals into the arms of the suffrage leaders, betraying as it did the masculine premise that women's role was primarily sexual.

A new generation prepared to challenge these regressive tendencies appeared on college campuses near the turn of the century. The feminist youth movement crystallized in 1899 at Radcliffe College, where discussion of suffrage was formally forbidden but where in practice antifeminist propagandists enjoyed the run of the campus. Out of curiosity, Maud Wood, soon to graduate summa cum laude, attended an off-campus suffrage rally featuring Alice Stone Blackwell. Readily converted, she joined a fellow student, Inez Gillmore, in forming a club to proselytize among students and graduates in the vicinity. In 1900 the first College Equal Suffrage League was formed, its manifesto declaring that, since the feminist movement had opened the doors to higher education, it was their duty to acknowledge the "obligation of opportunity" by taking "a positive stand" on the suffrage issue. The idea spread to Bryn Mawr, then to other campuses, especially those where antifeminist prejudice abounded.

As their members grew, their elders in NAWSA auxiliaries, chary of their jurisdiction over recruitment, looked with much disfavor on the youth groups whose members stubbornly insisted on independence of action. Not until the 1906 convention were the leagues officially recognized, and only then because Dr. Carey Thomas, president of Bryn Mawr College, had been won over to

active participation in the suffrage cause. Two years later the National College
Equal Suffrage League was given formal status as a NAWSA auxiliary. Thomas
was named president, but the prime mover remained Maud Wood Park, later
to become the first League of Women Voters president. Operating with a min-
uscule budget but with the steady support of the older feminists in the academic
profession and a group of energetic young women, Park carried on her missionary
work in the face of administrative resistance on many campuses, and overt
harassment on some. After the 1912 election, the League designed an intellectual assault on the antifeminists by devising a "Traveling Library"; books could
penetrate where speakers were forbidden. The library represented an experiment
in intellectual subversion to accelerate social change, touching all the points
where the feminists were pressing hardest against the institutional barriers.[30]

As a massive reaction against the status quo, the Progressive movement by
the turn of the century had embraced the suffragists, the social justice and urban
reform groups, and the agrarian and neodemocratic reformers, uniting men and
women, farmers and workingmen, humanitarians and liberals across both parties.
Insurgent Republicans in Congress after 1900 were strongly prosuffrage, and
many of their wives were, or had been, activists in their home states. Inevitably,
the disruptive conflict within the Republican Party between the insurgents and
the old guard would surface within NAWSA; this it did at the stormy 1912
convention, when the prominent support given by Jane Addams, one of its
vice-presidents, to the newly formed Progressive Party provoked a heated debate
over NAWSA's existing policy of nonpartisanship.[31]

The elections of 1912, in sparking the Progressive breakaway from the Republican fold, were indeed to leave their imprint sharply etched in the subsequent
history of the League of Women Voters. Jane Addams had been among eighteen
women delegates to the Progressive Party's inaugural convention, and seconded
the presidential nomination of Theodore Roosevelt. William Allen White
named her "the prize exhibit"; when she came down the aisle, "the delegates
. . . rose and cheered. . . . I saw [Roosevelt's] eyes glisten with pride and exultant
joy that she was fighting under his banner."[32] At the peak of her fame, Addams
was the most admired and influential woman in America; Roosevelt had insisted
that she be named a member of the Platform Committee as an "ambassador of
industrial reform." The Progressive platform endorsed woman suffrage as well
as the objectives of the neodemocratic and social justice reformers, erecting
"mileposts that the American progressive movement would follow for the next
fifty years."[33] The first program of the League of Women Voters caught up in
one capacious bag most of these reforms.

Women were on the political scene more visibly than ever before: voting for
the first time in California and Washington, and conducting successful referenda
in Arizona, Kansas, and Oregon. The Illinois state legislature, controlled by
Progressives after the election, hastened to grant women presidential suffrage,
the first breakthrough east of the Mississippi. Jane Addams campaigned actively
in eight states; later confessing to twinges of conscience at violating NAWSA

policy, she nonetheless felt it inevitable that a party pledged to social justice should "draw upon the great reservoir of [women's] moral energy so long undesired and unutilized in practical politics."[34] Her comments reflected the increasing difficulty of adhering to a nonpartisan policy as opportunities for direct political involvement increased.[35]

Though nearly a million women were able to vote, the 1912 elections diminished early prospects for a federal suffrage amendment. Roosevelt failed to rally the broad progressive coalition he sought; in defeating the Republican old guard, he assured a massive Democratic victory, and a Congress dominated by Southerners traditionally hostile to woman suffrage. As for the new Democratic president, Woodrow Wilson had entered politics as a Jeffersonian liberal, with Southern attitudes toward woman's proper sphere; the process of exchanging the presidency of Princeton University for the New Jersey governorship had shifted his views to a modified progressivism, but had not won him to the suffrage cause.

Soon after Wilson's inauguration, Alice Paul, the new head of NAWSA's Congressional Committee, arranged for a delegation to seek his support for the Anthony suffrage amendment, as had been done with every president since Rutherford Hayes. They were received courteously, but Harriet Upton found it a chilling experience; suffrage petitions signed by thousands would not influence him, he assured them. Dr. Anna Howard Shaw, as NAWSA president, subsequently led another delegation of over fifty influential women (with a score of congressional wives) to inquire bluntly why Wilson's State of the Union message in December that year had made no reference to woman suffrage. Wilson maintained that whatever his private views, he had no mandate to press upon Congress "policies which have not had the organic consideration of those for whom I am spokesman."[36]

The seeds of Wilson's eventual conversion had already been sown, however, through the association that began in August 1912 with Louis Brandeis, the progressive Boston lawyer. Through Brandeis he had met social justice reformers like Florence Kelley, Lillian Wald, and Brandeis's sisters-in-law, Pauline and Josephine Goldmark; they helped enlarge his understanding of the role women were playing in bringing about the social changes with which he himself was sympathetic.[37] Soon after his election, he invited a group of social workers to outline the measures they desired to become legislative recommendations; his Inaugural Address echoed their views, though the gap between sharing the social reformers' aspirations and being willing to apply his own resources of leadership to achieving such goals was to remain for some time unbridged. Yet Wilson did gradually warm toward the suffrage advocates, helped by the tactful diplomacy of Helen Gardener, and of others within the cabinet circle.[38] He sought their views, asked questions, appeared capable of changing his mind. When New Jersey held an unsuccessful suffrage referendum in October 1915, he journeyed to Princeton to cast his ballot in favor. Other signs hinted that the Southern traditionalist and the practical politician were moving in the direction in which strong tides of public opinion were now flowing.[39]

Fresh currents of activism were to be released within the suffrage movement by Alice Paul and her friend Lucy Burns. As graduate students in England, both had participated in the militant suffrage campaign there, suffered arrest, and joined in prison hunger strikes. Recently returned, the two proposed to Dr. Shaw in 1912 that a major suffrage parade be organized in Washington, D.C., to coincide with President Wilson's inauguration. In January 1913, Paul was made chair and Burns vice-chair of NAWSA's Congressional Committee, with instructions, however, to raise their own funds.[40] Personal magnetism fired by zeal quickly attracted a remarkable group of women eager for action. On the afternoon before Wilson's inaugural in March, an orderly procession of eight to ten thousand suffragists was beset on Washington's Pennsylvania Avenue by an unruly mob of onlookers; troops were required to restore order. The attendant publicity created a surge of public interest focused on Paul and her followers that she never permitted to die down.

The following month Paul established the Congressional Union for Woman Suffrage to assist the campaign for the federal amendment. By December, as Paul reported to the 1913 convention, it claimed over a thousand members and was publishing a weekly paper; Paul herself noted that it had become difficult to separate the activities of the Union and the Congressional Committee. At a national board meeting after the convention, it became clear that the Union was intended to be national in scope and to operate parallel to, but essentially independently of, NAWSA state organizations on behalf of the federal suffrage amendment. When Paul rejected proposals that the leadership of the two groups be separated, and that the Union be made accountable to the board, she was relieved of responsibility for the Congressional Committee.[41]

The breach between NAWSA and the Congressional Union was formalized in February 1914, and proved lasting.[42] The Union insisted on concentrating energies exclusively on the federal suffrage amendment, a tactic NAWSA saw as premature. From 1914 the Union applied the British suffragist strategy of holding the party in power responsible for the fate of such an amendment. Its electoral efforts henceforth to punish Democratic Party candidates—even those sympathetic to the suffrage cause—appalled NAWSA leaders as impractical and unnecessarily antagonizing supporters in Congress; it also endangered the movement's delicate nonpartisan status, which NAWSA had long nurtured. Nonetheless, despite its limited membership, the Union contributed measurably to the forward thrust of the suffragists by its newsworthy and often dramatic activities during Wilson's first term, although opinions differ over the value of the militant tactics that the Union (recast after 1916 as the National Woman's Party) adopted thereafter.

Alice Paul's successor as Congressional Committee chairman was Ruth Hanna McCormick, the dynamic Illinois suffrage leader. To all appearances an excellent

choice, she soon embroiled NAWSA in a new conflict and left a difficult legacy
for the League of Women Voters. In an attempt to outflank congressional states'
rights opponents of the Anthony amendment, her committee drafted a new
constitutional amendment seeming to herald a shift of focus of suffrage activity
to the state level.[43] On the eve of its introduction in Congress in March,
McCormick persuaded the national board to endorse the scheme without waiting
for convention authorization. The 1914 NAWSA convention witnessed a bitter
debate on the merits of the so-called Shafroth-Palmer amendment, widely
viewed as implying abandonment of the federal suffrage amendment and com-
mitting NAWSA to a wasteful and interminable series of skirmishes in the
states.[44] The 1915 convention voted to withdraw support for it, provoking
McCormick's resignation (to devote her energies to recruiting women into the
Republican Party, with consequences as yet unforeseen). The internal strife
opened the way for a shakeup that brought Catt back to the leadership with a
board of her choosing.[45]

As the 1916 elections approached, politicians showed signs of heeding the
shift in political currents. Women in twelve states now had at least presidential
suffrage. Both presidential nominating conventions were enlivened by spectac-
ular suffragist parades; both party platforms endorsed woman suffrage, though
not by federal amendment. The annual NAWSA Convention was summoned
in September; Catt invited both presidential candidates to Atlantic City to
address the assembly. The Republican nominee, Charles Evans Hughes, was
campaigning in the West, and could not attend.[46] Wilson's perception of the
opportunity was possibly keener; his appearance with his wife on the evening
of September 8, accompanied by several prosuffrage cabinet members and their
wives, was a triumph for him as well as for the suffragists.

Wilson's speech was a retrospective summary of the evolution of the suffrage
movement, as he saw it. Its "cumulating force" in recent decades was "one of
the most astonishing tides in modern history." Women had first come forward,
he noted, over the slavery issue, "which . . . was at bottom . . . nothing but a
question of humanity." Since the Civil War, political questions had become
"more and more . . . social questions . . . with regard to the relations of human
beings to one another"; women had played an increasingly significant role. The
suffrage movement was "*something which has not only come to stay but has come
with conquering power. . . . [It is]* a very superficial and ignorant view . . . which
attributes it to mere social unrest." "We feel the tide," he added, "we rejoice
in the strength of it, and *we shall not quarrel in the long run as to the method of
it.*"[47] While Wilson stopped short of endorsing a federal suffrage amendment,
it remains difficult to argue with those who date his conversion to the suffrage
cause to this address.[48]

The decision by both major party presidential nominating conventions to
relegate the woman suffrage issue to state action proved an opportunity that
Catt skillfully seized to rekindle NAWSA's campaign zeal and reshape its stra-
tegic design. The Atlantic City meetings—called two months earlier than

usual—were presented as an emergency convention. At a closed preconvention meeting of the national board and state chairs, she laid out an ambitious, highly detailed plan intended to force their opponents to fight on all fronts at once, and to win the suffrage amendment from Congress by 1920 (and its state ratification by 1922). Catt's "Winning Plan" was not revealed in public.[49] Convention debate was centered on securing agreement that the federal suffrage amendment would have priority, that campaigns in the states would be harmonized with this objective, and that the national board would be granted new powers to coordinate activities at state and national levels as much as possible.[50]

Woman suffrage was now a major issue with which both parties would have to deal. Three women had stood for Congress, though only Jeannette Rankin of Montana emerged victorious, running on a Republican ticket, a Progressive platform, and in support of Wilson's candidacy. This unorthodox mix of loyalties was widely noted; when she routed the Republican machine, she was hailed as a symbol of a new era. Her example in running for Congress promptly after leading the successful Montana suffrage campaign was regarded by many politicians as a warning of things to come.

On April 2, 1917, with women filling the galleries of the House of Representatives, Rankin was sworn in as the first elected congresswoman. That evening Wilson asked Congress for a declaration of war against Germany, posing difficult new commitments for the suffragist movement.[51] As were many other NAWSA leaders, Catt was deeply opposed to war; the international feminist movement with which she had worked actively since 1902 was closely intertwined with the movement toward peace, and when Jane Addams had organized the Woman's Peace Party in January 1915, Catt had lent support. But as prospects for continued American neutrality diminished, Catt reluctantly brought her colleagues to accept that a more direct response to the looming crisis was required; on February 25, 1917, NAWSA offered its services to the government should war be declared. And to the subsequent war mobilization, NAWSA did make a major contribution, though Catt insisted that "suffrage must remain their number one *war* job."[52]

NAWSA's support for the war effort did not spare it fierce attacks—from Alice Paul's National Woman's Party as well as from its traditional antisuffrage foes—but the danger of political isolation was avoided; and its activists did sustain the forward momentum of the suffrage campaign. During 1917 five state legislatures allowed women presidential suffrage, and Arkansas granted primary suffrage, the first breakthrough in the South. In November, a second referendum campaign in New York was victorious, adding five million women to the electorate.

The following month Catt convened the 1917 NAWSA Convention. The air was full of talk that NAWSA could now "schedule itself out of business," sharpening the critical importance of ideas long germinating in Catt's mind. She outlined a plan to reactivate auxiliaries in the enfranchised states, hinting at a continuance of the suffrage army now sweeping to victory.[53] Then she delivered her presidential message, addressed not to the audience but to Congress.[54] The message was a long and unsparing analysis of the political situation, and in conclusion she fired a warning shot: "We know, and you know that we know, that it has been the aim of both dominant parties to postpone woman suffrage as long as possible. . . . The party machines have evaded, avoided, tricked and buffeted this question from Congress to Legislatures, from Legislatures to political conventions. . . . Many of us have a deep and abiding distrust of all existing political parties . . . our doubts are natural. . . . [The] parties we also know have a distrust and suspicion of new women voters. Let us counsel together. Woman suffrage is inevitable—you know it. The political parties will go on—we know it. Shall we then be enemies or friends?"[55]

When Congress convened in December 1917, suffrage opponents had the New York victory to ponder; women's votes would now affect the choice of nearly 45 percent of the presidential Electoral College. A Woman Suffrage Committee had been secured in the House with Wilson's overt help, and had set January 10, 1918, as the date for a vote. On January 9, Wilson finally made a public commitment to the suffrage amendment's passage; the House vote just met the required two-thirds majority. In the Senate, a stubborn struggle continued until October; turning a deaf ear to a presidential message urging favorable action, the Senate rejected the amendment by two votes. This slender gap was narrowed in the November elections.[56]

Soon after the Armistice, Catt summoned a meeting of several women's groups to demand the inclusion of women on the American delegation that would help negotiate the peace. "The peace conference is the herald of a new order, and in that order women are to be represented not by men but by themselves."[57] Her view that the world's problems were the joint concern of men and women was accurate enough, but her hopes were unrealized; no woman sat at the negotiating table at Versailles.

Before leaving for Paris in December 1918, Wilson again urged congressional action on the Anthony amendment. The outgoing Sixty-Fifth Congress would be in Democratic hands until March, and the expediency of seizing credit for passage was indisputable. But Southern Democrats joined hands in the Senate with Republican conservatives to prevent a vote; postponement was now their only recourse. Despite the frustrating delays, Carrie Chapman Catt went ahead with plans for a Jubilee Convention to be held in St. Louis in late March 1919, to celebrate the near approach of victory and a doubly significant anniversary: the fiftieth year since the grant of suffrage in Wyoming and the fiftieth birthdays of the National and American Woman Suffrage associations. She had plans for ushering in the new era she had not yet fully divulged to anyone.

Jane Addams and Carrie Chapman Catt represented major aspects of the Progressive movement, and both were infected with the virus of reformism that set the tone for the period. Both believed that evolution had brought Western society to the point where the brute strength of the male in a society organized for survival had been rendered obsolete by technology. The social skills of women had functions outside the home rendered necessary by the blind stumblings of the male, whose selective attributes were best fitted for competitive struggle. Women's primary mission was to carry society toward a higher station of development. Both had faith in social politics—defined by Charles E. Merriam, their friend and associate, as "the systematic control exercised by the government over the economic and social life of the given society"—in preference to a noninterventionist government that merely exercised police power to protect property and prevent violence or fraud. Each possessed great intellectual breadth and strong inner compulsions; yet their differences were greater than their similarities.

Catt was the prototype of the professional career woman, successfully integrating her private and public lives by the strength of her adaptive intelligence and resolute will, though not without severe struggle. Her innate talents were strongly executive, developed and disciplined by a succession of obstacles in the path to their realization. Gifted and ambitious to leave her mark on events, she found herself balked by convention and denied status by law. Life held out prizes, only to snatch them away because of her sex; a keen sense of deprivation was deepened by successive layers of experience, in turn facing her with personal challenges commonly shared by other women in her day. Her talent for analysis and problem solving eventually shaped a personality that was "victory organized." But Catt's incomparable gift for leadership in her mature years was an achievement of self-discipline and control, reinforced by a firm grasp of reality. In retrospect it can be seen that she never blundered into success. Her battles were won in her head before she won them in the field.

Jane Addams' complex personality was at once archetypal and symbolic. To her own generation she seemed to stand for the whole of which the rest were but imperfect parts. Intellectually she saw things in large relations; and offered a lens through which others could read their own minds and hearts. William James expressed this when he wrote her that she was "not like the rest of us, who *seek* the truth and try to express it. You *inhabit* reality."[58] Unequalled in her social intuition and vigor of imagination, she was also a brilliant political activist and promoter of social inventions. She carried into the field of practical action a strong belief that society was discovering deeper and more potent impulses for common understanding and cooperation. Her vision of what might be accomplished by moral enterprise was united with a militant courage and a high order of administrative and political capacity in getting things done. Action was the sole medium of expression for her social ethics. Her vision was always that of a woman, and her concept of woman's role began with her need to apply her special knowledge to those fundamental problems with which she was best fitted to deal. Her extraordinary spiritual grace magnetized those drawn into her orbit to emulate her compassionate understanding and generosity of spirit.

Jane Addams' influence in shaping the ideas and releasing the moral energies of the leaders in the last phases of the suffrage movement can scarcely be overstated. From the brilliant circle of women in her orbit, the League of Women

Voters drew not only a large part of its program but a majority of its early officers. The first two presidents acknowledged their discipleship. The greatest of the early vice-presidents, Julia Lathrop, was her closest associate. Her conviction that the community in the traditional sense was in a state of disintegration motivated the general concern for social and economic amelioration that dominated the League's early program. Nevertheless, these concerns, however keenly felt, would not necessarily have eventuated in the League of Women Voters. If Jane Addams was its spiritual godmother, Carrie Chapman Catt was its true founder. Almost singlehandedly she transformed the major wing of suffrage movement into a parapolitical organization on the eve of enfranchisement and phrased its initial political-educational goals. Her farsighted purpose was to shape a political role for women.

NOTES

1. See Frances Wright (D'Arusmont), *Views of Society and Manners in America . . . during the Years 1818, 1819, and 1820* (New York: E. Bliss and E. White, 1821); Alexis de Tocqueville, *Democracy in America*, trans. G. Lawrence and ed. J. P. Mayer (New York: Doubleday, 1969); and Harriet Martineau, *Society in America*, 3 vols. (London: Saunders and Otley, 1837). See also Una Pope-Hennessy, *Three English Women in America* (London: Ernest Benn, 1929).

2. The discussion of developments prior to 1890 draws heavily on Louise M. Young, "Women's Place in American Politics: The Historical Perspective," *Journal of Politics* 38 (August 1976): 295–335; reprinted in *200 Years of the Republic in Retrospect*, eds. William C. Havard and Joseph L. Bernd (Charlottesville: University Press of Virginia, 1976).

3. The New Jersey Constitution of 1776 had enfranchised all inhabitants worth £50 or more; in 1790 the legislature confirmed that such rights extended to women, reversing itself in 1807 after women emerged as an important source of Federalist electoral support. The male monopoly of the franchise was not breached until 1838, when Kentucky granted school suffrage to white widows with children in school. See ibid., 303, 311.

4. Church-sponsored women's societies already existed, and had, on occasion, become active over public issues. But such groups normally operated under pastoral supervision, and devoted themselves to fund-raising, charitable, or educational activities. As Kraditor notes, the convention's initiative produced an "unplanned and unanticipated coalescing of the hitherto separate spheres of work of men and women members." See Aileen S. Kraditor, *Means and Ends in American Abolitionism: Garrison and His Critics on Strategy and Tactics, 1834–1850* (New York: Pantheon Books, 1969), 42.

5. Quoted in Otelia Cromwell, *Lucretia Mott* (Cambridge, Mass.: Harvard University Press, 1958), 125.

6. Flexner observes: "It was in the abolition movement that women first learned to organize, to hold public meetings, to conduct petition campaigns" (Eleanor Flexner, *Century of Struggle: The Woman's Rights Movement in the United States* [Cambridge, Mass.: Harvard Univ. Press, Belknap Press, 1959], 41).

7. Though members of a wealthy South Carolina plantation family, Sarah and Angelina Grimké had become active abolitionist campaigners in 1836, and a tour they made of the Boston area in 1837 attracted considerable attention. When the state Congre-

gational General Association censured their appearances before audiences including men, the sisters provided a forthright defense, bonding the slavery question with women's rights. The controversy over women's role in the antislavery agitation was to be prominent among the divisions that caused the AASS to split in 1840. See Gerda Lerner, *The Grimké Sisters from South Carolina: Rebels against Slavery* (Boston: Houghton Mifflin, 1967), chap. 3; Kraditor, *Means and Ends in American Abolitionism*, chap. 3; and Edward T. James, Janet W. James, and Paul S. Boyer, eds., *Notable American Women, 1607–1950: A Biographical Dictionary* (Cambridge, Mass.: Harvard Univ. Press, Belknap Press, 1971) 2: 97–99.

8. So read, in part, the announcement placed in a local newspaper on 14 July 1848; quoted in Elisabeth Griffith, *In Her Own Right: The Life of Elizabeth Cady Stanton* (New York: Oxford University Press, 1984), 52.

9. Accounts of the Seneca Falls Convention are provided in Flexner, *Century of Struggle*, chap. 5; and Griffith, *In Her Own Right*, chap. 4. The Declaration of Sentiments is reprinted in Anne F. Scott and Andrew M. Scott, eds., *One Half the People: The Fight for Woman Suffrage* (Philadelphia: J. B. Lippincott, 1975), 56–59.

10. In May 1870, in a conciliatory gesture toward its rival, the NWSA abandoned its antimale stance, and elected a man as president; the first head of AWSA had been Henry Ward Beecher, the well-known minister and abolitionist. See Griffith, *In Her Own Right*, 142.

11. The investment of confidence by Stanton and Anthony in an eccentric speculator and would-be politician, George Francis Train, had been rewarded with a subsidy for a short-lived but notable journal, *The Revolution*, which offers as brave a display of feminist enterprise as is available to social historians of the period; between 1868 and 1870, the blistering editorials by Stanton phrased the ideology of feminism as a revolutionary movement intent on changes far more sweeping than enfranchisement. Early in 1870, as the *Revolution* was ailing financially, the AWSA came forward with an alternative, the *Woman's Journal*; with its successor, the *Woman Citizen*, this was to serve as the most influential organ of the feminist movement for the next sixty years.

12. Voting rights for women had been discussed, though not conceded, when the New York State Constitution underwent revision in 1867; the same year the first popular referendum on the question was held in Kansas, a woman suffrage initiative being heavily defeated.

13. For an account of these initial successes, see Carrie Chapman Catt and Nettie R. Shuler, *Woman Suffrage and Politics: The Inner Story of the Suffrage Movement*, rev. ed. (New York: Charles Scribner's Sons, 1926), chap. 6; Flexner, *Century of Struggle*, 159–63, 177–78; and Alan P. Grimes, *The Puritan Ethic and Woman Suffrage* (New York: Oxford University Press, 1967). Wyoming was eventually admitted to statehood in 1890 despite congressional opposition to the inclusion of women as voters. Utah's admission in 1896 restored voting rights to women there after Congress had stripped these away in 1887.

14. In the forty years after 1870, seventeen referenda took place on the woman suffrage issue in eleven states, eight of these west of the Mississippi. See Flexner, *Century of Struggle*, 175.

15. Despite the introduction of the Franchise Department, the WCTU was unable until 1914 to give national endorsement to woman suffrage, to avoid internal division on this issue; see Young, "Women's Place in American Politics," 329 and n.

16. On Willard's career, see Mary Earhart (Dillon), *Frances Willard: From Prayers to*

Politics (Chicago: University of Chicago Press, 1944); and James, James and Boyer, *Notable American Women* 3: 613–19. After the mid-1890s, as influence shifted to more conservative WCTU leaders concerned to stress the temperance issue, many of those trained by Willard in the Franchise Department transferred their commitment to the suffrage movement—among them Dr. Anna Howard Shaw, Zerelda Wallace, and Belle Kearney.

17. Flexner, *Century of Struggle*, 244–47, 249–53; and Aileen S. Kraditor, *The Ideas of the Woman Suffrage Movement, 1890–1920* (New York: Columbia University Press, 1965), 123–62. Useful biographical discussion of Harriet Stanton Blatch may be found in James, James and Boyer, *Notable American Women* 1: 172–74.

18. Mabel Newcomer, *A Century of Higher Education for American Women* (New York: Harper & Bros., 1959), chaps. 1 and 2.

19. Arthur M. Schlesinger, Jr., *The Crisis of the Old Order, 1919–1933* (Boston: Houghton Mifflin, 1956), 26–27.

For useful biographies of these four, see Margaret Tims, *Jane Addams of Hull House, 1860–1935* (London: Macmillan, 1961); James W. Linn, *Jane Addams: A Biography* (New York: Appleton-Century, 1935); Jane Addams, *My Friend, Julia Lathrop* (New York: Macmillan, 1935); Dorothy R. Blumberg, *Florence Kelley: The Making of a Social Pioneer* (New York: A. M. Kelley, 1966); Josephine C. Goldmark, *Impatient Crusader: Florence Kelley's Life Story* (Urbana: University of Illinois Press, 1953); and Edith Finch, *Carey Thomas of Bryn Mawr* (New York: Harper & Bros., 1947). Excellent short biographies of each may be found in James, James and Boyer, *Notable American Women*.

20. Born in Ripon, Wisconsin, in 1859, Carrie Lane grew up on the Iowa frontier near Charles City. Despite her father's reluctance and the family's limited means, she attended Iowa Agricultural College, a land-grant institution whose faculty was much influenced by Darwin's evolutionary doctrines and Spencer's social Darwinism. She was furnished an education in the sciences and a rationalistic faith in evolutionary progress that became for her both an interpretation of history and a philosophy of action. Graduating in 1880, she worked in a law office before accepting a high school principalship in Mason City, Iowa, to earn money for law school; her success won appointment as city school superintendent instead. Marriage in 1885 to Leo Chapman, owner and editor of the *Mason City Republican*, ended her career in education, and she joined her husband's paper as assistant editor. Plans to purchase a newspaper in California were abruptly terminated by her husband's death in San Francisco in 1886. After spending a year there working for a newspaper, she returned to Iowa and, with earlier involvement in organizing Mason City women in support of an Iowa municipal suffrage bill, she became active in the Iowa Woman Suffrage Association. She remarried in June 1890; her husband, George William Catt, a civil engineer, supported woman suffrage, and they signed a contract permitting her four months each year to devote to suffrage activities (though in fact she worked almost full time on the suffrage campaign). His early death in 1905 left Catt financially independent, and she devoted the rest of her life to the suffrage cause, and to world peace and disarmament. See Mary G. Peck, *Carrie Chapman Catt: A Biography* (New York: H. W. Wilson, 1944); James, James and Boyer, *Notable American Women* 1: 309–13; and Robert B. Fowler, *Carrie Catt: Feminist Politician* (Boston: Northeastern University Press, 1986).

21. Peck, *Carrie Chapman Catt*, 61–65; and Catt and Shuler, *Woman Suffrage and Politics*, 114–17. For a discussion of the role of the liquor lobby during the suffrage struggle, see Catt and Shuler, *Woman Suffrage and Politics*, chap. 10; and David Morgan,

Suffragists and Democrats: The Politics of Woman Suffrage in America (East Lansing: Michigan State University Press, 1972), 157–66.

22. The Kansas campaign "acquainted women with new phases of American politics," Harriet Upton was to recall. "We learned many things, mostly about men, mainly about political men." Harriet Taylor Upton, "Random Recollections," Women's Archives, Arthur and Elizabeth Schlesinger Library on the History of Women in America, Radcliffe College.

23. The New York Constitutional Convention in 1894 finished the cycle of Catt's education by laying bare the fact that a minute minority of well-placed political leaders could frustrate an overwhelming preponderance of informed opinion. A small group led by Elihu Root and Joseph Choate prevented a woman suffrage provision from reaching the convention floor for a vote; Root's speech on this occasion became famous in suffrage annals. See Susan B. Anthony and Ida Harper, eds., *The History of Woman Suffrage* (Rochester, N.Y.: Susan B. Anthony, 1902) 4: 847–52.

24. Formed by over ninety women's civic and literary groups, the GFWC was rapidly to become among the largest and most diverse of American women's organizations; see Young, "Women's Place in American Politics," 328; and Flexner, *Century of Struggle,* 179–80.

25. Fowler suggests that during this first phase of Catt's leadership, Anthony's continued influence from the sidelines, the role of established groups of organizational notables, and the presence of potential rivals like Lillie Devereux Blake and Anna Howard Shaw meant that she failed to acquire the ascendancy she was to achieve after her return to the presidency in 1915. Fowler, *Carrie Catt,* 20–24.

26. The first of these needs she had attacked in 1895 by offering "A Course of Study in Political Science" to every auxiliary. Five hundred sets were sold and study groups set up. Later, a more comprehensive course was made available, and laid the groundwork for the emphasis on civic training that was to characterize the infant League of Women Voters.

27. In 1904, ill health—her own and her husband's—forced Catt to step down from the presidency. She became vice-president-at-large, and when her health was restored, she devoted an important part of her energies to the International Woman Suffrage Alliance. Formally launched in 1904, the Alliance built on the foundations laid by the International Council of Women formed in 1888 by Susan Anthony, Julia Ward Howe, Frances Willard, and Belva Lockwood. Catt served continuously as the Alliance's president until 1923, and saw its membership swell from eight national affiliates to thirty-two. Peck provides extensive coverage of Catt's international efforts in *Carrie Chapman Catt,* 121–25, 137–43, 147–67, 173–215, 347–97. Catt also built a Women Suffrage Party in New York City constructed from the precinct base upward, which was to play a key role in the 1915 and 1917 state suffrage referenda.

28. Ida Husted Harper, ed., *The History of Woman Suffrage* (Washington, D.C.: National American Woman Suffrage Association, 1922) 5: 178–79; see also Jane Addams, *Twenty Years at Hull-House* (New York: Macmillan, 1910), 339–40; and Jane Addams, *The Second Twenty Years at Hull-House* (New York: Macmillan, 1930), 88–94.

29. Harper, *History of Woman Suffrage* 5: 193–212.

30. The library's collection of twenty-seven works explored the social and economic as well as the political dimensions of woman's sphere. The writers included ranged from Mary Wollstonecraft and John Stuart Mill to playwrights and novelists like Ibsen, Shaw, and Olive Schreiner, critics like Charlotte Gilman and Thorstein Veblen, sociologists

like William I. Thomas and Helen Bosanquet, and leading feminists like Jane Addams and Florence Kelley.

When the Association of Collegiate Alumnae (later the American Association of University Women) firmly endorsed woman suffrage in 1917, the NCESL considered its work done. Many members were absorbed into the main body of the suffrage movement; others joined the National Woman's Party formed the previous year.

On the college leagues, see "Reminiscences," Maud Wood Park papers, files 694–700, Arthur and Elizabeth Schlesinger Library on the History of Women in America, Radcliffe College; Harper, *History of Woman Suffrage* 5: 167–74, 226–30, 660–64; and Ethel Puffer Howes, "The National College Equal Suffrage League," *Smith Alumnae Quarterly* (November 1920).

31. Serious divisions within NAWSA had first surfaced at the 1910 convention and were to continue, over various issues, until 1916. Initially, these had found expression in dissatisfaction over the lack of organizational direction supplied by Anna Howard Shaw, Catt's successor as NAWSA president. The Progressive surge in the 1910 congressional elections had carried Washington State into the suffrage column—the first state to grant suffrage since 1896—and readied the ground for California's inclusion in 1911; yet the national organization had seemed preoccupied with the need for cautious tactics to avoid antagonizing regional interest blocs (particularly the South). On these developments, see Harper, *History of Woman Suffrage* 5: 282–83, 341–42; Flexner, *Century of Struggle*, 257–58; Kraditor, *Ideas of the Woman Suffrage Movement*, 226n–27n; and Andrew Sinclair, *The Better Half: The Emancipation of the American Woman* (New York: Harper & Row, 1965), 296–301.

32. William Allen White, *The Autobiography of William Allen White* (New York: Macmillan, 1946), 484.

33. Arthur S. Link with William B. Catton, *American Epoch: A History of the United States since the 1890s*, 2d ed. (New York: Alfred A. Knopf, 1963), 120.

34. Addams, *Second Twenty Years at Hull-House*, 33.

35. As Kraditor observes, NAWSA's policy of nonpartisanship reflected the antipartisanship of the period as well as the unhappy memories of suffragists at recurring instances of party opportunism over the suffrage question and a pragmatic desire to avoid antagonizing one or another of the partisan camps. By 1912 there was another concern: the expansion of opportunities for women's political participation over the previous generation—both Democratic and Republican women were by now organized in partisan clubs—meant the need to avoid introducing party divisions within NAWSA's own ranks. Kraditor, *Ideas of the Woman Suffrage Movement*, 221–31.

36. Harper, *History of Woman Suffrage* 5: 373–76. Indeed, in February 1914, the Democratic Caucus in the House of Representatives not only refused to support a proposal for a standing woman suffrage committee—though there had long been one in the Senate—but resolved that the woman suffrage question should be dealt with at the state rather than the federal level. Ibid., 412–13.

37. Goldmark, *Impatient Crusader*, 140.

38. Helen Gardener (1853–1925) was an author, suffragist, and socially prominent Washington figure. An astute advocate for feminist causes, Gardener's help as a behind-the-scenes lobbyist during the Wilson administration proved invaluable. Maud Park, who directed NAWSA's congressional lobby from January 1917 until the passage of the Anthony amendment in 1919, described her as "a woman of genius who was to teach me almost everything of value that I came to know during those years in Washington."

President Wilson was to appoint her to the Civil Service Commission in 1920, the highest federal post yet held by a woman. See Maud Wood Park, *Front Door Lobby*, ed. Edna L. Stantial (Boston: Beacon Press, 1960), 22; and also James, James and Boyer, *Notable American Women* 2: 11–13.

39. Unsuccessful suffrage referenda were held in three other key eastern states in November; as in New Jersey, the prosuffrage vote had been comfortably over 40 percent in New York and Pennsylvania, and 35 percent in Massachusetts, testifying to the increasing organizational effectiveness of the suffragists and the growing popular appeal of their cause. See Flexner, *Century of Struggle*, 270–71; and Morgan, *Suffragists and Democrats*, 97–98.

40. Paul's predecessor as Congressional Committee head had received $10 from NAWSA in 1912 to cover her expenses; using NAWSA stationery and a list of possible donors given her by the national board, Paul raised over $27,000 by the end of 1913. See Flexner, *Century of Struggle*, 262–63; Harper, *History of Woman Suffrage* 5: 378; and Catt and Shuler, *Woman Suffrage and Politics*, 241–42. The Congressional Committee itself had been set up in 1910 to give new impetus to efforts to obtain passage of a federal suffrage amendment, but initially had had only limited impact; Harper, *History of Woman Suffrage* 5: 377.

41. Burns and the other members of the Congressional Committee then resigned. See Harper, *History of Woman Suffrage* 5: 381n.

42. The differing approaches of the two groups, and the difficult relations between them, have been the subject of several useful though contrasting accounts; see Harper, *History of Woman Suffrage* 5: 675–78; Catt and Shuler, *Woman Suffrage and Politics*, 240–48; Flexner, *Century of Struggle*, 263–70; Sinclair, *The Better Half*, 326–32; Kraditor, *Ideas of the Woman Suffrage Movement*, 226–48; Morgan, *Suffragists and Democrats*, 86–98; and Fowler, *Carrie Catt*, 145–53.

43. The proposal would have facilitated the holding of state referenda on the suffrage issue, and removed the constitutional and political barriers the suffragists often faced in obtaining these, by stipulating that petitions signed by 8 percent of a state's registered voters at the previous general election be sufficient to require that a referendum on woman suffrage be held; the exact wording is given in Harper, *History of Woman Suffrage* 5: 416.

44. Technically, the new amendment was intended to have a supplemental role; nonetheless, the expense in terms of political resources and energies of pursuing both this strategy and the federal suffrage amendment would have been considerable. While state suffrage referenda were seen as crucial for increasing leverage on Congress, they also were often costly efforts, and where defeat followed large-scale and well-organized campaigns—as in New York in 1915—there was risk of a corrosion of suffragist morale. Moreover, there was some danger, once the amendment was ratified, that Congress might simply shuffle the suffrage issue off its own agenda. While Catt and Shuler would describe the Shafroth-Palmer amendment as "a bomb . . . thrown into the national suffrage camp by its own Congressional Committee," they also noted: "Many suffragists believed that while it had precipitated an agony of differences, on the whole the proposal had been good interim strategy, for the arguments for and against had served to bring the question of suffrage by federal amendment still more prominently to the front. Moreover, state suffrage auxiliaries had been solidified in their allegiance to the National Suffrage Association's policy by the agitation." See *Woman Suffrage and Politics*, 246, 247–48.

45. Shortly before the 1915 convention, Dr. Shaw had announced her resignation

as NAWSA president. A strong movement quickly developed to draft Catt as her replacement. Fresh from defeat in the New York referendum (which she had directed) and determined to launch preparations immediately for another attempt, Catt was most reluctant to serve—"I am an unwilling victim" she told the convention—but she acquiesced in return for agreement that she could nominate her own national board. Shaw, who had favored Catt as her successor, became honorary president. Harper, *History of Woman Suffrage* 5: 445–47, 455–59; and Flexner, *Century of Struggle*, 271–74.

46. Hughes had already strengthened his party's position by personally endorsing the Anthony amendment.

47. See Harper, *History of Woman Suffrage* 5: 496–98; italics in original.

48. During the 1916 campaign Wilson was to make two major speeches to audiences of women. In Chicago, with Jane Addams on the platform, he declared: "The whole spirit of the law has been to give leave to the strong. . . . Society now has another element . . . the element which women are going to supply. It is the element of mediation, of comprehending and drawing the elements together. It is the power of sympathy, as contrasted with the power of contest." A week later he spoke to the Women's City Club in Cincinnati, pleading for a postwar society of nations to bring about a civil order based on justice, but also acknowledging that "there are things we ought to see to that we have not been seeing to—the health, the moral opportunity, the just treatment of ordinary citizens." In emphasizing the harmony of his views with theirs, he was no doubt seeking their influence, and the election's outcome justified his effort. Ten of the twelve enfranchised states were to be in the Wilson column; in seven, including California, women's votes appeared to have tipped the balance in his favor.

49. The details of Catt's speech remained secret for some years; see Catt and Shuler, *Woman Suffrage and Politics*, 260–62; Peck, *Carrie Chapman Catt*, 256–57, 261–63; Park, *Front Door Lobby*, 15–17; Flexner, *Century of Struggle*, 279–82; and Fowler, *Carrie Catt*, 143–45.

50. See Harper, *History of Woman Suffrage* 5: 486–87, 488–89, 510–11. The reforms bolstering the position of the national board were lent added weight by the prospect of a dramatic increase in the financial resources available to the national leadership. In September 1914, Mrs. Frank Leslie, a wealthy New York publisher, had died, leaving her considerable estate to Catt to use for suffrage work. Though litigation delayed access to this bequest, in early 1917 Catt was able to establish the Leslie Woman Suffrage Commission to manage a fund that eventually came to $900,000. See Harper, 755; Peck, *Carrie Chapman Catt*, 224–27, 265; and Fowler, *Carrie Catt*, 118–19.

51. Not least for Jeannette Rankin. Her first significant congressional vote was against American entry into the European conflict. Her attempt to justify her action was brusquely ruled out of order by the Speaker. Though only one of fifty House members opposing the war resolution, newspaper coverage singled Rankin out for criticism; reports that she had burst into tears—Park for one did not observe this from the House gallery—were cited as proving women's unfitness for public office. Addams was later to comment that such events had "demonstrated that it is much easier to dovetail into the political schemes of men than to release the innate concerns of women, which might be equivalent to a revolutionary force." Addams, *Second Twenty Years at Hull-House*, 110; see also Park, *Front Door Lobby*, 76–77.

52. Flexner, *Century of Struggle*, 289; italics in original. For a summary of NAWSA's services during the war, see Harper, *History of Woman Suffrage* 5: 720–40.

53. The text of Catt's remarks is given in League of Women Voters, *Forty Years of a*

Great Idea (Washington, D.C., [1960]), 8; this speech contained Catt's first public reference to the phrase "National League of Women Voters."

54. Carrie Chapman Catt, *An Address to the Congress of the United States* (New York: National Woman Suffrage Publishing Co., 1917). A copy was delivered to every member of Congress by a constituent, and during the subsequent campaign to ratify the Nineteenth Amendment, to every state legislator in the country.

55. Ibid., 18–19.

56. Catt had warned in her presidential address to the 1917 convention that the suffrage movement's forward tide might "soon engulf the resisters." Following the Senate vote, NAWSA swiftly organized campaigns to block the election of four opponents, carefully selecting two from each party. Two senators were indeed toppled—Willard Saulsbury (D., Del.) and John Weeks (R., Mass.); but NAWSA also lost an old Senate ally, John Shafroth of Colorado. See Park, *Front Door Lobby*, chap. 7–15.

57. Quoted in Peck, *Carrie Chapman Catt*, 302.

58. William James to Jane Addams, December 13, 1909; quoted in Christopher Lasch, ed., *The Social Thought of Jane Addams* (Indianapolis: Bobbs-Merrill, 1965), 84.

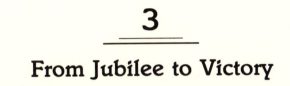

3

From Jubilee to Victory

As NAWSA's Jubilee Convention opened in St. Louis on March 24, 1919, Carrie Chapman Catt challenged the nearly victorious women to stay on the battlefield as an army of women citizens to "finish the fight" for the changes in "custom, laws and education" so imperatively needed.[1] She outlined three immediate goals: to complete the enfranchisement of American women, to remove legal discriminations against them, and to reach out a helping hand to their sisters in other lands. Indicting the "organized reactionary minority . . . knowing commercial America only," who had for so long opposed their liberation, she charged them with furnishing "the spirit, the funds and the motives" while the political machines had supplied the votes to further their "selfish demands." Appealing to the liberal tide of public concern over corruption and party manipulation of democratic institutions, Catt saw the "political restoration" of democratic processes as the real field of opportunity for women, unencumbered as they were by "bad political habits." They would have to rid the country of the general contempt for the electoral process, "lift this incubus from our public life," by improving the electorate through compulsory education laws in the states, adult education at public expense, and higher qualifications for naturalization: "This opportunity will last only a few years and it can never come again."

In a charged atmosphere, the convention voted to launch an auxiliary organization in the enfranchised states, and to dissolve NAWSA when its task was completed. Anticipating this outcome, Catt was ready with proposals that the new body, to be called the League of Women Voters, would be governed by a council of state league presidents, with Mrs. Charles Brooks of Kansas as chair; this council would adopt and implement all policies.[2] Provision was also made for standing committees—similar to the "suffrage service committees" existing during the war—to be responsible for particular subject areas.

The convention had scarcely closed before controversy began to swirl around the embryonic body. Returning to New York, Catt stopped in several cities for speeches urging support for the League of Nations, and was appalled by the evident suspicion with which professional politicians and much of the press viewed the proposed League of Women Voters. Congress had not yet passed the Anthony amendment, and hostile editorial comment quoted charges by political leaders that the suffragists were guilty of ingratitude, even treachery in setting up an organization to compete with the parties.[3]

In a joint statement in the *Woman Citizen* of April 26, 1919, Catt and Brooks explained their intent: "a union of all intelligent forces within the state" to attack "illiteracy, social evils, industrial evils." It would be political but not partisan, and certainly not a woman's bloc; men would be welcome as members. Catt noted: "The politicians used to ask us why we wanted to vote. They seemed to think we meant to do something particular with it . . . something we were not telling about. They did not understand that women wanted . . . to help make the general welfare. . . . We are not radicals."

In mid-April, the Women's Republican Club of New York had sent a reso-lution to major newspapers as well as suffrage leaders in the enfranchised states denouncing the new organization as a "nonpartisan party" that, by "encouraging dissension between men and women voters whose interests are identical," would constitute a "menace to our national life." Besieged by reporters, Catt had been caustic: "The League . . . happens to be everything you think it is not, and none of the things you think it is . . . what interests me is your willingness to announce . . . that you are at war with those who won you the vote. This is the inducement you offer to come into the Republican Party." Repeating the League's purposes, she added that its job could be completed within five years.[4]

Catt's plan for reconstituting the suffrage battalions was understandably threat-ening to some politicians. The radical tone of the Jubilee Convention resolutions revealed deep dissatisfaction with the political status quo, even if the threatened invasion of the party strongholds had less power to evoke terror. Nearly doubling the number of voters in itself held possibilities of unpredictable electoral shifts. The potential for fundamental change in the distribution of power seemed immense, as the interests that had opposed women's suffrage for so long feared.

Yet it was partisan women leaders who were in fact the driving force in trying to prevent the formation of the League of Women Voters. The Republican Party was the natural home of many active suffragists, and to Ruth Hanna McCormick of Illinois, leader of the GOP's Women's Division, the proposed organization appeared a duplication of effort.[5] Her antagonism was communi-cated not only to the women whom she attracted into party work but also to the Republican leadership; misrepresentation led to hostility that was not allayed for many years. Partisan women in the Democratic Party were fewer and less well organized; but several of them also objected to the new group. Mrs. George

Bass, an outstanding suffragist and Illinois Democratic women's leader, joined hands with McCormick in seeking to block the formation of a state league out of the existing NAWSA organization. Mary Morrisson took the lead in frus- trating this maneuver.[6]

The House of Representatives passed the Anthony amendment, 304 to 90, on May 21, 1919. Senate irreconcilables blocked action another two weeks, delaying ratification by assuring that most state legislatures had adjourned. The final Senate debate included hostile attacks from every element comprising the coalition of opponents, but principally from Southern Democrats and Eastern establishment Republicans. The Senate finally acted on June 4, 1919; the amendment passed with two votes to spare, forty years after its introduction into Congress. From Paris, President Wilson sent a cable of congratulations. Millicent Fawcett, longtime president of the National Union of Suffrage So- cieties in Britain, cabled "Glory Hallelujah." But all was not over. The battle for ratification by the states did not end until nearly fifteen months later, on August 26, 1920, on the eve of the presidential election.

In mid-June, 1919, the League's governing council held its first meeting in New York. There was no real organization yet, and the discussion became a series of questions: How would authority be organized within the council, and how should the committee structure function? How and by whom would the new organization be financed? What relation would state leagues have to the national organization? In enfranchised states where no suffrage organization now existed, how might they activate networks of leaders and members? How might rival claimants be accommodated in states with several suffrage associations? How should they cooperate with other women's groups? Some of the standing committee heads present wanted immediate action on pressing legislative is- sues—who had the power to make decisions?

All questions were referred to Catt, the source and symbol of authority. She designated a committee to draft a constitution, and proposed that Brooks tour the already enfranchised states with Julia Lathrop, director of the U.S. Children's Bureau, whose bill to provide federal aid for maternal and infant health was likely to attract grass-roots interest and help shape a public image for the new organization. To revive enthusiasm among women in these states, she also suggested urging that they prepare to enter the "immense field of correction" by identifying deficiencies in state laws relating to education and women's legal status. Only two committees had been authorized at the Jubilee Convention: American Citizenship and Women in Industry. They might press for legislation, she felt, though the League would have to keep its skirts clear of controversial issues until firmly established.

Dr. Valeria Parker, chair of the Committee on Social Hygiene (not yet formally authorized), wanted to bring state league representatives to a pioneering conference on social morality—at which women physicians from many countries would discuss "the revolution in sex relationships." Catt warned her that women from church-related groups should be closely involved, since questions of birth control, sterilization of the unfit, and control of prostitution were likely to be major concerns. Mabel Costigan, head of the new Food Supply and Demand Committee, pressed for authority to activate it, but was reminded that the convention had authorized no such action.[7] Following this discussion, as was characteristic of Catt's working methods, Brooks issued a circular letter to state presidents and committee chairs, summarizing her advice[8]—the first link in a continuous chain of communications from the nerve center of the embryonic organization to its outlying parts.

The Nineteenth Amendment was ratified by eleven states within four weeks of its passage by Congress, and by February 1920, the month the Victory Convention met, by thirty-three; only three more states had to be won. At the NAWSA Executive Council's final meeting before the convention, Catt pressed for a decision over the proposal for a continuing organization, dividing the issue into a series of questions: Should NAWSA dissolve when its work was finished, or make plans for an ongoing organization? How should NAWSA's financial responsibilities be liquidated? What body should it designate to represent American women in the International Woman Suffrage Alliance? What plans should they make for the education of new voters?[9]

The organization created by the Jubilee Convention had been intended only for the enfranchised states, and had had a partly tactical purpose in sustaining a nationwide suffrage momentum; thus the decisions now to be taken were of fundamental concern. The Council agreed that the last question was the key, but several disagreed that the body Catt envisioned was the best vehicle for politically educating the new voters. Mary Hay, Harriet Upton, and Narcissa Vanderlip, all Republican Party officials, argued that the road to civic competence lay through the political parties; Bass and Anna Pennybacker, both Democratic leaders, agreed. Others argued that the General Federation of Women's Clubs furnished both civic education and a worthwhile program serving women's interests.

The discussion was prolonged, but Catt was not easily overborne. The suffrage movement, despite having more than two million members, was a composite army united only in pursuit of a single goal. Women's present solidarity, she feared, might quickly dissolve. Those who had fought so long for political citizenship should not be permitted to sink into new forms of subjection under party tutelage, as appeared to have happened in the enfranchised states. Women had to be trained for their political role; while obtaining the rudiments of a political education as petitioners, they had acquired a tendency to be moralistic and censorious, and a fondness for indirect methods. Victory might be hollow if women did not shape an effective role in political life grounded in self-confidence and independent habits of mind.

The eventual vote was unanimous for an ongoing organization to secure political education and improved legislation in the shortest possible time. The new organization was to be firmly nonpartisan, though there was debate about the implications of this stance. Some felt "independence of mind" required eschewing party affiliation; but more favored active entry into party work, with all this implied of loyalty and responsibility. Catt was confident they were strong enough to avoid succumbing to "party sophistries," and that those with a natural bent for politics would make their voices heard within the parties as representatives of the new voters.

The Victory Convention, meeting in Chicago's La Salle Hotel in February 1920, brought together a remarkable assembly of women: presidents of women's organizations, college presidents, scholars, doctors, lawyers, social workers, teachers, directors of settlement houses, society leaders, philanthropists, wives of men eminent in political and business life, and plain housewives. They were presiding, as Catt told them, over "a mighty experiment."[10] The Anthony amendment was not yet part of the Constitution, but hopes were high, and the mood was exuberant.

Catt's final address reminded the delegates that "the real struggle for emancipation is yet to be won . . . on the inside of the political parties." She outlined the prospect:

> Perhaps, when you enter the party . . . you will find yourselves in a sort of political penumbra where most of the men are. These men will be glad to see you . . . you will be flattered . . . think how nice it is to be free at last . . . think how charming it is to be partisan; but if you stay longer . . . you will discover a little denser group . . . the umbra of the . . . party. You won't be so welcome there. Those are the people . . . planning the platforms and picking the candidates . . . that is the place to be. And if you . . . are active enough you will see something else—the real thing in the center, with the door locked tight . . . there is the engine that moves the wheels of your party machinery. . . . If you really want women's vote to count, make your way there.

The convention formally agreed to reconstitute NAWSA as the National League of Women Voters, and adopted a constitution and bylaws providing for a Washington headquarters and a four-member executive board comprising a chair, vice-chair, secretary, and treasurer.[11] From the ten names presented by a nominating committee, the delegates chose four: Maud Park, Edna Gellhorn, Marie Edwards, and Pattie Jacobs.[12] The new board members were asked to agree among themselves the office each would hold. None wanted to head the new organization, but after lengthy debate, Park was left with fewer excuses than the others—she had no family commitments, and lived closest to Washington. As she later recalled, she was "prevailed upon to accept the undesired office," and when she was introduced to the convention, "felt as if an avalanche of work had fallen" on her.[13]

While the distribution of offices was being decided, the delegates briefly debated and endorsed the programs of the standing committees—numbering more than sixty items. Margaret Robins, chairing the Committee on Women in Industry, won acceptance for all the protective labor legislation sought by the National Women's Trade Union League, of which she was president.[14] Pennybacker, head of the Committee on Child Welfare, and (besides being a Democratic Party activist) a past president of the General Federation of Women's Clubs, proposed a dozen items of social legislation, including what became the Sheppard-Towner Act of 1921. Catharine McCulloch's Committee on the Unification of Laws Concerning the Legal Status of Women ended its list of statutory discriminations requiring amendment with a demand for independent citizenship for women.[15] Mrs. Frederick Bagley's American Citizenship Committee concentrated on the electoral and educational reforms cited in Catt's speech to the Jubilee Convention. Mabel Costigan secured adoption of various consumers' demands, including tariff revision, antitrust law enforcement, municipally owned markets and utilities, and cooperatives.[16] Dr. Valeria Parker's program attacked the double standards of sex morality embodied in prostitution and vice-abatement laws.

Nor was this all. Delegates also passed a variety of resolutions from the floor. Several related to education: support for a federal department of education, an increase in teachers' salaries, vocational education, compulsory physical education, and an end to compulsory military training in schools. Two sought to defend freedom of speech and the press.[17] The resolution supporting entry to the League of Nations was sharply debated before passing. A final resolution, introduced by Mrs. John Pyle, South Dakota state league president and head of the Women's Division of the state Republican organization, and seconded by Harriet Upton, soon to be vice-chair of the GOP National Committee, offered aid to New York women in their fight against the reelection of Republican senator James W. Wadsworth, a diehard suffrage opponent; this passed unanimously.

The program scope and variety underlined the diverse character of the delegates. As presiding officer, Catt made no effort to direct the convention's course, believing that the infant body must find its own way, divorced from its parent. The result was "a kettle of eels," as Park later noted. With ratification still uncertain, there was a common interest intensely shared; yet discernible in the emotional atmosphere were many conflicting interests and concerns. How the organization would develop the cohesion essential for its survival was a problem at least partly understood by its new officers, but one still to be faced.

Several hundred women remained after the convention to attend the political education school Catt had organized to prepare a cadre of women to train the new voters in communities all over the country, once the amendment was secured. In eighteen sessions over six days, they heard lectures on the structure of government, the electoral process, and the functions of parties by Charles Merriam, P. Orman Ray, and Ernst Freund; interspersed were seminars on practical politics conducted by Catt, Park, Jane Addams, and others. Dozens of women were readied for the nationwide program of citizenship schools already planned for the weeks between ratification and the November elections.

Concurrent with the school, the League Executive Committee held its inaugural meeting, joined by the standing committee chairs, the seven regional directors, and several state presidents. The major problem facing them was the ambitious program adopted by the convention. The standing committees had worked independently, and, with one exception, none had considered means of reaching their goals. The hopelessness of satisfying such a mandate was evident. It was agreed that the leadership must assume executive responsibility for specific legislative projects, concentrating on what was feasible.

The bylaws were unclear about other matters—for example, the relation of the national standing committee heads to the national Board of Directors and to the state boards: where lay the appointive power?[18] Mabeth Paige of Minnesota sought clarification of the powers and duties of the regional directors, of whom she was one.[19] There was also the question of finance. NAWSA had underwritten the first year's budget. The budget for the coming year totaled $180,000; an appeal for subscriptions from convention delegates had produced promises of $50,000. But the bylaws made no provision for exacting payments. The suffrage association had relied on donations and large gifts, but such dependence appeared neither feasible nor desirable for the daughter organization. Catt had wanted a dues-paying requirement written into the bylaws. Marie Edwards, as treasurer, argued not only for members' dues but state assessments based on size of membership and ability to pay. Minnesota's president, Marguerite Wells, sought state quotas rather than national dues.[20] Resistance to these proposals came from state presidents who feared that most of their potential members would simply have little disposable pocket money.

The meeting also discussed the urgent need for a research department to help prepare public statements and educational materials on national issues. It was proposed that the women's colleges might act as "research laboratories"; Dean Virginia Gildersleeve of Barnard College and President Carey Thomas of Bryn Mawr had offered help. In fact, the national headquarters soon proved a lodestone attracting trained college women as staff researchers. In no area did the League develop sophisticated techniques more rapidly than in the preparation of materials in support of its program.

During the discussion of the standing committees, Pennybacker announced her resignation as chair of the Child Welfare Committee to devote her energies to Texas Democratic politics. She also proposed that the committee be abolished, since its work overlapped that of other organizations; all were aware that as past president of the GFWC, she foresaw rivalry between the League and this body.[21] Margaret Robins chose this moment to state that she was resigning from the Committee on Women in Industry, acknowledging that she had assumed the chair to make certain of the inclusion of the NWTUL's own program in the League's agenda; she was too busy as NWTUL president, she said, to give further time to the League.

The action of these leaders underlined the problems inherent in the League's composite character, emphasizing the prime necessity for an autonomous structure capable of defining coherent purposes and programs. Pennybacker had struck at an especially vulnerable point. Child Welfare had the deepest roots and greatest appeal of all the social needs with which women had been involved; how could the League be denied usefulness in this field? On the other hand, protective labor legislation had far less intrinsic interest to rank-and-file members. The NWTUL was a relatively small, urban, middle-class organization with a settlement house base that had furnished some outstanding suffrage leaders; it had helped fix public attention on the exploitation of women and children in sweatshops, factories, and service industries, winning support for the principle of collective bargaining as well as for an extensive program of protective legislation.[22] Moreover, the concerns of labor were outside the experience of most early League members. It was under the persuasive leadership of Robins' successor, Mary McDowell,[23] and particularly after the National Woman's Party in 1921 introduced the equal rights amendment, which threatened all protective legislation, that the League became actively involved in correcting the economic inequalities suffered by women along with other forms of discrimination.

NOTES

1. Catt, *The Nation Calls* (New York: National Woman Suffrage Publishing Co., 1919). The phrases were quoted from President Wilson's speeches on behalf of the League of Nations, and convey a meaning quite lost today.

2. Mrs. Brooks, of Wichita, was representative of the community-oriented midwestern state leaders who dominated the last phase of the suffrage movement. Besides being president of the Kansas Suffrage Association, she chaired the Kansas Division of Women's Oversea Hospitals, the Kansas Women's Committee of the Council of National Defense, and the Council of Reconstruction, and was historian of the Kansas branch of the Colonial Dames.

3. Friendly editors on the *Christian Science Monitor*, the *St. Louis Post-Dispatch*, and the *New York Evening Post* emphasized instead the "novelty" and "independence" of the proposed organization, which likewise did not accurately convey Catt's conception of its role. See Peck, *Carrie Chapman Catt*, 309; and "Woman Suffrage Scrapbooks," Manuscript Division, Library of Congress, Washington, D.C.

4. *Woman Citizen*, 19 April 1919. At the Jubilee Convention, Catt had spoken rather of a five-year trial period to establish whether such a League might have a useful role to play; see Peck, *Carrie Chapman Catt*, 307.

5. The daughter of Mark Hanna, the redoubtable Republican leader and Ohio senator, and herself a veteran suffragist, her own extensive political experience made it difficult to realize how remote from the political world most women were, and how great their need to develop a political identity.

6. Mary Morrisson (1882–1969) was the daughter of civil service reformer William D. Foulke. A graduate of Bryn Mawr College, she rose to leadership in NAWSA after 1912; she was a member of the Catt Board in 1916 and, subsequently, a League founder. A woman of great intellectual distinction, with a sharp, logical mind that was excellent in debate, she became a lifelong League leader in Illinois and Connecticut. She was also an active Republican; a delegate to the 1920 convention, she seconded the nomination

of Herbert Hoover. See *Woman Citizen*, 11 December 1920, for her account of the founding of the Illinois League.

7. Mabel Costigan (1881–1947) and her husband, Edward, had been leaders in the Colorado Progressive Party. When President Wilson named him as a member of the first Tariff Commission in 1917, Mabel Costigan transferred her abundant energies to Washington. She became a leader in the D.C. Suffrage Association, president of the Consumers' League, and chaired NAWSA's Committee on Food Supply and Demand after 1919. An exceptionally able and forceful woman, she was a League founder and, as the first chair of the League's Committee on Food Supply and Demand, set the organization's goals in the economic field.

8. On June 20, 1919. League of Women Voters Papers, Minutes and Related Records, Ser. 2, Box 4, Manuscript Division, Library of Congress, Washington, D.C.

9. Account pieced together from reminiscences of Harriet Taylor Upton and Maud Wood Park, Arthur and Elizabeth Schlesinger Library on the History of Women in America, Radcliffe College.

10. Proceedings, Victory Convention, February 12–18, 1920. LWV Papers, LC. See also *Woman Citizen*, 21 February 1920.

11. NAWSA leaders were very conscious of the significance of handing over the keys to their "child and inheritor," whose "great task" would be to achieve "the aims and aspirations of women who had longed for, prayed for and fought for political freedom." The final resolution declared:

> WHEREAS, millions of women will become voters in 1920, and whereas the low standards of citizenship found among men clearly indicate the need of education in the principles and ideals of our government and methods of political procedures, therefore be it
> RESOLVED, that the National League of Women Voters be urged to make the political education of the new women voters (but not excluding men) its first duty in 1920.

After the first year, the chair and vice-chair offices were retitled president and vice-president respectively. The Executive Committee was soon to be expanded with the addition of a second and third vice-president; its role was to exercise executive responsibility in the periods between the thrice-yearly meetings of the national Board of Directors, which consisted of the same officers as well as the seven regional directors.

12. Catt's personal choice for chair was not among them; see "Reminiscences," Maud Wood Park Papers, files 694–700, Arthur and Elizabeth Schlesinger Library on the History of Women in America, Radcliffe College.

Maud Wood (1871–1935) was born in Boston. She took her degree from Radcliffe College in 1898, one of the first women to graduate summa cum laude. She had secretly married Boston architect Charles Park in 1897 and, after his death in 1904, divided her time between suffrage and settlement house work. A lecturer in economics and political science, she earned her living on the lecture circuit. Handsome, gracious, and tactful, she proved an excellent choice for the League's first president. Her papers formed the nucleus of the Woman's Rights Collection in the Schlesinger Library, Radcliffe College.

Edna Fischel Gellhorn (1878–1971) graduated from Bryn Mawr College. The daughter of a physician (and wife of another), she carried forward a tradition of community achievement in St. Louis established by her mother. An officer of the Missouri Suffrage

Association before joining the first League national board as vice-chair, she was a lifelong League leader at both state and national level.

Marie Stuart Edwards, a graduate of Smith College, was president of the Indiana Women's Franchise League before becoming first treasurer and later vice-president of the League at national level. An able businesswoman, her organizational skills were an indispensable asset.

Pattie Ruffner Jacobs (1875–1935), of Montgomery, Alabama, was the NAWSA auditor from 1916 to 1918, and was influential in holding together the Southern auxiliaries after key Southern leaders broke away from NAWSA in 1916 over the states' rights issue. Besides becoming the League's first national secretary, she also joined the Democratic National Committee the same year.

For further details of the careers of Park, Gellhorn, and Jacobs, see, respectively, Barbara Sicherman et al., eds., *Notable American Women: The Modern Period: A Biographical Dictionary* (Cambridge, Mass.: Harvard Univ. Press, Belknap Press, 1980), 268–70, 519–20; and James, James, and Boyer, *Notable American Women* 2: 266–67.

It had been Catt's hope that those who would assume leading roles within the new League would be drawn from among the younger, rising group of NAWSA leaders, rather than from its existing senior leadership. She herself was to turn her energies increasingly in other directions—initially to international woman suffrage work and then, after the mid–1920s, mainly to questions of world peace and disarmament; see Peck, *Carrie Chapman Catt*, 326 and pts. 6 and 7. Catt did, however, retain significant links with the League, and remained its honorary president until her death in 1947.

13. Park, "Reminiscences." That Park had remarried in 1908, to a New York theatrical agent, Robert Hunter, was known only to her closest friends.

14. Margaret Dreier Robins (1868–1945), suffrage leader, social reformer, and early member of the National Women's Trade Union League, was head of NAWSA's Committee on Women in Industry. A Progressive in 1912, she became a member of the Women's Division of the Republican National Committee in 1916. See Mary E. Dreier, *Margaret Dreier Robins: Her Life, Letters and Work* (New York: Island Press Cooperative, 1950); and also James, James, and Boyer, *Notable American Women* 3: 179–81.

15. Catharine Waugh McCulloch (1862–1945), lawyer and suffragist, was a Rockford Seminary friend of Jane Addams, a lifetime associate of the Hull-House group, and an outstanding expert on women's legal disabilities. As chair of the Committee on the Unification of Laws Concerning the Legal Status of Women, she laid the groundwork for the League's achievement in the removal of such disabilities between 1920 and 1932. See James, James, and Boyer, *Notable American Women* 2: 459–60.

16. Costigan became the League's first representative to appear before a congressional committee. Speaking on behalf of the National Consumers' League as well, she pressed for passage of legislation regulating the meat-packing industry before the Senate and House Agriculture committees; see *Woman Citizen*, 10 April 1920.

17. The United States was undergoing its first "Red scare." The Wilson administration—and notably Attorney General Mitchell Palmer—had reacted with a campaign against "subversives" that constituted a substantial attack on civil liberties.

18. A tempest had already been stirred when Catharine McCulloch appointed a Pennsylvania representative to her committee on women's legal status of whom the state board did not approve. It was decided that the directors of national standing committees would be appointed by the national board, while the heads of equivalent state-level bodies would be appointed by the state boards. The powers of those chairing national

committees were further defined by agreeing that copies of all their communications must be sent to state presidents and regional directors for information.

19. It was decided that the regional directors were primarily liaison officers, connecting links between the state boards and the national board, who would provide intelligence channels, shore up weak leagues, and undertake organizing work in underdeveloped regions. Like other officers, they would be unsalaried, but their traveling expenses would need to be met.

20. Wells conceived of the League as a relatively small organization capable of expanding to embrace large numbers on specific issues, then contracting when these had been dealt with. Born in Milwaukee in 1872, Marguerite Wells was a graduate of Smith College. A leader of the Minnesota suffrage movement, she was to be the League's third national president (1934–1944), and the last to have come out of the suffrage campaign.

21. This issue had surfaced as the Victory Convention had neared adjournment. Catt was informed that Alice Winter, the Federation's current president, was concerned about the League's intrusion into its own fields of interest. Catt brusquely advised finding a way to work together, and a resolution was quickly passed calling on the League to make its purposes "immediately clear to local groups," to form alliances with organizations doing similar work, and to set up a committee in Washington composed of representatives of the major women's organizations to coordinate activities—an initiative that was to lead to the creation of the Women's Joint Congressional Committee; see chap. 5, esp. n. 11. Despite efforts at cooperation at the national level, friction between the League and the General Federation remained a problem at the local level for several years.

22. On the NWTUL, see J. Stanley Lemons, *The Woman Citizen: Social Feminism in the 1920s* (Urbana: University of Illinois Press, 1973); and Philip S. Foner, *Women and the American Labor Movement: From Colonial Times to the Eve of World War I* (New York: Free Press, 1979), esp. chap. 16 and 17.

23. Mary E. McDowell (1854–1936) was director of the University Settlement in Chicago and a close associate of Jane Addams. Trained by Frances Willard in the young women's division of the Woman's Christian Temperance Union, she had been a founder of the NWTUL, and called herself a "social politician." She and Jane Addams persuaded President Theodore Roosevelt to appropriate federal money to investigate working conditions in the stockyards after the stockyard strike in 1904. She also furnished Upton Sinclair with material for *The Jungle* (1906), a novel that prompted Congress to pass the first Pure Food and Drug Act the same year. See Howard E. Wilson, *Mary McDowell, Neighbor* (Chicago: University of Chicago Press, 1928); and James, James, and Boyer, *Notable American Women* 2: 462–64.

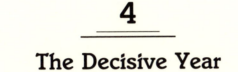

4

The Decisive Year

The fourteen months elapsing between the Victory Convention and the first convention of the National League of Women Voters was marked by a succession of events that tested the infant organization's viability. On May 14, 1920, it was announced that the League had opened its Washington headquarters, and was "destined to play an important part in the next few months" in promoting social legislation. A fortnight later, President Maud Park issued the first of a series of press releases stating the specific demands of organized women that the League would present at the approaching party presidential nominating conventions.

Thirteen platform planks, with carefully drafted supporting statements, had been winnowed from the program adopted at the Victory Convention as having primacy at the national level. Heading the list was the Sheppard-Towner bill for infant and maternal health. This was followed by calls for a constitutional amendment to abolish child labor, adequate funding for the Children's Bureau, a federal department of education, federal aid for combating illiteracy and raising teachers' salaries, compulsory civic education in the schools, federal regulation of food marketing and distribution, increased federal aid for home-economics training, women's representation on federal commissions dealing with women's work, the creation of a federal-state employment service including women's departments headed by qualified women, an end to discrimination against women in the civil service, continued funding for public education in sex hygiene, and independent citizenship for American-born women married to aliens as well as identical naturalization procedures for men and women.[1]

The decision to press forward with these initiatives, despite the fact that the Nineteenth Amendment was not yet ratified, demanded a forceful presentation of the planks before the respective resolutions committees at the party conventions. President Park led an impressive delegation of League officers and prominent Republican women to the Republican Convention in June. Despite considerable press attention, their impact was hardly satisfactory; only five of the thirteen were adopted, and only one of those was among the important "social justice" planks.[2] Two weeks after the disappointments in Chicago came the Democratic Convention in San Francisco. The hard-pressed Democrats were eager to woo potential voters, and endorsed all the proposals save that for a federal department of education. Park was invited to address the convention after the reading of the platform; she declined, but agreed to sit on the rostrum along with others who had appeared before the Resolutions Committee—a precedent-setting interpretation of the League's relation to the parties. Yet in reality, the League's moderately advanced social views found warm response in neither party. The change in public mood had been drastic; Progressive ideals now raised few echoes among the ruling powers.

After San Francisco came the final battle for ratification. By August 1920, some thirty-five states had accepted the Nineteenth Amendment, and hopes for the crucial thirty-sixth centered on Tennessee, a border state with a foot in both parties and a traditional cleavage within suffrage ranks over the states' rights issue.[3] The story of that hot summer's skirmishes in Nashville had all the shadings of a satire on American political mores, from low comedy to melodrama. Catt personally led the campaign. After the amendment quickly passed the Tennessee Senate, opponents made a strenuous effort to prevent a vote in the lower house, a handful finally exiling themselves to Alabama to deny a quorum; many in both parties indeed devoutly wished ratification could be postponed until after the elections. Finally, on August 18, the Tennessee assembly ratified with one vote to spare; on August 26, the Nineteenth Amendment was proclaimed part of the Constitution.

The bizarre close to the ratification struggle had generated immense press coverage. Never before, nor since, have women been so prominent on the political scene, so frequently in the headlines. A mass meeting held in Washington was attended by four thousand people, including many officeholders; when Catt returned to New York, she was met by Governor Alfred E. Smith and a regimental band. No other amendment to the Constitution had taken so long to secure, been resisted so implacably, or been so widely regarded as an event of historic significance when it was finally ratified. All of this took its inevitable toll. The wave of sanguine expectation swept the women along in its course.

Many suffrage leaders were soaring aloft on partisan pinions in the summer of 1920. Two of the four members of the national board—Marie Edwards (Republican) and Pattie Jacobs (Democrat)—were on national party campaign committees. At least a dozen state board officers held senior party posts, while many more were on advisory committees. Will Hays, GOP national committee chairman, assured Republican women that the "just rule for a political party is that the right of participation in the management of the party's affairs must be and remain equally sacred and sacredly equal." Notwithstanding his pledge, the New York Republican organization endorsed James W. Wadsworth for another Senate term, despite the warning of Mary Garrett Hay, the party's state vice-chair, that such an implacable foe of their enfranchisement was unacceptable to women. Forced to choose between being a rubber stamp and an independent "party woman," she resigned her post and organized an anti-Wadsworth committee made up of women's groups, labor unions, civic organizations, and the Anti-Saloon League.[4]

The letters exchanged among League leaders that summer were full of troubled questions. "I think that all the politicians dread a floating vote which can be . . . thrown from one party to the other," wrote Marie Edwards from the Republican national headquarters to Park.[5] Party leaders could not forgive avowedly Republican women for attempting to overthrow Wadsworth and Senator Frank Brandegee in Connecticut. From Texas came complaints over women being taught how to split their ballot to topple their ancient enemy, gubernatorial candidate Joseph Bailey—which they did. Harriet Upton, now vice-chair of the Republican National Committee, wrote Edwards of the awkward situation in St. Louis, where the newly organized League was seeking to defeat three controversial judges as a way of teaching the local GOP machine to offer better candidates. The League's "very future is at stake," Edwards replied, if this was to be the pattern of their behavior.[6]

Almost as troubling as the partisan friction among former allies was the disappointment of Republican League members over the party's treatment of their platform demands. Upton, Edwards, and Cornelia Pinchot pressed Will Hays to have Warren Harding amplify his views on their cherished concerns, especially the Sheppard-Towner bill. Hays responded by arranging a Social Justice Day, when a delegation of women, including Catt and the League's national board, journeyed to Marion, Ohio, to hear the candidate talk blandly of his warm support for Sheppard-Towner. Harding also endorsed the Women's Bureau and the Children's Bureau, and declared his enthusiasm for elevating education and welfare to cabinet status in a new department he referred to as "social welfare"; he thought a woman should head such a department, thus appearing to affirm his intention, if elected, to name a woman to his cabinet. On the League of Nations, however, he was silent.

If Harding's promises reassured the party faithful, they disappointed those, like Catt, who considered the League of Nations the crucial campaign issue. While avoiding a partisan stance earlier, Catt had made an extensive speaking tour in support of the League of Nations. With Harding's failure to define a clear stance on the League question, Catt concluded that the path toward international cooperation did not lie down the crooked lane of Republican ambiguities. Warning her Republican friends that she could stay silent no longer, she gave an interview to the press in Lincoln, Nebraska, in late October declaring her support for James Cox, the Democratic candidate.[7] For this "betrayal" of her neutrality, the Republicans never forgave her.

Then came the climactic event of the extraordinary year: the November elections, on which such expectations had focused. An estimated twenty million voters had been added to the electorate; yet less than half of those registered went to the polls as Harding was elected. There were numerous reasons for the turnout, and voter apathy characterized both sexes. But League leaders saw it as no less than a tragedy. The naïve confidence that millions shared their own desires had led to exaggerated hopes, enhanced by their own high visibility during the campaign; this was succeeded by a correspondingly exaggerated despair over the outcome. Shock waves of disappointment—at the turnout and paucity of women elected to office—and the public criticism of the League by partisan women washed over the organization, and would have capsized a frailer craft.[8] Yet the experience, if dismaying, only confirmed their sense of the need for an organization of women voters, to preserve their solidarity until they could reassess their objectives.

In an effort to correct misunderstandings, President Park prepared answers to "Five Crucial Questions," which the *Woman Citizen* published in late November and the League thereafter issued in thousands of copies.[9] Realistic self-appraisal was the prime order of business at a somber November board meeting. With its first major deposit of experience, the League had to set about reconstructing its self-image as representing all women. While there was concern over ways to increase the number of successful women candidates at all levels and to secure real representation for women within the parties, the realities of the narrow stage on which the League could perform were reflected in the sharp discussion of the problems inherent in maintaining a nonpartisan image when leading members and officers had taken part in such bitter statewide campaigns as those in New York, Missouri, and Texas (and numerous local campaigns from which reports were trickling in).

Some political leaders had clearly been expecting that women would play a role commensurate with their numbers, and had promised to establish the principle of fifty-fifty representation within the party organizations. Both parties had done so at the national level, where it least mattered. For the Republicans, however, the conciliatory promises of Will Hays had only been honored in a few states where the suffrage organization was large and prestigious. The Democrats had named over a hundred women to the San Francisco convention, though mainly as alternate delegates and very few, as was quickly noted, from the pioneer suffrage states. The *Woman Citizen* had observed scornfully that women could not be satisfied with "places assigned to them because they are women"; changes in party structures had to be won to assure that women might gain on their own merits a voice in party councils corresponding to their political ambitions.

The national board empowered Marie Edwards, a senior Republican figure, to seek an explanation of what, to League leaders, was the party's underlying "hostile attitude"; likewise Elizabeth Hauser, to whom the Democrats were indebted, undertook to urge a more friendly approach in these quarters. Opposition from such sources "shows our value," said Mary Morrisson, but it also showed the parties' dismaying power to create a distorted image that might crush the life out of the infant League. It was agreed that a careful statement of national policy on partisan activity should be presented to the 1921 convention;[10] and that state and local league presidents should "be advised" to avoid partisan commitments.[11]

If the tangle of circumstances surrounding the elections forced on the League leadership a clarification of nonpartisanship, it also laid the groundwork for what became a searching inquiry as to their basic purpose. Following the elections, Catt wrote each board member suggesting that the next convention eliminate "women" from their title and, with suggestive overtones of a third party, invite progressive-minded men to join in formulating "an independent political policy for the nation."[12] Catt brought the matter up again at a joint session of the League and NAWSA boards several weeks later. The League's future was a matter of grave concern to her; while it must work out its own destiny, she felt impelled to observe that it lacked an outstanding objective: "Nobody knows what it stands for." The obvious remedy was to define a primary aim, curtail the program and perhaps abandon some of the standing committees.[13] In short, the League should focus its energies on political education and the improvement of political institutions.

Catt had a broad, even inspiring vision of women collectively serving as an agency to revitalize the country's political life. She conceived of the League as an organization to train women in civic competence, and to win for them a representative share in the shaping and execution of public policies; instead of pursuing legislative panaceas for social ills, they should gradually improve the political society by participating in its governance. League leaders shared her desire to translate statutory equality into psychological reality with the least friction in the shortest possible time; but the younger women knew that her vision plunged beyond the feasible. In any case, the Victory Convention had phrased a controlling idea of larger scope; the League's purpose was to be dual: "Foster education in citizenship and support improved legislation." This was interpreted to mean—in a succinct statement of its guiding ideology—that the League was to be an organization of women to help "develop the woman citizen into an intelligent and self-directing voter and to turn her vote toward constructive social ends."[14]

Criticism similar to Catt's came from Lucy Miller, president of the Pennsylvania League, one of the most effective of the new state organizations. Miller pressed for state autonomy over program and policy, and a program limited to women's political education. The League's dual aims, she argued, were conflicting. Fostering political education implied reaching out for the greatest possible membership. If, at the same time, they insisted on pursuing politically controversial legislation, the results would inevitably narrow the League's membership base.

The result of Catt's discontent and Miller's criticisms was the appointment of a committee, headed by Katharine Ludington, to explore the problems of fashioning consensus over the League's dual role as this affected both program and policy, and to report on ways of "simplifying, coordinating and emphasizing advance consideration and study of the program and improving convention procedures"—a large and unfocused assignment, but one entrusted to an able and imaginative group of women.[15] There was general recognition that the program did not receive sufficient consideration before adoption, and also that League aims must be clarified and persuasively interpreted. Subsequently called the Committee on the Simplification of the Program, it became the longest enduring and most important of all the committees that shaped the League's character.

The real issue between Pennsylvania and the national board, however, had been the division of power, in turn underlining the League's problems in superseding a body that had been only a loose federation of state auxiliaries. NAWSA conventions had resembled pure democracies, incapable of coping with conflicting interests and local passions save by schism. Catt had wrestled with the difficulties of a powerless NAWSA board, and only succeeded in forging a centralized authority in 1916 by unusually forceful leadership and the bonding effects of a passionately felt common purpose. Skilled in statecraft, Catt had adroitly implemented her resolve to establish a continuing organization, and had proposed a continuance of the standing committees to furnish incentives for sustaining the coalition after ratification by providing for the ongoing interplay of competing interests. She also showed foresight in dividing the nation into seven regions to cushion the divisive effects of cultural differences and supply a source of liaison between the national board and state leagues until a conception of shared purpose developed.

Park spent much time during the first year of her presidency in travel and lecturing. Lacking a private income but determined to fix the precedent that no League officer should receive compensation for her services, she felt compelled to carry out lecture engagements already contracted for, and made it her aim to "carry Congress to the women." Her audiences heard lucid explanations of the way bills were passed; she aroused their interest in legislative issues—made them taste the tariff in their tea, and taught them not to be surprised that those legislators who had opposed suffrage also opposed protective legislation for women and children. She communicated her own conviction that a new political day would dawn when women began to perceive how their own concerns were related to the political process. In the course of her journeys she visited infant leagues and renewed their involvement, conveying her own sense of the significance of their work. Her vigor and warmth of personality had a restorative effect on many whose enthusiasm was flagging.

The records of Park's trips contain ample evidence of the difficulties the young League faced. Hostile pressures were exerted by the parties at state and local levels, and through the parties by a variety of business interests. What was the justification for this organization? Why insulate the women from the parties?

Moreover, in areas in the Midwest and South where the General Federation of Women's Clubs had deep roots, the League's efforts were viewed coldly; no essential dissimilarity was seen between what the League proposed and what the General Federation was already doing.

The expectation that state and local suffrage associations would speedily reconstitute themselves as leagues had been a large one. Fulfillment depended on the vigor of the leadership and the degree of political tension the long struggle had engendered. States where suffrage had been vigorously opposed saw the appearance of infant leagues in sturdy health. Their leaders had acquired political experience, and their opponents were readily identifiable. These were mainly the urban states east of the Mississippi.

Pennsylvania had carried over its structure, leadership, and membership virtually intact from NAWSA—in fact the only state to do so; and had a claimed membership of 25,000.[16] The activism of the New York City League marked it as a prototype of the organization envisaged by Catt. Its leaders held office in the League and also in the executive ranks of the parties. They pressed for fifty-fifty representation for women in party management and sought to secure the nomination of women to run for public office (though their candidates in 1920 were all defeated). The emphasis placed on "direct action"—compiling and distributing data on candidates records, holding public meetings for candidates, and developing an active speakers' bureau—underscored the realization that the most available points of access to the political process were in the community and precinct. Their representatives attended every meeting of the New York City Board of Aldermen and the state legislature. At the state level, Eleanor Roosevelt became the chief legislative observer, and with the aid of Elizabeth Read, a lawyer, she analyzed every major piece of state legislation in the 1921 session—an innovation widely noted and eventually adopted by other Leagues.[17]

In neighboring New Jersey, suffragists also had reformed as a strong League. And in Connecticut, with leaders of the caliber of Katharine Ludington and a large pool of experienced activists, the League was developing methods of work that were to serve as a model for other states. Connecticut's urban, compact nature permitted an integrated state organization and well-staffed headquarters. In 1921 the state league published a handbook *The Successful Conduct of a Local League*, which was the precursor of the now standard *Local President's Handbook*. It also issued a *Legislation Bulletin* summarizing and evaluating the 1921 state legislative session. The national board placed an observer in the Connecticut state office to get ideas on how state leagues could best be organized.

Along with Missouri, the states bordering the Great Lakes promptly transformed their suffrage associations into leagues under the spur of energetic leadership. Cities like St. Louis, Chicago, Detroit, Cleveland, and others had been staging areas for municipal reform movements, and were still charged with moral electricity. Out of this atmosphere came nearly a score of national board members in the first decade, including Park's successor, Belle Sherwin.

On the other hand, Louisiana remained unorganized, and likewise Wyoming, ironically the first enfranchised state. In seventeen largely rural states, League organizations were reportedly struggling to survive; farmers' wives lacked mobility and small-town women were involved in other organizations. Nevada and Utah had fine state boards but almost no members. In Kansas Mrs. Charles Brooks organized a promising state league, but only Lawrence, Emporia, and Wichita survived the first years.[18] In the Dakotas, officers had played dual roles in the League and on party committees, with frustrating consequences. In Colorado, two suffrage bodies claimed to be the state league, while in Montana there were paralyzing divisions between radical and conservative leadership factions. Altogether, organization was claimed in forty-six states, but hope outdistanced the reality in more than a third.

NOTES

1. League of Women Voters, *A Woman's Platform Presented to the Political Parties* (Washington, D.C. [1920]). A fourteenth plank, calling for the creation of a Women's Bureau in the Department of Labor, became unnecessary when Congress passed legislation establishing this agency in June 1920.

2. See the report by Anna S. Richardson, *New York Times*, 11 July 1920.

3. The ratification struggle in Tennessee is explored in several illuminating accounts; see Catt and Shuler, *Woman Suffrage and Politics*, chap. 30; Peck, *Carrie Chapman Catt*, 320–43; and A. Elizabeth Taylor, *The Woman Suffrage Movement in Tennessee* (New York: Bookman Associates, 1957), chap. 7.

4. The campaign was to prove a bitter one. Wadsworth was reelected in November, though running half-a-million votes behind Warren Harding in New York. His opponents were not finished with Wadsworth, however; in 1926 a similar coalition defeated him.

5. Marie Edwards to Maud Wood Park, October 1920. LWV Papers, Ser. 2, Box 4, LC.

6. Vendettas against the political machines occurred elsewhere in 1920, though on a smaller scale. Few were successful, but no one should have been surprised—least of all the politicians—in view of the reservoir of resentment that had been filling up for decades. Such vindictive behavior, however, was not to characterize the League again.

7. *Lincoln Sunday Star*, 23 October 1920. Her declaration was, given its timing, unquestionably the "bombshell" the press called it.

8. Not the least disappointing had been the defeat in New York of two handpicked Democratic candidates, Harriet May Mills and Bertha Rembaugh. Of the eight women who had run for Congress, only the acerbic antifeminist Alice Robertson of Oklahoma won; she remained a sore trial during her two-year incumbency, for she consistently opposed women's issues (including the Sheppard-Towner bill). For her biography, see James, James, and Boyer, *Notable American Women* 3: 177–78.

9. *Woman Citizen*, 24 November 1920. Park hoped to reassure the politicians that the League did not intend to become a separate political bloc, but rather saw its role as supplementary to that of the parties; members would be urged to join political parties and work "inside party lines" to win acceptance for League-supported measures. As to other women's and civic associations, Park admitted that the League might duplicate their concerns in part, but stressed that no other organization was devoting its energies exclusively to education in citizenship and the interests of women as voting citizens.

10. In the meantime Park reported her seemingly contradictory decision to deny official support for the appointment of their mutual friend, Pauline Goldmark, to the new Railway Commission Board, despite strong pressure from Florence Kelley and others. Such endorsements, however worthy the candidate, could not become the policy of the national board, she argued, if it was to sustain a nonpartisan image for the League. Not yet had the distinction been made between supporting individual women being considered for appointive office and partisan support for a political party or a person running for office.

11. Other board members at these levels remained free to assume partisan roles if they deemed it expedient.

12. Catt-Park correspondence, LWV Papers, Ser. 2, Box 4, LC.

13. The Committee on the Unification of Laws Concerning the Legal Status of Women, she suggested, could be turned over to the party women, since civil disabilities could be most easily removed by women working inside the parties; the child-welfare subject should be turned back to the General Federation of Women's Clubs, and women in industry to the labor unions; social hygiene, she thought, could be abandoned.

14. Both statements are taken from early League publications: respectively, *The National League of Women Voters: What It Is, Why It Is, How It Works* (Washington, D.C. [1920]); and *Principles and Policy of the National League of Women Voters* (Washington, D.C. [1920]). The latter pamphlet added that the League believed that women "should study public questions, not as good citizens only, but as WOMEN citizens; that there are matters for which women are peculiarly responsible; and that organization of women is necessary in order to give these matters the emphasis in government that their importance demands."

15. LWV Papers, Ser. 2, Box 18, LC. In naming Ludington as chair, Park was acknowledging the considerable gifts of this Connecticut League leader, one of the small group who were the foundation pillars of the League. Almost single-handedly, Ludington secured the League's financial base during its early years, though of parallel importance was her service in moulding the League's public image through her successive interpretations of its principles, policies, and educational aims.

16. If the largest state league in numbers and influence, it was already deviant, and destined to become more so. Its leaders, Lucy Miller and her sister, Eliza Smith, of Allegheny County (Pittsburgh), sought to perpetuate the independence of the suffrage auxiliaries, providing the national board with organizational problems for years to come.

17. See Joseph P. Lash, *Eleanor and Franklin: The Story of Their Relationship Based on Eleanor Roosevelt's Private Papers* (New York: W. W. Norton, 1971), 260–62.

18. The success in Lawrence illustrated a pattern that was to be reaffirmed elsewhere: academic communities offered fertile ground for local leagues. The failure in Topeka underlined what became another truism: the political environment in state capitals did not provide optimum conditions for new leagues.

5

Possibilities, Hopes, Dreams

The announcement of the League of Women Voters' first annual convention was sent to groups representing two million women, and confidently referred to the "exalting and holy crusade" that had endowed women with "power." "How best shall we use this power to become a vital . . . force in our community?" it asked. "How best to continue the work of educating a conscientious, well-informed electorate?" When pressed by journalists to spell out the League's intentions, President Park had indicated that several courses were open. They could use their power directly by training women for their citizens' function and by pressing for "needed legislation." Indirect measures were also available—for example, spreading knowledge of the "great lacks in our social structure"; the technique of lodging uncomfortable facts in the public consciousness was one in which they were skilled. She saw many opportunities to improve local and state laws relating to the schools, public health and welfare, elections, and local government; eventually, women would "humanize political activity."[1]

As the 1921 convention approached, the *Woman Citizen* had solicited the views of congressmen on the new organization.[2] Most who responded had been suffrage advocates, and all anticipated that women would inject a new note in politics. Senator Morris Sheppard (Tex.) voiced the view of several that there was "a distinct woman's interest, just as there [was] a manufacturer's interest or a farmer's interest," though "there [would] always be other interests and objectives to drown the voices of women." Congressman George Tinkham (Mass.) viewed welfare issues as generally nonpartisan, and said it was good to see "nonpartisan women" supporting them; Senator Joseph Ransdell (La.) also approved their nonpartisan policy. Senator Miles Poindexter (Wash.), however, observed acidly that special legislation for women and children was "class legislation," and unjustifiable unless it benefited everyone. Senators Charles Curtis and Arthur Capper of Kansas accepted the League's role as "supplementary," but urged women to retain their partisan ties; while Utah's Reed Smoot thought the difficulties in the path of a nonpartisan but avowedly political organization almost insuperable.

Critical doubts in any quarter regarding the League's role only sharpened the painful soul-searching that continued among leaders over both aims and responsibilities. They were aware of a certain pharisaism in the concept of nonpartisanship, giving rise as it did to the image of the unattached citizen. "To wish political ends is to wish political means," they were fond of saying; and undoubtedly the political parties were the indispensable means for concerted political action. Yet their first year's experience had shown how difficult it was to wear the armor of party ideology and still bear the shield of independence. As was evident in the discussions at the preconvention board meeting, a growing conviction of the practical limitations of their political goals warned them to tread warily until they had attained more competence.

Nearly a thousand delegates from forty-six states and representatives from nine women's organizations attended the six-day convention in Cleveland. Park's presidential address candidly reviewed their difficulties.[3] Reaffirming their faith in the power of the ballot offered no answers to the tangled problems of finance, or of creating administrative machinery, allocating responsibilities, dealing with internal differences over the program, moderating the hostility of the parties, establishing cooperative links with other interest groups (especially those which saw no need for their existence), and pressing toward their legislative goals. After fourteen months work, the fruits of their pursuit of federal legislation had been hardly impressive. The League was criticized for supporting "costly" and "interventionist" measures. Their efforts to train voters were viewed as an invasion of the parties' prerogatives. Their desire to inform themselves of candidates' qualifications was called "pestering."

The various state reports proved a gloss on Park's speech. True, leagues in North and South Carolina had wrested from their legislatures their initial demand: raising the age of consent from ten to fourteen years (the South Carolina women had been barred from the debate since the subject was not "fit for ladies' ears"). North Dakota and New Jersey had won jury service for women, and in both the Dakotas and Iowa campaigns to introduce compulsory education had succeeded. But the new state leagues were also facing determined opposition. Maryland reported their efforts frustrated by litigation testing the validity of the Nineteenth Amendment. In Delaware women had been prevented from registering for the 1920 party primaries; when the League drew up a list of legislative demands and sent these to the legislators asking their views, the Delaware legislature had passed a law making it illegal to "intimidate" candidates and legislators with questionnaires. The New York League, having seen the defeat of a long list of "desired bills," declared that their goal was "the political regeneration of the state"; so likewise did Minnesota.

Pennsylvania's report struck a different note, and opened the convention's major policy debate. Backed by a delegation of forty-eight, Lucy Miller announced that political education would be their primary task. Sustaining a large membership ruled out the promotion of controversial legislation. Her league had concentrated on a single bill to raise teachers' salaries and a campaign to elect women to school boards. They had successfully pursued selective goals; New York and Minnesota, with their lengthy agenda, had won nothing. By putting its own construction on the League's stated aims, Pennsylvania raised in concrete form the question of how far states were free to act, or not act, on the national program. What degree of independence could be tolerated in a national organization desiring to speak with one voice on national issues?

In reporting the work of the special committee on aims and methods, Katharine Ludington had anticipated the Miller challenge by proposing that priority be given to political education; the need was for a steady increase in members capable of the disciplined activity necessary for the achievement of legislative goals. Following Miller's comments, Marie Edwards offered further conciliatory suggestions that the avenues to building state leagues not be restricted; but she reminded Miller that new members were being recruited through shared concern over important public issues as well as through citizenship schools, and rejected her assumption that the League had to choose between being a pressure group or a civic organization. Others sought to provide a suitable balance between working for legislation "along the lines of women's interests" and developing a better method of adopting the program, reflecting a widely shared impulse to resolve the dilemma by focusing discussion on the program itself.

Catt had listened with seeming patience to the state and committee reports. When it came time for her report on the Election Laws and Methods Committee, she said simply that it had not yet been organized. There were too few who had the expert knowledge necessary, though in her view the electoral process was the key point of access to the political stage. She suggested casually, as if an afterthought, that they drop the word "women" and become a League of Voters: "The men will be experienced and the women interested." Lashing out at the parties, she declared that "there must be a revolution in every aspect of the electoral system." None of their reports of legislative achievements, she added, had related to the "malfunctioning of their local and state government."

Catt's intervention caused the session to do an about-face in laying homage at their old leader's feet. Several followed in Miller's wake in arguing for a program designed to get political power rather than social reform; they had devoted their time, one said, to "binding up the scratches when the body politic was being devoured by cancer." Mary Morrisson brought the ship back on course:

> This country is in a state of tragic indecision . . . and yet I think there is a profound hunger in the souls of most people . . . for an intelligent attempt to make our government function; to help develop a constructive program to put us back on the path of progress. The League of Women Voters has such a program, and if we believe in that program passionately . . . we will

go forward with the old crusading spirit . . . that we are working . . . to make the country worthwhile.

In the wake of these discussions, the convention accepted Catt's proposal that her Committee on Election Laws and Methods be replaced by a more broadly focused Department of Efficiency in Government. Steps were also taken to revise the League's bylaws to straighten out lines of authority and improve the method of program adoption. The practice of introducing resolutions from the convention floor on substantive issues was eliminated. Revisions also defined the degree to which the national program was binding on state leagues; in the future they would not be required to actively support a program item, but they might not oppose it.[4] Yet the actual presentation of the program in 1921, despite the urgent directive of the national board, did not show a great advance over 1920, either in clarity or uniformity of style. The distinction between affirmation of a cherished principle and endorsement of a course of action remained blurred, as did also the difference between endorsement of a specific legislative proposal and active support of such a proposal.

Among the speeches interspersing the convention's working sessions was a moving indictment of the horrors of war by Will Irwin, a well-known war correspondent. Catt was to follow with a talk on the psychological aspects of politics; but so stirred was she by Irwin's remarks that she dramatically tore up her prepared text and made an extemporaneous plea for an all-out campaign for peace. Since the politicians had rejected the League of Nations, new solutions would have to be fashioned. "The women in this room can do this thing," she cried. "Let us do it."[5] Thus the League entered the field of foreign policy formation, destined to be among the most fruitful of its intellectual dominions. So aroused were the delegates that the convention reaffirmed the strong resolution passed by the Victory Convention calling for a reduction of armaments and an end to military training in the schools, and gave overwhelming approval to the creation of a Special Committee on the Reduction of Armaments, which in 1922 became the permanent Committee on International Cooperation to Prevent War (acquiring departmental status the following year).

After the convention, Park called on President Harding to inform him of the delegates' action and remind him of his campaign promises. At the same time, Elizabeth Hauser, the new committee's chair, began energetically organizing public meetings to elicit support for the amendment that Senator William Borah (Idaho) had offered to the current naval appropriations bill calling for a naval conference on the limitation of armaments. By June Congress had approved the amendment, Hauser's improvised campaign marking the League's initial public effort to influence foreign policy.

In August, Park led a League delegation to Harding's office to formally request recognition of women as "an integral part of government" (and to balance military representatives) in his selection of U.S. representatives for the conference on naval armaments which the administration had decided to convene in

Washington in November. Harding agreed that "the influence and intuition of women" should be utilized, and promised to name qualified women to the advisory committee of the delegation—a promise he kept by appointing four senior Republican women.[6]

Another event of this fateful year requires mention. The militantly suffragist National Woman's Party had viewed winning the vote as only a "tiny step" toward complete equality—which, indeed, it was. After initial uncertainty over its aims following the Nineteenth Amendment's ratification, the NWP early in 1921 called for concerted action to eliminate state and federal legislation imposing legal disabilities on women; by November this program had sharpened to a demand for a federal equal rights amendment that would level all distinctions in law between men and women. The prospect of such an amendment alarmed women's groups seeking protective legislation for working women.[7] Park had an "unproductive" interview with the NWP leader, Alice Paul, in the autumn, and in early December saw her again, accompanied by Marie Edwards, Florence Kelley of the National Consumers' League, Lida Hafford of the General Federation of Women's Clubs, Lenna Yost of the Woman's Christian Temperance Union, and Ethel Smith of the National Women's Trade Union League.[8] Despite Park's attempts to persuade her to phrase the proposal so that protective legislation might be exempt, Paul remained adamant; her party would not yield its demand for blanket statutory equality. Protective legislation was an implicit "recognition of the inferiority of women," Paul maintained; rather than restricting their freedom of contract to protect them in their weakness, women in industrial employment should be encouraged to strengthen their capacities by competing freely in the labor market with men.[9]

The League board debated actively whether to oppose an equal rights amendment if it were introduced. The issue had been adopted "for study" at the Cleveland convention, and the 1922 convention was to resolve to reject the proposal, a position at that time shared by most women's organizations. Some had believed a compromise might be achieved in the shape of state equal rights amendments, especially in the South, where legal disabilities on women were extreme. State leagues were meanwhile encouraged to accelerate their study of state codes so that legislative remedies for specific disabilities might be proposed, and then to work with vigor for their adoption; in the long run, it was felt, this strategy might prove more feasible than running headlong into both law and custom with a blanket demand for juridical equality.

The first major federal legislative victory for organized women after ratification was the passage of the Sheppard-Towner Maternity- and Infancy-Protection Act in November 1921. The decision to single this out as the first legislative target had been made at a national board meeting held between the presidential nominating conventions in June 1920.[10] The final NAWSA convention had left the League the responsibility for bringing together women's organizations to work for legislation in which they shared an interest. This was a task ideally suited to Park's diplomatic gifts, and she summoned the heads of major women's organizations to a meeting in Washington in November 1920. Ten responded, and the Women's Joint Congressional Committee (WJCC) was established, with Park as chair.[11]

Park promptly organized a subcommittee of the WJCC, with Florence Kelley as head, to coordinate a major congressional campaign for the bill; all WJCC members joined.[12] The League had already pressed the parties to promise support for the measure at their national conventions, and Park asked the state league presidents to send a letter to all congressional candidates asking their stand. After the inauguration, President Harding was treated to some plain talking by Harriet Upton and, acting on his campaign pledge, he dispatched a special message to Congress—timed to coincide with the Cleveland convention—supporting the bill's passage. Despite an intensive lobbying effort and a major campaign to elicit grass-roots backing, strong opposition delayed final approval by the House of Representatives until November.

In many respects the Sheppard-Towner Act involved no great concessions either of funds or of principles; and in the light of Children's Bureau surveys showing maternal and infant mortality rates that were considerably higher than in most European countries, it seemed as sensible as it was morally justified. The law was an enabling act that provided for federal-state cooperation through matching grants for the purpose of promoting maternal and infant hygiene. An annual appropriation of slightly over $1 million was authorized for five years, not more than $50,000 of which was to be spent annually by the Children's Bureau on administration. The states themselves would carry out work under the act, but their plans and budgets were to be approved by a federal board composed of the director of the Children's Bureau, the surgeon-general, and the director of the Bureau of Education.

Though the principle of federal aid for the states had become firmly grounded since the 1860s, the act clearly represented a significant extension of federal involvement into the sphere of social welfare, traditionally a preserve of the states and local communities (or of private charities). Moreover, since its introduction in 1911, the matching-grant formula—entailing an obligation by participating states to achieve specific, nationally defined goals as well as federal supervision of the disposition of their grants—had provoked mounting concern over federal encroachment upon state responsibilities. When the attempt was made in 1926 to extend the act's period of authorization, its opponents were able to impose a crippling amendment that continued federal funding until 1929, but then terminated the act itself.

If the Sheppard-Towner Act was significant as a constitutional landmark, it was also to have considerable educative value to the League during its years in force. The League's collective sense of responsibility for the act was evidenced in the painstaking effort to see it properly implemented. Soon after its passage, Dorothy Brown, the Child Welfare chair, wrote all state presidents outlining a program of action: first winning the cooperation of state health officials, making a survey of hospital and medical facilities at the community level, and then holding League meetings to familiarize the public with the act's provisions; with these steps taken, they were to bring pressure on the state legislatures from all angles to ensure appropriation of the matching grant. In emphasizing the League's role both as mediator and "public educator," these instructions were revelatory of incipient procedures that gradually became institutionalized as time confirmed their value.

Few reports in the League records offer more interesting reading than those detailing the experience with the enforcement of this act. Altogether forty-four states took advantage of the federal funds for maternal and child health, but not all did so to equal effect. Some states used only a fraction of the funding available, while others required constant public pressure to assure even moderately effective administration; especially painful to League activists were reports of official hostility directed toward woman doctors attracted to public health jobs under the act. From 1922 until 1930, every League convention echoed concern over the Sheppard-Towner Act. It was the first legislative achievement that provided in Jane Addams' phrase, "education by the current event," spelling the difference between profound commitment and a superficial concern. This commitment spilled over into other areas relating to children—health, education, child labor, judicial treatment—and constituted the bulk of the League's work at the community level during the first decade.

NOTES

1. *Cleveland Journal*, 10 April 1921.

2. *Woman Citizen*, 8 January 1921.

3. Proceedings, Cleveland Convention, April 11–18, 1921. LWV Papers, Minutes and Related Records, LC. Unless otherwise noted, the Proceedings furnish the substance of this chapter.

4. The Ludington committee had addressed both these concerns in its report, conceding that there had been too little time for deliberation on the program at the 1920 convention—with the result that what had been adopted was the program "of the Convention rather than that of the League of Women Voters"—and also that the national board had no power to coerce the states over policy; on the other hand, it had suggested, while state leagues would have freedom to choose state programs, that adopted by the national convention was a "national program," and therefore obligatory, though the meaning of "obligatory" would have to be tested by experience.

5. Quoted in League of Women Voters, *Ten Years of Growth*, by Belle Sherwin (Washington, D.C., 1930) 5; for a fuller account of Catt's speech, see Peck, *Carrie Chapman Catt*, 406–8.

6. LWV Papers, Ser. 2, Box 7, LC. To the fury of League leaders, the maverick congresswoman Alice Robertson had called on Harding the day before their interview, and issued a statement that her advice had been sought on women's representation at the conference, and that she had to acknowledge that no women possessed the qualifications.

Of those Harding appointed, three had been prominent in the suffrage movement and one, Katherine P. Edson, had subsequent League associations that included service on the national board in 1932–33, after her retirement from the California Industrial Welfare Commission.

7. Of particular concern in this period was the use of legislation to improve women's wage levels, limit hours of work, and restrict their recruitment for night work or jobs considered unhealthy for women employees.

8. LWV Papers, Ser. 2, Box 6, LC.

9. Early drafts of the amendment had in fact included a clause exempting protective legislation; but, with lack of agreement with other women's organizations over its wording, this had been dropped. Florence Kelley, who had been a member of the NWP's National Council, had by now broken with the NWP over the issue.

10. This program was initially recommended by Julia Lathrop, head of the Children's Bureau, in 1917; the original bill was introduced in Congress in 1918 by Jeannette Rankin.

11. Park's main coup had been to get the GFWC's president to cooperate with her in a statement of intention, expressing the belief that the two organizations should work together without friction or duplication. This was sent to all branches of both groups. With a membership that varied over time, the WJCC quickly established itself as a highly effective lobbying agency. Any federal bill supported by at least three (subsequently five) members became the responsibility of a subcommittee, which was to elect its own officers, plan and finance its own strategy, and dissolve when the work was finished. A useful account of the WJCC may be found in Lemons, *Woman Citizen*, 55–58.

12. LWV Papers, Ser. 2, Box 7, LC. See also Lemons, *The Woman Citizen*, 153–80, and "The Sheppard-Towner Act: Progressivism in the 1920s," *Journal of American History* 55 (March 1969) 776–86.

6

The Pan-American Convention

The idea of broadening the base of the League's third annual convention by inviting delegates from the member countries of the Pan-American Union is traceable to Lavinia Engle, a young feminist from Maryland's Montgomery County. She was encouraged to promote the idea by a handful of Baltimore League members, who raised a substantial sum of money with the help of the Baltimore Board of Trade. The time for planning was short, but Helen Gardener won the cooperation of Dr. Leo Rowe, director of the Pan-American Union, and he in turn gained the support of Secretary of State Charles Evans Hughes by pointing out the diplomatic value of such a gesture at a time of strained relations with Mexico.[1] As president, Maud Park had doubted the plan's practicality until Secretary Hughes had been won over, and Carrie Chapman Catt was at first reluctant to provide financial support from the Leslie Commission. Nonetheless, the ambitious affair proved a success.[2]

The League issued a convention call to its own membership to gather first in Baltimore and then Washington for ten days of conferences and special events; delegates from twenty Latin American states and Canada attended. The keynote was friendly cooperation among the women of the Americas toward feminist goals, though feminism was little developed in the South American states; in none were women fully enfranchised. The fillip given to feminism in South America by the undertaking's success persuaded Catt that a permanent Pan-American women's organization could be formed, with the League as a nucleus—an idea which later materialized, though in a somewhat different form, in the Inter-American Union of Women. The convention's real legatee, however, was to be the Carrie Chapman Catt Memorial Fund, now the Overseas Education Fund.

Interspersed among the special events were the working sessions of the League's third annual convention, the Pan-American activities furnishing welcome interludes in what was otherwise a difficult week. A national board meeting beforehand foreshadowed the debates lying ahead. As criticism of the Sheppard-Towner Act had not ceased with its passage, and was accompanied by complaints that women's welfare demands threatened to escalate the costs of public bureaucracy, the board chose not to support any forthcoming federal legislation, save for the bill for independent citizenship for married women, an important feminist grievance and, usefully, one requiring no appropriations. The meeting was enlivened by the presence of Catt, who urged the board to devote more convention time to discussing ways of increasing women's presence in public office at all levels of government. She also reopened earlier arguments that the League might enhance its impact by dropping "women" from its title and drawing in like-minded men. Her criticisms, if pragmatic in their thrust, revealed dissatisfaction with the profile the young organization was assuming.[3]

Park's presidential address to the convention struck a challenging note.[4] In the national tour of local and state leagues, she had seen a tapestry being woven by hundreds of hands in hundreds of small episodes. Yet, alluding to the welcome extended to the League by the National Municipal League—as a "big, dynamic organization with a vision and a fixed purpose to improve things"—she asked how far their achievements justified such praise. As for the suggestion that they join with men in a broad progressive bloc, she made her disagreement clear. If the League had a special purpose, such a membership base would not serve it; they must preserve the right to choose their own path, use their own techniques, and fashion their own political role. Men would continue to solve problems in terms of their "distinctive experience in the economic world," and women to believe that education, public health, and public morals should be "reckoned with quite as fully as . . . business interests." Nor did she deem it enough to concentrate solely on the machinery of government. "Efficient machinery may be a profound menace. . . . Despotisms have their own terrible kind of efficiency." No woman possessed civil competence until she comprehended public needs on the basis of her own independently acquired standards of social and economic justice. The League's entire program, therefore, was "training in citizenship."

The forceful speech was the board's answer both to Catt and Lucy Miller, and prompted an immediate response. Miller introduced a resolution to make the Department of Efficiency in Government the League's chief department, and to abolish the committees on Living Costs, Social Hygiene, Women in Industry, and Legal Status of Women as other organizations dealt with their subject matter. The League's long program was wasteful and irresponsible she argued; no one could be adequately informed on all subjects, and convention debates often lacked relevance. The Pennsylvania League had tried to voice this criticism in Chicago and again in Cleveland, and had failed. They had resolved not to implement such a committee structure themselves, but to concentrate instead on political work. They were carrying out Catt's intentions, and appeared alone in doing so.

A sprinkling of delegates voiced agreement, but the sturdier feminists among the League leaders argued that the social issues Miller rejected were the main incentives to membership for many women; their political education grew directly out of their concern for specific legislation. Belle Sherwin brought the majority view into focus by observing that she could not give her life to such a concentration on means without reference to ends.[5] The discussion had laid open for inspection the conservative social and economic views of the Pennsylvania leadership; but the debate, if warm, was inconclusive, for the changes proposed were sweeping and the ideological conflicts threatening. Miller herself suggested that the issue be referred to a special committee of five: one from the national board, one standing committee chair, and three named by the Executive Committee; this would report at the next convention. The proposal seemed a fair way to test League sentiment regarding its program and purpose, and was adopted; Sherwin became its chair.

Since Catt's name had been invoked, delegates demanded her views. She seized the opportunity to reaffirm what she had already urged on the national board. Though seeking to avoid influencing policy, she felt impelled to acknowledge, regretfully, some responsibility for the creation of the standing committees. At the Jubilee Convention she had sought to transform the suffrage movement into an effective political organization of women that would continue to supply the argument of numbers, most coercive of all threats to politicians. The reform groups represented within NAWSA that had formed a powerful network of leadership, commitment, and resources had been invited to bring their programs to the convention to ask delegates to choose what they wanted to sponsor. As presiding officer, she had refrained from interfering. The convention had to make the decisions; the new organization had to proceed from its own initiative and develop its own rationale. She was now sorry that several of the committees had been created, for they appeared to "befuddle the general mind," and even to confuse members as to why the League had been called into being:

> I regret to say it, but I believe these Committees have spent the character of the League. The average person knows of the League because of Sheppard-Towner, or of social hygiene, or the minimum wage . . . more than for its political activities. . . . I do not agree that social welfare is training in citizenship; getting rid of venereal disease has no more to do with the quality of citizenship than getting rid of the common cold. But that is for you to decide. Thinking it over for a year is a good idea . . . to Pennsylvania I say that whether Mrs. Park is right or I am right will be shown by the kind of work the states do. If Pennsylvania does better political work; gets more people out; better officials elected; more members; then her method is best. If social legislation is better, that too will be revealed.

The split within the League received widespread attention. Miller had alerted Pennsylvania papers that she intended "to force the issue," and expected Catt's support (though the latter insisted she had had no advance notice of Miller's plans). *The Christian Science Monitor*, always generous with publicity, headlined the divisions in an article declaring that others among the "politically experienced women"—naming Mary Garrett Hay and Harriet Upton—had supported Catt.[6] Commenting editorially, the *Monitor* complimented Catt for her strictures on the League, and for her "statesmanlike grasp of political situations."[7]

The astringency of Catt's criticisms should not be misunderstood. While personally less sympathetic toward humanitarian concerns than Park or Sherwin, she did not share Miller's views, and certainly understood that to secure the enactment of desirable legislation was political education of the most valuable kind. If she made too little allowance for the difficulty of securing full membership in the political society for the millions who had not been culturally conditioned to consider a concern for public affairs as a major life function, she agreed with the League leadership that education was the place to begin. Her speech, apparently unpremeditated, appeared rather to have been a rueful acknowledgment of a tactical error. Yet she well appreciated the need for the offspring body to maximize the gains inherent in preserving the coalition of interests in the parent NAWSA, and was not the first contriver of a coalition in political history to discover that, in the end, the ideological network by which it was threaded together would prove intractable for her purpose.

About this purpose she remained starkly candid: the overthrow of a governing group basing its legitimacy on its sex, and its replacement by one drawn from the whole electorate with no gender-linked qualifications. The special mission of the League as representative of the newly enfranchised sex was to furnish the educational and political training to qualify its members for participation within the larger political society. But a parallel aim must be to solicit and encourage those naturally disposed toward the exercise of political power to enter the lists, and then to support them. The suffrage leadership had contained many who, in Catt's view, possessed this ability for public stewardship.

The Special Committee took up its difficult task immediately after the convention. To Sherwin's dismay, Miller left for several months in Europe before a meeting could be arranged. Not wanting to lose time, Sherwin asked the Pennsylvania League to prepare a survey of their civic educational work as to volume, subjects covered, and methods used in order to appraise operating methods without the apparatus of standing committees. The Pennsylvania League declined to cooperate, saying that the committee had been appointed to consider reorganization at the national level, not Pennsylvania's methods of work.

On Miller's return in mid-August, she wrote Sherwin asking her "to consider the facts."[8] How many standing committee chairs had any knowledge of political work? How many convention votes represented real working leagues? The financial statements revealed the truth: equal votes but grossly unequal payments.[9]

Pennsylvania and the "stronger Leagues" had been outvoted in three conventions. The national board had not met the issue fairly, in fact had manipulated the votes of inexperienced delegates to get its own way. The question before the committee was in reality the survival of the League; Pennsylvania could not continue unless there was a change of policy and program.

Yet at the committee's three meetings, Miller's arguments found little resonance. The concept of "good and efficient" government, the committee concluded, was not only an abstraction but one that might permit evasion of their mission to educate women for citizenship. The standing committees were seen as serving a vital role in identifying concrete problems, defining legislative means of coping with them, and preparing materials for educational use. So far from being "kindergarten training," their work concerned "the very subject matter of government."

Agreement was unanimous, on the other hand, that each state should retain its freedom of initiative, provided its program did not conflict with League principles; and also that the role played by the standing committee heads at annual conventions should be de-emphasized. There was likewise consensus that more of the League budget should be devoted to field work, and that the bylaws needed further revision to state the League's purpose not as twofold but fourfold: training for citizenship, needed legislation, efficiency in government, and international cooperation. In addition the committee took an important step toward the unified program of the future by recommending that hereafter this be presented in two parts, a platform of League principles and a program of recommended federal legislation and suggested state activities. The League's organizational structure was to be strengthened by assigning standing committee chairs an advisory role and elevating department heads to membership on the national board; all would be safely incorporated within the lines of authority spinning out from the board, which had the power to abolish, regroup, or rename substantive fields.[10] Nevertheless, the Pennsylvania League continued to be dissatisfied, and to go its own way.[11] The Special Committee recommendations, however, were adopted at the 1924 Buffalo convention.

NOTES

1. Helen Hamilton Gardener was one of the League's greatest benefactors, though never an officer. For further details concerning her contributions to NAWSA as well as the League, see *supra*, chap. 2, n. 38.

2. Coinciding with preparations for this event had been the move, two months earlier, of the League's national headquarters from a cramped office on Pennsylvania Avenue to Washington's historic Barton House, for many years the residence of Clara Barton and cradle of the American Red Cross.

3. LWV Papers, Minutes and Related Records, Ser. 2, Box 9, LC. Catt's dissatisfaction had recently found expression in a sharp disagreement with Park that nearly caused the latter to resign from the League presidency. On January 28, 1922, the *Woman Citizen* had published an article by Catt crediting the League with the key role in the

campaign for the Sheppard-Towner Act. When this angered other groups that had participated in the WJCC's efforts, Park was forced to write a conciliatory piece underlining the joint nature of the WJCC campaign. Catt was greatly vexed—at the rebuke implicit in Park's article, but far more so over what she perceived as the League's defensive immersion within the WJCC, evidence to her that the hostile pressures the League had faced from the party (especially Republican) politicians had taken their toll; there was real risk, she felt, that the League's larger role might be blunted, even that other women's groups might succeed in crowding it from the stage. When Catt's displeasure was communicated to other members of the national board (though not directly to Park), the League president wrote her a dignified letter of regret that their paths seemed to be diverging, and offered to withdraw from the leadership. Catt answered promptly, insisting that no one could match Park for her "masterly, tactful and wise management of things," and also stressing her confidence in the national board. Catt continued: "I do not like the way the League is drifting but that does not matter. . . . I have the utmost confidence in the Board . . . supreme confidence in the President. . . . The League is going in a direction it had to go, doubtless, and if the rest of you see no breakers ahead . . . the fact that I think I see them is of no concern . . . your continued judgment must be right." LWV Papers, Ser. 2, Box 3, LC; letter from Catt to Park, April 16, 1922, Carrie Chapman Catt file, Woman's Rights Collection, Arthur and Elizabeth Schlesinger Library on the History of Women in America, Radcliffe College. For additional discussion see Lemons, *The Woman Citizen*, 167–69.

4. Proceedings, Baltimore Convention, April 20–28, 1922. LWV Papers, LC. Unless otherwise noted, the Proceedings furnish the substance of this chapter.

5. Belle Sherwin (1868–1955) was the daughter of a Cleveland industrialist, and graduated from Wellesley in 1890. She became associated with Cleveland urban reform during the regime of Mayor Tom Johnson. She founded the Cleveland Consumers' League, was the longtime president of the Women's City Club in Cleveland and of the Cuyahoga County Suffrage Association, and became vice-president of the National Municipal League. Belle Sherwin served as vice-president of the League of Women Voters from 1921 to 1924, and as president from 1924 to 1934; more than any other individual, she fashioned the League's guiding philosophy. See Sicherman et al., *Notable American Women*, 646–48.

6. The convention proceedings failed to note this. See *Christian Science Monitor*, 27 April 1922.

7. *Christian Science Monitor*, 2 May 1922.

8. LWV Papers, Ser. 2, Box 18, LC.

9. Many of the delegates at the 1921 convention had indeed come from states that had not paid their annual dues as provided in the bylaws; the legitimacy of their credentials was thus open to question. California, Maine, Texas, and Idaho had "forgotten" to pay; fifteen other states had only paid half the money owed. The financial record also revealed where the League could claim unquestioned vigor: Connecticut, Illinois, Indiana, Massachusetts, Minnesota, Missouri, Ohio, New Jersey, New York, and Pennsylvania. Four of these were the home states of members of the national board.

10. "Report of the Committee on the Plan of Work," LWV Papers, Ser. 2, Box 18, LC.

11. In these initial years, the national board also faced criticism verging on rebellion from several local leagues which doubted the League's wisdom in seeking to speak with one voice on federal legislation when not all local groups were in agreement. The board's

patience with those who failed to grasp the implications of a cohesive national organization intent on collective political action is revealed by the correspondence Belle Sherwin had in the early 1920s with the Ohio state president over such complaints by the Oberlin League. See LWV Papers, Ohio file, Ser. 2, Box 27, LC.

7

"An Every Woman's Organization"

An afterglow of enthusiasm generated by the Baltimore convention was still evident when delegates gathered in Des Moines, Iowa, in April 1923.[1] President Maud Park swiftly struck a sobering note. The convention she likened to a mirror, an apt symbol for those early years. The president's duty was to hold up the mirror and invite delegates to examine their collective self-image. While she could proclaim that "we are now 'an every woman's organization' and our future is assured," Park's own exercise of this duty was not conducive to complacency, and no doubt helped shape the League's ongoing inclination toward critical self-examination.[2] She asked them to judge themselves in terms of civic competence in discharging their "special responsibilities" as women citizens, in the search for peace, and in their vigilance regarding law enforcement.

"Practical politics" was the main concern of the 1923 convention. The state legislative reports showed the impact of the 1922 elections. The assigned homework had been to study state electoral laws; the exercise proved educational. Three state leagues had found that unnaturalized aliens were still allowed to vote, though their attempts to amend this by statute had failed. Several had been involved in efforts to secure direct primary laws, or protect such laws from attack. The Georgia League, seeking to compile that state's electoral statutes, had been told: "We ain't got no laws . . . just customs."

State leagues were beginning to enjoy some success in redressing women's grievances. Several had won laws raising the age of consent, a nearly universal feminist complaint. Some had obtained equal guardianship laws. Married women in Illinois and Colorado could now make contracts without their husbands' consent. Several legislatures had responded to pressure to end common-law discriminations relating to dower and curtesy, separate domicile, and division of property in case of divorce. In Maryland, Delaware, and Missouri women

League presidents—the suffrage generation. *Upper left*, Maud Wood Park, 1920-24; *upper right*, Marguerite M. Wells, 1934-44; *below*, Belle Sherwin, 1924-34. (Maud Wood Park: Underwood & Underwood, Washington, D.C.; Belle Sherwin: Underwood & Underwood, Washington, D.C.)

acquired the right to hold public office, and in Iowa to sit in the state legislature; New Jersey women could no longer be denied the privilege of serving as overseers of the poor; in Kentucky they could now serve on the state university's governing board. In March 1923, there was also an important federal legislative victory with the passage of the Civil Service Reclassification Act, though this measure was to prove only a small start toward improving the discriminatory civil service system.

The fate of women candidates in the 1922 election was also reported in detail. Sixteen women had run for Congress, including two state league presidents. The only winner among them was Winifred Mason Huck of Illinois, elected to finish the unexpired term of her father. Eighty-four women were elected to state legislatures, nearly double the number in 1920. Among them was League officer Mabeth Paige, one of eight women elected to the Minnesota legislature.

Paige noted that her campaign rivals had mocked her for being unable to command the support of her own organization, given its nonpartisan commitment. Emily Newell Blair, soon to be vice-chair of the Democratic National Committee, was prompted to scold delegates severely for not supporting women candidates. If politics was to remain a game played mainly by men, it was partly women's own fault.

Many delegates who had engaged in party work complained that politicians had lectured them about "loyalty." Other partisans voiced disappointment with the participant's role, and missed the "exaltation" of the suffrage crusade; some confessed their disillusion at discovering the raw facts of boss-controlled politics. In a major address, Cornelia Pinchot, fresh from assisting her husband become Pennsylvania's governor, expressed doubts that the aim of fifty-fifty representation in the parties would prove meaningful; "women's contribution" would not duplicate that of men. "The sources of power are still largely in men's hands, and will not be readily surrendered." Different sources of influence must be fashioned by developing "new patterns of consent." The field of opinion formation and selective pressures was open to them.

President Park reaffirmed the national policy of nonpartisanship, but reminded delegates that state leagues were free to determine their own policy. She urged members to be as active in parties as possible without hampering League work. All were agreed on the prime necessity of securing able and qualified women in public office. Marguerite Wells was appointed to chair a committee of three to identify ways of penetrating the parties, including methods of encouraging women to attend political and party meetings and opening communications with political leaders. Plans were also made for a pamphlet analyzing party structures and functions, *Know Your Parties*, the first of many League publications on practical politics.

As an immediate step to declare its intent, a paragraph was added to the Preamble of the League's program:

> The League believes that qualified women in administrative office, upon boards and commissions and in legislative bodies will contribute a necessary

point of view to government in the United States and to its international relations. The League therefore urges the election and appointment of qualified women to positions in national, state and local government.

The concern with women candidates was only one part of the problem. The sagging turnout in the two national elections in which women had already participated was disquieting. The nation seemed hardly a functioning democracy. President Park called for a major get-out-the-vote campaign for the 1924 elections, urging a thorough grass-roots survey of nonvoters[3] as well as outlining proposals for what was to become the Voters Service, perhaps the League's best-known activity. Lists of eligible voters were to be compiled to remind them to register, and voter qualifications and places and dates for registration and voting published; information on candidates and issues was to be assembled; candidates' meetings were to be held; and voting canvasses made of each precinct. A program never before attempted on such a scale by a citizens' organization, inevitably it was to fall short in practice. It was also to prove, initially, a source of friction with the political parties. Yet this enterprise was to offer a greater field for direct political participation than any other aspect of the League's work.

President Park utilized the early conventions for "experience sessions" to encourage delegates to discuss their trials of new and unaccustomed political activities. The Des Moines convention included one on candidates' questionnaires, suggested these were not always being wisely used. Questions were sometimes censorious in tone or lacked relevance. Many delegates had little notion of a reciprocal exchange between themselves and the candidates. Some saw questionnaires as a means of satisfying a sense of duty while avoiding "the disagreeable politics of partisanship." Others confessed an "irresistible urge" to "investigate the qualifications of candidates." While a few Leagues had found questionnaires a means of establishing constructive ties with the parties, some reported decidedly counterproductive experiences. Mrs. Glenn Waters of Minneapolis ended the session by warning against "overindulgence in the imperative mood," and against the presumption that political institutions and officeholders did not merit public confidence.

After the convention, the national board acted promptly to frame a model plan for compiling information on candidates. The questionnaire was a key point of entry to the political process, one intimately shaping the character of the League's relationship with elected officials. Questions had to be relevant to the League's program and confined to issues on which the League could reasonably seek candidates' opinions. Candidates should have clear explanations of the League's positions. Attention should also be given to disseminating such information among local league members. Those undertaking interviews should be carefully trained; nothing could be left to chance.

If the League had not yet perceived the full dimensions of what it had undertaken, it was nonetheless charting its course. Under the formative leadership of Maud Park, essential choices had been identified which were to have a

profound bearing on the League's organizational character and on the development of its distinctive methods for realizing the larger aims involved in the
struggle for women's suffrage. In later years, the convention marking the close
of the Park era—held at Buffalo in April 1924—was often referred to as the
high-water mark of the League's early self-confidence. While the convention
was in session, word came that the House of Representatives had passed the
child labor amendment and sent it to the Senate, where prospects for approval
were bright. The delegates could listen with satisfaction as President Park enum-
erated their successes: The Sheppard-Towner Act, the Cable Act,[4] the Packers
and Stockyards Control Act, the Voigt Act,[5] the Civil Service Reclassification
Act, and the establishment of the Women's Bureau and the Bureau of Home
Economics.[6]

State leagues had been even more successful. In a swiftly gathered harvest of
seeds sown over the two preceding decades, some 420 "needed" laws had been
won, and 64 undesirable laws successfully opposed. The largest number had
been in the fields of child welfare, where 45 states had enacted a total of 130
laws. But important incremental gains were also recorded in enhancing women's
legal status through the removal of legal disabilities and the striking down of
discriminatory statutes.

Park's valedictory presidential address underlined the League's developing
objectives. "I doubt that many of us believed that there was anything wonderful
in being able to put some marks on a piece of paper. . . . We thought of the
ballot as a tool. . . . We are working for ends now and that is a glorious thing
to be doing." Aiming a verbal shot at the Pennsylvania leadership, she added
that the League had chosen to be a "middle-of-the-road organization in which
persons of widely differing political views might work out together a program
of definite advance." It had not resolved to "lead a few women a long way
quickly, but rather to lead many women a little way at a time." The League
had begun with a "creative attack" on ignorance and indifference by citizen
education and support of needed legislation. It would now take a further step
toward direct participation by education for action in practical politics. Qualified
women were needed in legislative bodies and administrative offices to contribute
"a necessary point of view."

Important organizational questions still faced the League. The national body
had now been legally incorporated; state leagues were urged to apply formally
for membership to establish their own corporate status. Katharine Ludington,
for whom problems of finance were a perpetual concern, reminded delegates
that a system of financial quotas for state leagues, and the regular discharge of
these assessments, was essential to reduce the League's dependence on large
gifts. Another problem, the method of choosing delegates to League conventions, was partly budgetary, partly the result of having to unlearn old suffrage
habits. Ideally, it was agreed, every state league should be represented by its
president, finance chairman, state heads of committees and departments, and
at least one delegate from each congressional district. But such representation

was far beyond the capacity of states to finance; the task of finding delegates still rested on the state presidents' abilities to locate individuals able to go at their own expense.[7]

Park, in her presidential address, had likened the League's first four years to the "critical . . . danger-fraught" years of human infancy. Certainly chill winds were blowing, and an undercurrent of doubt and vexation was evident in the convention proceedings. Antisuffragist bodies had regrouped and were showing rekindled energies in mounting vituperative attacks against the peace and social-reform concerns of leading women's organizations. In the political mainstream, newspaper editorial writers, stimulated both by the approaching national elections and the evidence of corruption in Harding's cabinet and in the enforcement of the Volstead Act, engaged in speculation over the results of women's emancipation. Did they count in public life? Had public morals improved? Did women really want the ballot? With the same lack of balanced judgment that had characterized the press in voicing extravagant expectations in 1920, editors were now scanning the political horizon in pained amazement that no women political leaders had emerged; nor had the anticipated moral revival taken place.[8]

By far the most serious attack on the League's existence had occurred in December 1922, when an article appeared in the *Woman Patriot* claiming that all fifteen member organizations of the Women's Joint Congressional Committee and the National Council for the Prevention of War were "socialistic," "red," "radical," or "internationalist"—interchangeable terms of opprobrium.[9] The defamatory allegations were subsequently combined with a spider-web chart purporting to show the interlocking directorates of these bodies by connecting them with some fifty women, including the presidents of all the women's organizations involved and an additional dozen who had no formal positions in these groups but were widely known; among the latter were Carrie Chapman Catt, Belle Case La Follette, Helen Gardener, Florence Kelley, Rose Schneiderman, and Jane Addams. All were charged with being members of the "Socialist-Pacifist Movement, an integral part of International Communism."

The creator of the spider web proved to be a woman librarian employed in the U.S. Army's Chemical Warfare Service. Once in print, the Service's head, General Amos A. Fries, an already outspoken critic of the NCPW, used the allegations in a speech charging that all the legislation sponsored by the WJCC, and particularly the Sheppard-Towner Act, had been drafted in Moscow. With coverage in the *Washington Post*, the consternation at League headquarters was considerable. Maud Park, on a lecture tour, wired Secretary of War John Weeks demanding an immediate retraction, and Harriet Upton called upon him personally to condemn the charges. Weeks demurred, saying he had no power to censor speeches by career officers not made in the line of official duties.

The "preparedness" bloc in Congress, senior War Department officials, and many career officers were greatly concerned about the demand for reduced military budgets, and viewed the peace-minded women's organizations unfavorably. General Fries continued his speeches. On March 22, 1924, the *Dearborn Independent* carried expanded charges, this time including Senator Thomas J. Walsh, a World Court advocate and currently newsworthy as the investigator of the Teapot Dome Scandal. Conducting his own inquiry, he discovered that the materials had been widely distributed within the army, under its franking privileges, to warn that "pacifists" and "reds" were trying to undermine America's defenses. The Associated Distillery Industries of Kentucky, an old suffragist foe, also reprinted the *Dearborn* articles, as did the Manufacturers Association of Kentucky and the Allied Industries of New York.

Maud Park and Katharine Ludington called on Weeks again, demanding that General Fries retract his statements, send a retraction to everyone who had received the original spider-web chart, and destroy the charts in his files. By this time, the secretary had evidently begun to feel pressures from other sources, and promised the charts would be destroyed. But the elimination of the charts in the War Department's possession, if indeed it occurred, could hardly have mattered, so widely had they been distributed. Nor had the last been heard of them. The allegations continued throughout the twenties and thirties, enjoyed a reincarnation in "the Red Network" during the McCarthy period of the early fifties, and are still regularly cited in the publications of the Liberty League and other conservative pressure groups.

The end of Park's presidency marked the close of the League's novitiate. Mary Morrisson's tribute, on behalf of the delegates at the Buffalo convention, underlined Park's role in giving breadth to the League's social concerns. Initially, the membership had been unsure of what they wanted, knew only that they would not become a woman's party. Having given her life to the furtherance of women's political equality, Park was convinced that women had a "peculiar responsibility" for the "social welfare" realm of government, hitherto neglected. This she had communicated to them, along with a glimpse of political realities. Personal qualities of intellectual integrity, forbearance, and generosity of spirit had given her a measure of detachment rare among individuals as determined as she to bring about radical change. She had served, in short, as a fine representative of the "new woman."

Yet her four years as leader had not been easy. Crises and internal struggles had determined the task of the president, and had exacted an emotional toll. The problem of establishing the national board's authority, of creating a balance between the voluntary and the coercive, was unresolved, and would furnish grist for League history for many years. To Park herself, the gradual falling away of the once immense membership was discouraging; in her reminiscences, she confessed bitter disappointment over the League's failure to gain a majority of the estimated two million members allied with NAWSA in 1920.[10] The more complex challenges facing the enfranchised woman citizen seemingly failed to motivate into active membership as many as were mobilized in the NAWSA around the single concrete goal of suffrage.

NOTES

1. Proceedings, Des Moines Convention, April 9–14, 1923. LWV Papers: Minutes and related Records, LC. Unless otherwise noted, the Proceedings furnish the substance of this discussion.

2. See League of Women Voters, *A Record of Four Years in the National League of Women Voters, 1920–1924*, by Maud Wood Park (Washington, D.C., 1924); *Ten Years of Growth*, by Belle Sherwin (Washington, D.C., 1930); *A Portrait of the League of Women Voters at the Age of Eighteen*, by Marguerite M. Wells (Washington, D.C., 1938); *25 Years of a Great Idea*, by Kathryn H. Stone (Washington, D.C., 1946); *A History of the League Program*, by Kathryn H. Stone (Washington, D.C., 1949); *Forty Years of a Great Idea* (Washington, D.C. [1960]).

3. Initiatives resulting from this project led to two of the earliest electoral surveys, in both of which the League collaborated: Charles E. Merriam and Harold F. Gosnell, *Non-Voting: Causes and Methods of Control* (Chicago: University of Chicago Press, 1924); and Ben A. Arneson, "Non-Voting in a Typical Ohio Community," *American Political Science Review* 19 (November 1925): 816–25.

4. The Cable Act—for which the League had lobbied with particular vigor—was a significant step toward creating citizenship rights for American women that were independent of their marital status. Second to the Sheppard-Towner Act, it was the most publicized of the early legislative victories by women's groups; and when the act was signed by President Harding in September 1922, Maud Park received the pen as chair of the WJCC. If its passage had occurred despite overt opposition from the State Department, it had also provoked anguished cries from Hull-House that certain of its provisions might actually add new hardships for immigrants' wives. Indeed, the original act did have important flaws, one of which was dramatized in 1928 with the election to Congress of Ruth Bryan Owen, daughter of William Jennings Bryan. Her defeated opponent charged that her election was invalid; residence abroad after her marriage to a British army officer had disqualified her from citizenship, and while she had returned to the United States in 1919 and regained her citizenship in 1925, she had allowed insufficient time before standing for Congress. Owen provided a brilliant defense before the Elections Committee of the House of Representatives and was allowed to take her seat. Her case provided opportunity for the League and other groups to successfully press to have the act's shortcomings corrected.

The Cable Act in turn lay on the periphery of a much larger issue—immigration. At its 1923 convention, the League had found itself drawn into the ugly conflict over the limiting of further immigration to the United States when a group organized by Lucy Miller provoked heated debate in seeking support for restrictive legislation then before Congress. Recognizing that the issue would arise again, the national board appointed a Committee on Immigration headed by Frances Perkins (a member of the New York State Industrial Commission, and later the first woman federal cabinet member as Franklin Roosevelt's Secretary of Labor from 1933 to 1945). Intended to be representative of the League's conflicting viewpoints, the committee developed an extensive program of study. It was not until the 1938 convention, however, that the initial steps were taken toward clear support for non-discriminatory immigration policies.

5. The Voigt Act prohibited the interstate shipment of skimmed milk laced with coconut oil and sold as whole milk.

6. Proceedings, Buffalo Convention, April 24–29, 1924, LWV Papers, LC. Unless otherwise noted, the Proceedings furnish the substance of this section of the chapter.

7. See LWV Papers, Ser. 2, Box 46, LC.

8. Indicative of these editorial currents was a widely read article, "Is Woman-Suffrage a Failure?" by Charles E. Russell, a liberal journalist and former ardent champion of suffrage (and husband of a suffrage leader), see *Century Magazine*, 107 (March 1924): 724–30. The *Woman Citizen* kept a running inventory of the critical comments on women's political behavior during 1923 and 1924.

9. *Woman Patriot*, 1 December 1922. This publication was a short-lived revival of an antisuffrage paper, and was published by Alice Hay Wadsworth, wife of the New York senator who had been such a stubborn opponent of women's suffrage.

10. "Reminiscences," Maud Wood Park Papers, files 694–700. Arthur and Elizabeth Schlesinger Library on the History of Women in America, Radcliffe College.

8

An Experiment in Political Education

Belle Sherwin served as the League's president from 1924 to 1934—ten difficult years of political and educational experiment and continuous self-questioning, not unaccompanied by periods of doubt and threats of defeat. While strongly committed to action, and winning some notable legislative victories, the League in this period appears in retrospect self-contained and inward-looking, constantly shifting its reference from the outward reality to an open consciousness seeking to organize its own understanding of the complex experience it was undergoing.

Training women for their new civic role had been the League's initial task. But the experience had soon demonstrated that the essential lessons had to be learned, in Sherwin's words, "from the alphabet upward." A formal education approach had to be abandoned for methods more pragmatic and experimental. There were no models to follow in a political society that regarded the civic function as a cultural inheritance requiring no training. Collectively, though not universally, American women had experienced through their enfranchisement an awareness of a wholly novel relationship in life; upon that hinge of awareness—but also upon personal experience—their politicization had to turn. But Sherwin was confronted with a difficulty always facing those seeking to forge a new society: the fact that those with whom she had to work had already been trained to life in some other society.

In Sherwin's view, the purpose of political education must be to secure "relatedness"—not the mere acquisition of facts but the self-documented discovery of their relation to the individual's own experience. In correcting the deficiencies in their information about the political process, women had to be stimulated to ask: How does this relate to me? Drawing a municipal tax map or studying the local school system might result in the acquisition of knowledge, but such knowledge would be of little value unless it altered a woman's understanding of her own experience.[1] Perceiving relatedness would furnish the psychological basis for involvement, and help inculcate an individual sense of civic responsibility.

The stress on the League as an "experiment in political education" voiced Sherwin's belief that the role of study and fact-finding was to prepare the woman citizen to develop her own attitudes toward the political system.[2] The experience of viewing all sides of public issues would develop habits of fairness and sagacity as well as the capacity to perceive relationships; individuals would be enabled to do their own thinking and possess their own viewpoints, would be inducted into the civic culture by internalizing a self-conception as participants within the larger political society. Such a notion of civic responsibility, grounded in civic competence, was an ideal with implications the League has been exploring ever since.

The great project of Sherwin's administration was thus to demonstrate that the League's educational purpose and its program were inseparable parts of an organic whole. The League made its program; yet as it did so, the program made the League: "The program is the thing"—a program of work with its origins in the experience of its own participants. The League, for Sherwin, was like "a university without the walls . . . whose members enter to learn and remain to shape the curriculum."[3] The fulfillment of Sherwin's vision did not come during her tenure, nor during her successor's; but they pointed the way.

A spirit of philosophic inquiry illuminated all of Sherwin's institutional activities, and touched all who shared them with her. In board meetings and conferences she persistently explored the character and function of the League and how these were related to its stated aims and policies. She saw program making as the vital center. At what points did knowledge meet life and become politically effective? How might plans of study and action be devised that would express women's new relationship to the community through what they did, and how they did it, and what happened as a consequence? League records after 1924 reveal how searchingly she scrutinized the organization's developing procedures.

Key to the program-making process was the group of department and standing committee heads.[4] Summoned to an early conference, each reported the activity and measurable accomplishments of her group. The atmosphere of mutual understanding Sherwin encouraged assisted her efforts to enhance their advisory and tutorial role in policy formation. The national chairs were assumed to have a substantive mastery of their fields, be able to foresee incipient issues, and be ready with recommendations when the national board was formulating the program. Their responsibilities extended also to the state level, where they suggested legislative programs to state chairs and prepared them to enlist support from state boards.

A conference of state presidents found itself asking difficult questions: Was the League, in fact, a temporary organization to meet a historical exigency? If not temporary, why? Always beyond the officers Sherwin saw the members. How could they convey to local leagues a sense of their crucial importance? Clearly it was here that the experiment in political education had to take root. How could they induce members of local leagues to conceive of themselves as *participating* members? The revolutionary fires had been banked; in comparison with the activism the suffrage movement had achieved, many leagues were losing ground. Finance remained a widespread problem. Yet though dues had been kept low to attract a wider range of women, the membership was still heavily middle class.

It emerged that the states most advanced in institutionalizing effective methods of fashioning agreement on state programs had also evolved workable democratic procedures; this appeared likewise true of the stronger local leagues. At the same time, it was evident that the national program was still viewed as something coming down from on high; it was to be loyally supported, but did not directly involve members. As the conference revealed, many members never actually saw the program; the national board could not yet afford so extensive a distribution. As for the program proposals sent out two months in advance of the annual national convention, only in the best-organized leagues was there real discussion; some state presidents were remiss about getting these to local presidents because they lacked secretaries and offices; a few did not perceive the importance of doing so.

Sherwin appointed a Committee on the Realignment of the Program in quest of procedures that would knit together the parts into a more cohesive whole.[5] At an early stage in her tenure the six standing committees were loosely combined under one department—Public Welfare in Government; thereafter only the Committee on the Legal Status of Women remained a separate division. This regrouping was accompanied by sharper divisions between program content and method and between "study" and "support," and by ongoing efforts to strengthen the "Explanation of the Program."[6]

Even more important was the development of a publications policy for the systematic preparation of study materials designed for program needs. The discovery of an organic relationship between informed understanding and effective action had preceded Sherwin, and indeed antedated the League.[7] The necessity for objective accuracy as the basis of authority was also understood; but not until Sherwin's administration was a well-defined publications policy devised. In 1924 the nucleus of a research staff was recruited; in 1925 the national board assumed full responsibility for the caliber and authority of all materials; nothing could be published in the League's name without the board's approval.[8] Over the years, this exercise of executive authority has been a major channel for exerting national leadership. It became the policy to deal with subjects for study in the stages preparatory to action with publications that were factual, objective, and popularly written, so that members might be prepared to meet opponents' objections as well as to understand the League's own approach.

Sherwin's talent for administration did not exhaust itself on such concerns.

She sought to create in the League's national headquarters a functioning center, drawing in previously dispersed activities and systematizing communications and administration. She appointed an executive secretary; in addition to the research staff, she secured experienced staff to deal with publicity, legislation, and organization.[9] In 1933 Barton House was abandoned for more spacious quarters on Jackson Place, facing Lafayette Park and the White House.

While the administrative machinery was being set in motion, essential operational activities were taking place. In the early decades the League considered it an essential part of its function to define the issues most relevant to its own program and present them formally to the presidential nominating conventions of the major parties in order to publicize women's concerns. In 1924, in contrast to the thirteen demands of 1920, the League prepared four planks, each a model of careful phrasing; Julia Lathrop was selected to present them to both conventions, accompanied by a delegation of women. As in 1920, the party out of power treated the League's delegation more cordially than the party in power, though in both cases innovations were visible in the manner of their reception. The Republican National Committee named a committee of woman officials, none League members, to "screen" the planks before forwarding them to the Resolutions Committee. At the Democratic convention, Eleanor Roosevelt formed a Women's Advisory Committee of women leaders from several organizations; together they coordinated the women's planks and spoke with one voice.

Both parties had named more women as delegates and alternates to the 1924 presidential nominating conventions than in 1920.[10] At a national board meeting shortly after, the convention experiences were discussed, and agreement was reached that the nominating process appeared the most fruitful area of cooperation with the parties. Recommendations were formulated for greater involvement at this point. The League's unremitting efforts to establish a working relationship with the parties reflects how deeply the League leadership believed, with Catt, that the parties were indispensable instruments for achieving women's share in managing the "people's business."[11] Nevertheless, in assuming their educational and opinion-shaping role, they were consciously trespassing on party territory.

Some party leaders minced no words in telling them just that. Governor Nathan Miller, addressing the New York state league convention in January 1921, had remarked scathingly that there was "no need for a League of Women voters any more than for a League of Men Voters. . . . any organization which seeks to exert political power is a menace to our institutions unless it is organized as a political party."[12] The situation had not been improved by the public statements of some of the older League leaders who had carried over animosity from the suffrage conflict.[13] Moreover the legislative reforms the League advocated were threatening to party leaders; nonpartisan elections, direct primaries, the short ballot, civil service reform, council-manager municipal government—all were intended to trim the power of the parties. Politicians naturally regarded such measures as inimical to their interests, and took every step possible to thwart them.

The enthusiasm generated by the showing of women at the 1924 nominating conventions was considerably dampened by the election results, despite the effort expended on the "Get-Out-the-Vote" campaign.[14] While aggregate figures told nothing of who did not vote or why, and though the League's own precinct inquiry had been spotty, one fact was clear: among nonvoters, women were the worst offenders. Of several women who had run for Congress, only Mary Norton of New Jersey had been elected, and she with the help of the Hague machine.[15] Innumerable letters had come to national headquarters after the elections asking what women had accomplished, and an astringent reply was drafted. Christian Herter, editor of the *Independent*, wrote Belle Sherwin asking for guidance through the contradictory statements regarding the "actual contributions which women had made toward the political advancement of the United States . . . both in the exercise of the vote . . . and the election or appointment to positions of public trust." Since she was a woman of "wide experience and attainments . . . qualified to generalize on a situation which has had such a short life," he would welcome her views, particularly since "many foreign nations are genuinely anxious to learn the result of the experiment." Palpably tired of this mixture of condescension and complacency, Sherwin replied that women's votes "have undoubtedly affected political fortunes. . . . I wish to add that I am one of those who would not expect larger or more conspicuous results from the contributions of women in so short a time . . . though I agree with you that the subject calls for discussion."[16]

Many analytical soundings were taken in the choppy political seas. Questionnaires were circulated among selected universities to discover the number of women majoring in political science, or even enrolled in courses; and to investigate possible relationships between those elected to student offices and larger political concerns. Another questionnaire prepared by political scientists at the universities of Kansas and Oklahoma was designed to ascertain career choices, membership in campus political groups, and other forms of political participation: the results were largely negative. A survey at Ohio State University had women students rate a list of twenty-five career choices in order of preference; a career in politics came last. Such explorations, buried now in League records, not only underlined the League's genuine concern, but their certain knowledge that political socialization would not take place overnight. The evidence supported Belle Sherwin's theory that motivation to learn had to precede acquisition of political knowledge, and that the motivation to participate would not come until the knowledge was internalized. A generation might be needed, they were beginning to believe, before their great design would be etched clearly, and every woman be a participating citizen.

As so often in human affairs, circumstances beyond the control of League leaders played a major role in determining the nature of their options. Forceful currents below the surface of events—ones destined to bring the decade to a close in economic and political bankruptcy—were already generating regressive tendencies in the patterning of sex relationships. Such tendencies were reflected in the "flapper" and the "gold digger," creatures of the jazz age who got more space in the press than did women of achievement. By the late twenties, laws were being passed in many states denying married women the right to teach or hold public employment if their husbands were employed. Veterans' preference became increasingly discriminatory. Fewer women were privileged to attend college. As the great women educators of the previous generation were replaced (increasingly by men), the theme became "life adjustment" rather than "self-realization." The tidal wave of achievement had reached its crest just before the ratification of the Nineteenth Amendment, and had slowly ebbed. Even before the onset of the depression, women had lost part of their precarious footing in the economic world, and had not yet secured it in that of public affairs.

NOTES

1. John Dewey influenced Belle Sherwin's theory of education as a "continuous reconstruction of experience." See John Dewey, *Democracy and Education: An Introduction to the Philosophy of Education* (New York: Macmillan, 1916).

2. Proceedings, St. Louis Convention, April 14–21, 1926. LWV Papers, Minutes and Related Records, LC. Some state leagues, by contrast, were urging more emphasis on action, and less on study, to maintain momentum for needed legislation reforms affecting women.

3. President's Address, General Council Meeting, April 27–30, 1927. LWV Papers, LC.

4. At the time Sherwin assumed the presidency, there were at the national level two departments—Efficiency in Government and International Cooperation to Prevent War—and six standing committees: Child Welfare, Education, the Legal Status of Women, Women in Industry, Social Hygiene, and Living Costs. Each standing committee was made up of a national chair and the head of the relevant committee in each state league. Since from the outset each had reflected the interests of a significant component of the suffrage coalition, each had enjoyed substantial autonomy, with its own program and network of specialists.

5. Marguerite Wells emerged as the dominant member of this committee, which did not end its task until the eve of her assumption of the presidency in 1934.

6. Lemons suggests that the League was among the feminist social reform groups being pushed on the defensive at this time in the face of often virulent attacks by conservative politicians and economic interests: "The National League of Women Voters also developed a slower process of formulating positions. Belle Sherwin introduced the 'consensus method' to the league after she became president. Decision-making was stretched out and made more complex in order to assure maximum solidarity in the league on controversial issues before taking a public stand. A proposal required several trips between national and local levels, taking several years, before it could be adopted as a legislative objective of the NLWV." See Lemons, *The Woman Citizen*, 222. While external pressures on the League were a significant factor in this period, the League's

own internal dynamics remained the more important formative influence on the changes being discussed.

7. Fact-compiling methods of social investigation had been developed by the social justice reformers during the late nineteenth century, especially by those associated with the settlement house movement (from which in turn a significant number of suffrage leaders and early League officers had come).

8. By the end of 1929 there were some 155 League publications, ranging from a few to 140 pages in length; in 1929–30, nearly sixty-five hundred orders for League materials were received; see LWV, *Ten Years of Growth*, 11–12, 24. A report on adult education in the United States done for the Carnegie Corporation remarked: "Unlike the publications of the women's clubs, League materials are documented and supplemented with references that really guide. The literature of the League is as a whole sophisticated and admirably done; it has substance; and it is well adapted to the needs of the layman and nonstudent, without any dilution of content." See LWV, *National League of Women Voters*, by Nathaniel Peffer (Washington, D.C., National League of Women Voters, January 1927), 10; reprinted from his *New Schools for Older Students* (New York: Macmillan, 1926).

9. By 1936 the national headquarters had eighteen professional staff; another thirty-five were employed by nineteen of the state leagues, and a further twenty-nine by thirteen local leagues. See LWV, *The National League of Women Voters: An Achievement in Citizen Participation in Government* (Washington, D.C., October 1936).

10. Not until after 1948 would so many women be included again.

11. A view fortified by the formal and informal advice of their friends among the political scientists, especially Charles Merriam.

12. See *Woman Citizen*, 5 February 1921: 950–51; Peck, *Carrie Chapman Catt*, 403–5; Joseph P. Lash, *Eleanor and Franklin*, 261; and Lemons, *The Woman Citizen*, 98–99.

13. The politically powerful Pennsylvania League, for example, had declared itself a rival of the parties to free the public from control by "selfish and powerful minorities." Press release, Pennsylvania League of Women Voters, October 19, 1921, LWV Papers, Pennsylvania file, LC.

14. See reports and correspondence relating to the "Get-Out-the-Vote" campaign, LWV Papers, Ser. 2, Boxes 46–48, LC.

15. The New Jersey League had been preparing an electoral challenge to Mayor Frank Hague (of Jersey City), whose tight control of northern New Jersey had made him the very symbol of abhorrent bossism. Hague had astutely countered by arranging the nomination of Mrs. Norton, a young woman active in Catholic welfare work. When asked to run, she had demurred, insisting that she knew nothing about politics. "Neither do they," Hague said, "but you can learn. They can't, because they think they know already." Congresswoman Mary Norton, interview with author, January 1951. Norton enjoyed a long and successful congressional career.

16. Correspondence between Christian Herter and Belle Sherwin, June 1925, LWV Papers, Ser. 2, Box 48, LC. As hard to bear as their own disappointment with the showing of women in public life had been the criticism of close friends and champions like Anna S. Richardson of the *Woman's Home Companion*; she chided the League in print and in private for appealing only to women who were already aware of civic concerns, and for neglecting the masses of ordinary women. She urged them to make more emotional appeals to average women instead of ascending to the rarefied atmosphere where civic principles dwelt. See correspondence between Anna S. Richardson and Maud Wood Park, LWV Papers, Ser. 2, Box 47, LC.

9

Unfinished Business

The Richmond convention in 1925 was one of the most important in a decade of precedent-setting conventions.[1] For six days some five hundred delegates, including twenty-one from college leagues, debated program and procedures, listened to speeches and attended committee conferences.[2] Belle Sherwin's first presidential address underlined her view that the political rewards in solid achievement thus far had fallen short of hopes. The disappointing results of the "inventive, energetic, widespread" "Get-Out-the-Vote" campaign challenged them to reconsider their methods of election campaign activity. On the legislative front, they were currently struggling to win ratification of the child labor amendment; initial evidence of popular acceptance had concealed determined opposition, which had broken out in unexpected places. They had to learn to cope with the "aggressive publicity of partial facts," used so adeptly by their enemies, to counter criticisms that women's organizations "adopt measures they do not understand," were "socialistic," and supported the aggrandizement of federal power. How naïve they had been in 1920 to suppose that five years would see their goals attained; their education was only beginning.

Sherwin also summarized their experience with the early citizenship schools. When interest flagged after two or three years, some had said that "women were not smitten with being educated," but the fault had lain with the "educational stuff" of the schools. The Department of Efficiency in Government was redirecting both the substance and the emphasis of the schools toward recruiting and training members, and organizing new leagues, rather than teaching women how to mark a ballot. She had drawn up four models for citizenship schools designed to emphasize the points of the political system where the individual citizen made contact, and where access might lead to the heart of the governing process.[3]

Upper left, Katharine Ludington, Connecticut suffrage leader and member of the League's national Board of Directors, 1920-34. *Lower left*, Mary Morrisson, daughter of civil service reformer William Dudley Foulke, and a leading League activist in Illinois and Connecticut. *Above*, Louise Baldwin (Vermont), chair of the Committee on Living Costs, 1924-34. (Katharine Ludington: Ira L. Hill, New York; Louise Baldwin: Harris & Ewing)

Sherwin also called attention to the proposed Program of Work. Here for the first time was formulated the fundamental belief carried forward to the present: "The League of Women Voters understands efficient government to be representative, responsible and responsive government; stronger than any political or economic group; capable of rendering with the least waste and the lowest cost services adapted to the needs of all the people."

The convention's program had been carefully arranged to develop the triple idea of representative, responsible, and responsive government. Representative government was dealt with first. The meager results of the 1924 "Get-Out-the-Vote" campaign were analyzed by a succession of state presidents. In Wisconsin, voting schools had been held in twenty towns, voting instructions in several languages distributed, and innumerable speeches made by League members on the duty to vote. An unshakeable apathy had been evident, however; many women remained prejudiced against voting, and many more simply fearful of going to the local courthouse to register—suggesting a need to make registration and voting simpler which many delegates echoed. The California League reported its surprised discovery that responsibility for registration was legally a state concern; in many local jurisdictions the parties assumed this responsibility, exercising it in ways best calculated to serve their own best interests. In North Carolina sheer timidity had kept many women from the polls because of the absence of a secret ballot. A full report on the campaign was promised for the following convention, together with recommendations for future election campaign activities.[4]

League leaders were aware that the needs that had been phrased under the rest of the League's program—which belonged to the sphere of "responsible and responsive government"—were contributing toward the federal assumption of functions traditionally viewed as within the sphere of state and local initiative. They were not responsible for the trend toward interventionism, which had begun under the first Roosevelt; but the hostile resistance to many items on their program involved them inextricably with the forces working toward a shift in federal-state relationships. As president, Maud Park had tended to view these changes in political terms. Their demands unquestionably created expectations regarding what the federal government could and must do, and in 1924 she had warned that they might expect increasing opposition.[5] Sherwin took a different course. She saw the need to interpret their connection with the shift in federal-state relationships as part of educating their membership toward the goal of political maturity; they were playing a significant role in shaping an enlarged social consciousness, and their political education must embrace an awareness of this fact.[6]

The last annual convention was held in St. Louis in 1926.[7] In returning to the site of the Jubilee Convention, the League appears to have been symbolically severing its ties with the parent organization and declaring its selfhood. The suffrage heritage had been woven into their experience; the "deep intent" had been embodied in a living organization. Not a few members still yielded loyalty

Above, a citizenship school in Tampa, Florida, in March 1929. The initial preoccupation of such institutes with teaching women how to vote had by now been superseded by other concerns, especially improving citizen access to government. (League of Women Voters) *Below,* Katharine Ludington chairing the Radio Committee in 1932, the final year of its innovative efforts at developing radio as a medium of political education. (Mrs. W. Burden Stage)

to a tradition rather than an organization; but none of the standing committee chairs were those of 1920, and only six of the state presidents. The delegate body was the smallest of the seven annual conventions: 311 women from thirty-six states. Twenty-eight states sent three delegates or less, and eight states only one. Over half the votes were controlled by five states—Missouri, Michigan, Illinois, Ohio, and Pennsylvania. These tallies were partly a function of distance, partly an ominous warning. Organizations were claimed in forty-four states, but only twenty-four had fully functioning boards. With an estimated total membership of sixty-five thousand, eleven state leagues had four thousand or more members, twenty-two less than a thousand.[8] But the figures were unreliable.[9]

Katharine Ludington, in a gloomy treasurer's report, acknowledged the first deficit since 1922. The national budget had been increased in 1924–25 to $135,000 to implement Sherwin's plans for expanded activities, but $89,000 of this had come from wealthy supporters. After 1927 budget growth had to be curtailed. Even so, the deficit continued to mount, reaching a total of $18,000 in 1933. In the depression years of acute financial stress, many questioned the wisdom of continued existence, but none of those who had been among the founding members; they simply dug deeper into their own pockets to keep the League alive.

As had previous annual meetings, the 1926 convention included major sessions on practical politics. Several elected women officeholders spoke on "making democracy function through parties," and stressed the satisfactions they had found in partisan involvements; two admonished delegates to follow their concerns into municipal and state government, echoing Jane Addams. In a special conference on political techniques, speakers stressed the importance of seeking low-level party posts such as poll watchers or members of election boards—humble political tasks without reward, and not much sought after, but nonetheless vital for guaranteeing honest elections.

The Committee of Nine appointed the previous year to examine women's electoral participation reported to the convention on the results of its investigations. It had found that voting statistics were in key respects empirically crude. Eligibility figures, for example, relying as they did on census figures with estimated amendments for illiterates, aliens, and population shifts, were only approximations. Forty-six states required voter registration; though varying greatly in their requirements, registration systems, as well as curbing electoral fraud, clearly made voting more difficult. Few states had absentee voting laws; few citizens in those states knew about them in any case. On the other hand, it was evident that the enfranchisement of women was "largely responsible for the decline of the . . . average turnout to the fifty per cent level of 1920 and 1924." Many reasons could be advanced: "the novelty of enfranchisement" and the "unfamiliar and unanticipated responsibilities"; the effects of "dependent and confining" occupations like domestic service and homemaking, or of those outside the home where women worked long hours at low pay; and not least women's limited opportunities in citizen-related activities like jury service and public and party officeholding. Comfort was extracted from the fact that women voted in greatest numbers in the states enfranchised before 1920.

The committee was ready with specific recommendations for Voters Service activities, including furnishing information on literacy tests, providing ballot-marking classes, especially for young voters, and continuing the unremitting effort to improve the election laws; all state and local leagues were advised to appoint a Voters Service chair and make electoral activities a year-round project as a community service.[10] Energy and imagination have embroidered this original design with many details in the years since 1926, but the essential features of the League's enduring Voters Service program had been outlined.[11]

The St. Louis meeting amended the bylaws to provide for conventions on a biennial basis instead of annually, with General Council meetings in the off years. In its early years, the League had needed the convention for publicity as well as for organizational purposes; however, by now the stimulus of an annual national public event no longer justified the cost in time and money.

The first General Council meeting in 1927 marked a transition in League history.[12] Sherwin told council members that they "were beginning to find out what was the essential thing about the League." In the beginning members had not fully comprehended what "participation" might involve; but the League had become both a vehicle for political education and a "medium for a new political development." And if they had begun with multiple and often contradictory goals, with policies but no methods for implementing them, they were now "chastened and made lucid by experience."

The major policy discussion focused on the question of nonpartisanship as it was being implemented in various states. Some leagues insisted that their partisan activities were not interfering with League work; in a few states—New York and Missouri, for example—League officers also held party offices, though they "tried to preserve a 50–50 balance." Delegates from several states took issue, arguing that it was "very confusing to the public mind" to have state board members functioning as party officers.

Sherwin had already acted to bring clarification of an expanding concern by requesting the Committee of Nine to collect all available information on the League's sustained drive to activate women for party work. The national staff had also begun compiling a survey of women in public office, which it continued to publish annually until the women's divisions of the major parties assumed this task in the 1930s. The committee's final report was to appear after the 1928 elections, which witnessed a crescendo of partisan commitments on the part of League officers.[13] The committee concluded that the experience of partisan involvements had sometimes proved disruptive—in eleven states creating misunderstandings that might be hard to correct and giving rise to scepticism regarding the League's sincerity. In one state the partisan links had brought League work to a standstill and led to a loss of its leaders; in another they created serious dissension within the board, provoking criticism both within and without the League.

As for the party nominating conventions, those women delegates interviewed said women were conspicuously underrepresented on the important committees. They also found themselves handicapped by the size of the gatherings, acknowledging that they felt "uncertain both of their own ability as delegates and of the convention method of nomination"; the average delegate of either sex counted for little, it emerged. Regarding women's power within the parties, all agreed it was nominal; some noted they were solicited to offer "the woman's point of view," but only for information gathering, not policy making.[14]

The general conclusions were inescapable. The committee recommended that the League reaffirm its policy of nonpartisanship, and reconcile itself to coexistence with the parties. They concluded that it was women outside the parties and not those within who made themselves felt. Both public events and private experience had tended to give undue emphasis to the marked tension that their presence on the political stage seemed to create. The evidence was persuasive that they could define their political role without reference to the political parties; the many paths to direct participation in the future would lie in the direction of voters service activities. In the course of following such paths, they could hope to succeed in activating many women to seek public office.[15] A continuous and central concern for the League during its first decade had been the welfare of mothers and children. The Sheppard-Towner Act to promote the health and welfare of mothers and infants, discussed in Chapter 5, was due to expire in 1927; from 1925 onward the collective efforts of the League and several other women's groups were concentrated on the discouraging attempt to secure a renewal.[16]

The first bill had not passed easily; by 1927 the opposition was open and unashamed. Obdurate congressmen refused to listen to the argument that "the function of motherhood has an exchange value as well as a use value," deserving of federal aid on the same terms as the farmer's animals.[17] League supporters in Congress warned that a two-year renewal was nearly impossible; a one-year compromise might be difficult. The Coolidge administration had concerns more pressing than "the special responsibilities of women," though Coolidge himself declared support for a two-year renewal. Senator James Couzens wrote regretfully to the president of the Michigan League that despite his own backing, the Senate Education and Labor Committee was not favorable to renewal. He knew none who doubted the act's achievements, "but the question seemed to be how far the federal government should extend its hand in activities which could be done as well or better in the states, even though admittedly the backward states will do nothing at all." He admonished those "interested in this splendid work" to get busy and demand that the states prepare to do it themselves.[18]

The attacks came from many angles, but most damaging were those from the American Medical Association.[19] It kept up a ceaseless barrage, calling the act "socialistic" and destructive of family life, and alleging that "bureaucrats" determined on treatment over the objections of parents, that individuals were denied their own doctor's services, that pregnant women were examined for syphilis, and that the Children's Bureau had distorted statistics and exaggerated needs. Such allegations were used by business interests, which maintained a more covert opposition, and by the Catholic and Lutheran churches, always open foes of the measure. Also difficult to fend off were attacks based on the apparent logic of transferring the activities authorized under the act from the Children's Bureau to the Public Health Service, if appropriations were renewed. The Institute for Government Research of the Brookings Institution proposed the transfer "in the interest of efficiency."[20] Ann Webster, head of the League's Social Hygiene Committee, wrote a biting letter to the monograph's author, pointing out: "Women . . . look upon that Bureau as their particular stake in the federal government. Their demand created it . . . it has always been manned by great women and its name and work are better known to women than any other department of government. . . . Dismember the Bureau and you have lost something more precious than any plan ever set on paper . . . against the apparent gain in 'efficiency.' "[21]

A Senate majority was finally mobilized to vote for a two-year extension, though a handful of opponents conducted a bitter nine-day filibuster which revived the sex antagonisms of the suffrage battle.[22] The act was finally to lapse in June 1929. Despite many difficulties, its application did bring measurable improvements, particularly in rural districts. The Sheppard-Towner Act proved the forerunner of the Social Security Act of 1935, and was incorporated there as Title V. The attempt to coordinate federal and state action to aid mothers and infants was the first step toward the introduction of a comprehensive social security system.

Second to the welfare of mothers and young children among the neglected interests for which the League accepted responsibility was that of the child laborer, whose bleak fate impinged on the public welfare at so many points. Informed opinion had long held that the social costs of child labor were high in terms of poverty, illiteracy, juvenile delinquency, illegitimacy, and mental retardation. Before World War I, a bare handful of states had enforceable compulsory education laws or even mildly restrictive child labor laws. Congress passed the first child labor law in 1916 in response to public indignation over a Children's Bureau report on the wages and working conditions of child workers; this also underlined their economic insecurity and the incidence of industrial accidents among them. When the law was declared unconstitutional by the Supreme Court in 1918 (in *Hammer v. Dagenhart*), Congress tried again with a measure taxing the profits of firms employing children. After the second federal law was struck down in 1922 (in *Bailey v. Drexel Furniture Company*), women's organizations and the National Child Labor Committee joined with the American Child Health Association (launched by Herbert Hoover) in demanding a constitutional amendment to give Congress power concurrent with that of the states to regulate and prohibit child labor.

The League eagerly placed the question on its program in 1923, after a moving convention speech by Julia Lathrop. The following year, with Congress having passed the child labor amendment and sent it to the states for ratification, a subcommittee of the Women's Joint Congressional Committee was set up; chaired by Florence Kelley, eleven women's groups participated. An alliance was formed with other groups known as the Organizations Associated for Ratification of the Child Labor Amendment (known more familiarly as OAR). The 1924 platforms of both major parties dutifully carried planks calling for its approval. Support so widespread seemed certain to carry the amendment to swift and easy victory.

Initially, the visible opponents were conservative bodies like the Sentinels of the Republic and former antisuffrage groups like the Woman Patriots and the American Constitutional League.[23] While these familiar figures deflected the arrows of the proponents, a formidable opposition was mobilizing. Taking advantage of the rising tide of resistance to federal encroachment in the area of labor-management relations, the National Association of Manufacturers, the U.S. Chamber of Commerce, the National Grange, the American Farm Bureau Federation, and Southern textile interests blanketed the country with propaganda that the amendment was "communistic," that it would undermine the family and parents' control over their children, and that it would infringe states' rights.

The battle over ratification was quickly joined. Georgia, Louisiana, and North Carolina rejected the amendment. Then, in November 1924, came Massachusetts, where seventeen groups led by the League had carefully prepared the way for approval. On the eve of the legislature's debate, the advocates were alerted to a sudden hostile swing of opinion; so quietly had the Chamber of Commerce and the local Catholic hierarchy done their work that the amendment's friends remained unaware of the danger.[24] Their decisive defeat opened a Pandora's box of troubles. In Maine, the struggling League found its allies deserting, and the amendment lost. The experience in other New England states was similar. The Pennsylvania state league had refused to support ratification, and watched complacently as it was rejected. The president of the Washington state league suddenly switched sides and became a leader of the antiamendment forces. In California the issue became embroiled in the gubernatorial election; the amendment was ratified, but the cost in blood spilled in the League and elsewhere was high. In several states opposition increased so markedly that local leagues frantically reported losing membership; Ohio complained that resistance was growing to all its program. Since Florence Kelley was the amendment's most conspicuous champion, the ratification struggle in turn helped spur the circulation of the insidious allegations of the spider-web chart.

By early March 1925, only four states had approved the amendment, while seventeen had rejected it and one postponed consideration indefinitely. Sherwin sent Legislative Secretary Marguerite Owen on a nationwide tour to assess the situation. She found that in many states the League appeared to be the only organization pressing vigorously for ratification. The branches of the General Federation of Women's Clubs were almost uniformly opposed, despite the declared support of the Federation's national board in the WJCC.[25] Few of the other groups participating in the WJCC subcommittee had any significant network of local and state organizations. An agency such as the WJCC was valuable chiefly for pressing Congress to pass federal legislation; it had no levers of direct influence with state legislatures.

Even the League's board showed evidence of division. But Julia Lathrop, now a national vice-president, wanted to fight aggressively, and joined Kelley in trying to energize the amorphous OAR. The minutes of numerous OAR meetings between 1925 and 1929 show how earnestly the League expanded staff time and resources relative to the contributions of others.[26] In addition, with women's, church, and labor groups united in a legislative campaign, they often found themselves navigating in choppy crosscurrents of motive and method. Sherwin grew steadily more wary, and prepared the way for an eventual revision of policy with regard to collaborative efforts involving other groups. The futile campaign to win ratification of the amendment continued into the early 1930s; the issue of child labor in the end was left to be dealt with by a series of New Deal enactments.

Despite the discouragements on this front, the League found itself drawn into three other constitutional controversies at the time: over the equal rights and Wadsworth-Garrett amendments,[27] both of which the League opposed, and over the Norris lame-duck amendment,[28] which it strongly favored. As an institutional experience, the anguishing effort to secure ratification of the child labor amendment taught the League many procedural essentials for effecting constitutional change; and also inured it to the snail-like pace by which public attitudes are transformed.

The year 1930 marked a low point in the League's life. The general economic collapse after 1929 had dried up most of its private sources of funds and cost it thousands of members.[29] Belle Sherwin and others saw an opportunity to lift their spirits by making 1930 an anniversary year, marking the end of their first decade. They conceived of a memorial to the pioneers and the founders, one indeed that might properly be used as a means of raising an endowment in the form of an Anniversary Memorial Fund. Each state might honor its suffrage pioneers by proposing their names for a national role of honor, pledging $1,000 for each name nominated. An advisory committee consisting of Marie Edwards, Emily Blair, Cornelia Pinchot, Dorothy Canfield Fisher, Mabeth Paige, and Alice Hamilton was appointed to select names and remind forgetful state leagues of their neglected heroines; Edwards made a nationwide tour, rejuvenating the interest of many older members who had fallen by the wayside. Despite hard times the goal of $250,000 was almost reached, and the names of the "ancestors of the League of Women Voters" were duly inscribed on a handsome scroll.

At the League's 1930 Louisville convention, special sessions were devoted to nostalgic reminiscences by survivors of the suffrage crusade. Some were there who could trace an unbroken line of descent from the founders of the movement; dozens were present who had attended the Victory Convention in 1920. After a decade of hard work, trials and disappointments, along with some triumphs, the League achieved a sense of unity and historical continuity which added a cubit to its collective stature.[30]

The Louisville convention was to mark the disappearance of one of the major symbols of the suffrage struggle. The *Woman's Journal*—formerly the *Woman's Citizen*, and one of the longest lived reform journals in American history—had been kept alive by an annual subsidy from the League in return for two pages in each issue as a vehicle for reporting League concerns. After years of debate in board meetings about the need for a newsletter or bulletin of their own, League leaders had come to the conclusion that the sentimental ties with the *Woman's Journal* should be severed; the subscription list now numbered few of its activists. But older members could not bear to give the links up, and the 1930 convention voted to keep them for one more year, raising the money on the spot. This stopgap action saved the *Woman's Journal* momentarily, but served as the coup de grâce to the little magazine; its last issue appeared before the end of the year. Established in 1870, the column of this well-edited journal remains a storehouse of information regarding the emergence of women, both in the United States and abroad. In its files the first feminist movement lies buried.[31]

NOTES

1. Proceedings, Richmond Convention, April 16–21, 1925. LWV Papers, Minutes and Related Records, LC. Unless otherwise noted, the Proceedings furnish the substance of the discussion in this section.

2. Maud Park, the initiator of the College Equal Suffrage League movement a quarter-century earlier, had recently made an extensive tour of campuses to stimulate interest in forming college leagues.

3. In her presidential address five years later, Sherwin was able to cite a report by the Committee on Policy of the American Political Science Association: "The committee is . . . of the opinion that adult political education is one of the most important means of improving the quality of government in our democracy. The education of the electorate on public questions is too exclusively left to partisan effort in which not truth but distortions of the truth are the staple commodity. A very honest and well-conducted attempt at political education is being made by the League of Women Voters. This movement is, however, much limited by lack of funds, and there is no League of Male Voters." The League by this stage had organized nearly thirteen hundred institutes and schools on government and politics. See LWV, *Ten Years of Growth*, 17, 12; and also Peffer, *National League of Women Voters*.

4. The board appointed a Committee of Nine to study all aspects of participation in the political process, including the status of women in the parties as well as voting patterns, literacy and registration requirements, incidence of poll tax, provisions for absentee voting, and the frequency of elections.

5. LWV, *A Record of Four Years*.

6. Accordingly, Sherwin organized convention sessions to open up these topics and invited professors John Gaus and Arthur Macmahon to address delegates, asking them

specifically to give the League guidance in placing this set of changes in historical context. See Sherwin correspondence of May 2, 25, and June 4, 5, 1925, LWV Papers, Ser. 2, Box 55, LC.

7. Proceedings, St. Louis Convention, April 14–21, 1926. LWV Papers, LC. Unless otherwise noted, the Proceedings furnish the substance of the discussion in this section.

8. There were reportedly more than a thousand local leagues and eighty-seven college leagues.

9. Despite Sherwin's efforts to encourage this development, reasonably accurate membership records did not exist until 1930.

10. Two immediate offspring of the report were Gladys Blakey's *A Handy Digest of Election Laws* (Washington, D.C.: Department of Efficiency in Government, League of Women Voters, 1928), and a "campaign book" which laid out a skeleton plan for election campaign activities.

11. One significant new departure occurred the following year, when Merlin Aylesworth, president of the National Broadcasting Company, invited the League to conduct an experiment in political education by radio. He offered the League a free half-hour weekly to conduct a series of broadcasts devoted to the forthcoming presidential election campaign. NBC's Washington and New York stations were made available, with its other outlets welcome to use the program if the chose. Aylesworth, a friend of Katharine Ludington, was impressed by the League's commitment to political education, and also no doubt saw the potentialities of radio in election campaigns. Lasting five years, the venture enjoyed considerable success in exploring a new form of adult education, anticipating the revolution wrought by radio and television in political campaign techniques. See LWV Papers, "Voters' Campaign Information Service," Radio Series, 1928–1932, LC.

12. Minutes, General Council Meeting, April 27–29, 1927, LWV Papers, LC. The General Council meetings were designated as workshops, and traditionally have been held in Washington, D.C. The council includes the national board, the presidents of the state leagues, and one additional delegate per state; it is empowered to adopt a budget and make such modifications in the program as are necessary.

13. Of the fifteen members of the national board, four made public declarations in favor of a national candidate, and one served on a national party committee. All three of the counsellors to the board—Maud Park, Gertrude Ely, and Julia Lathrop—engaged in active campaigning, two for Herbert Hoover and one for Alfred E. Smith; Ely and Lathrop were given leaves of absence while Park officially resigned. Of the six national chairs of standing committees, three were actively engaged in the campaign (two having been given leaves of absence). Among state officers, thirteen of the forty-four state presidents declared for a candidate. Altogether, thirty-five officers or former officers of the national or state boards were actively partisan in the 1928 campaign, most of them for Hoover.

14. Committee of Nine, *Report*, 1929, LWV Papers, LC. The League's work on participation and its methods of empirical fact-finding did not go unnoticed. In 1929, Professor Edward Robinson of Yale University's Institute of Human Relations invited the League to cooperate with him on a survey of voters' attitudes in the next presidential elections; this pioneering project called for volunteers from forty-two local leagues scattered over the country to interview an extensive sample of voters on their reactions to issues and candidates. The project was the first such investigation in depth of voter attitudes. This massive undertaking—one that was ultimately to canvas over eighty-four-

hundred voters—was the subject of a debate at the 1930 convention before approval was given. The results of the project were published by Professor Robinson as "Trends of the Voter's Mind," *Journal of Social Psychology* 4 (August 1933): 265–84.

15. See, for example, Peggy Lamson, *Few Are Chosen: American Women in Political Life Today* (Boston: Houghton Mifflin, 1968). This analysis of the political careers of ten women who were serving (or had served) in state legislatures revealed that most had gained their first political insights in the League.

16. Child Welfare Committee, "Renewal, Sheppard-Towner Act, 1925–27," LWV Papers, Ser. 2, Boxes 65, 119, 120, and 121, LC.

17. Testifying before the House Interstate and Foreign Commerce Committee, Maud Park had been asked if furnishing such aid did not tend to pauperize people; her answer was swift: "Did it pauperize the farmer whose hog was sick to have the government send a veterinarian? Why should it pauperize the same farmer if his wife were ill, to have the government provide medical care within a hundred miles?"

18. Senator James Couzens (Mich.) to Mrs. Henry Sherrard, April 12, 1926, LWV Papers, Ser. 2, Box 54, LC.

19. See, for example, William C. Woodward, "The Sheppard-Towner Act: Its Proposed Extension and Proposed Repeal," *American Medical Association Bulletin* 21 (May 1926); and also *Journal of the American Medical Association* 86 (6 February 1926): 421.

20. James A. Tobey, *The Children's Bureau: Its History, Activities and Organization*, Brookings Institution, Institute for Government Research (Baltimore: Johns Hopkins Press, 1925).

21. Julia Lathrop, who had served as the bureau's director since its creation in 1912 and who initially proposed the program that became the Sheppard-Towner Act, had retired in 1921, the year the measure was passed. A pioneer among professionally trained administrators capable of applying the resources of science and technology to the business of government, she was to devote the final decade of her life to the League, and played a vital role in shaping the League's early program concerns as well as its methods of work. At the Children's Bureau, Lathrop was to be followed by three outstanding women administrators—Grace Abbott, Katharine Lenroot, and Katherine Oettinger.

22. Maud Park later described the filibuster in unsparing detail to the 1927 General Council meeting, preserving a record of the type of masculine prejudice that had thwarted women's political emergence for decades; see "Unfinished Business," General Council Meeting, April 27–29, 1927. LWV Papers, LC.

23. The Sentinels of the Republic had been established in the early 1920s to uphold states' rights, and included many prominent persons in its membership. The Woman Patriots and the American Constitutional League had descended, respectively, from the National Association Opposed to Woman Suffrage and the Man Suffrage Association Opposed to Political Suffrage for Women.

24. Mrs. Roland Baker, "Public Opinion vs. Manipulation," Proceedings, St. Louis Convention, April 14–21, 1926, LWV Papers, LC.

25. Faced with internal dissension on the question, the General Federation subsequently withdrew from the WJCC, though it continued its official support for the amendment; Lemons, *The Woman Citizen*, 146–47.

26. "Child Labor Amendment, 1924–29," LWV Papers, Ser. 2, Boxes 32, 52, LC.

27. The Wadsworth-Garrett amendment was first introduced in Congress in 1921 by Senator James Wadsworth (N.Y.) and Congressman Finis Garrett (Tenn.). A conservative riposte to the passage of the prohibition and woman suffrage amendments, this

measure would have greatly complicated the process of changing the Constitution. An attempt to slip the measure through Congress at the close of the lame-duck session in 1925 was only averted when Marguerite Owen of the League spotted the maneuver and quickly mobilized opposition; see Lemons, *The Woman Citizen*, 241–43. To assist in clarifying the League's views on the issues posed by the Wadsworth-Garrett amendment, the national board enlisted Judge Dorothy Kenyon, a distinguished lawyer and a League member, to prepare a short treatise which was to be one of the prototypes for the long series of educational publications the League has produced on public questions; see LWV, Department of Efficiency in Government, *Changing the Constitution: A Study of the Amending Process*, by Dorothy Kenyon (Washington, D.C., 1926).

28. An amendment to abolish the lame-duck term of office for the outgoing Congress and president was introduced in Congress by Senator George Norris (Neb.) in 1922; eventually receiving congressional approval in 1932, it was sent to the states for ratification, and became the Twentieth Amendment to the Constitution in February 1933. The League initially supported the proposal in 1925, but only gave active backing from the late 1920s. Lemons notes that the League, together with the American Bar Association, became Norris's principal allies; see *The Woman Citizen*, 133.

29. The severe shakedown resulted in a budgetary crisis, but Katharine Ludington saw the loss of their private contributions as ultimately beneficial, since it enabled her to press for an integrated budget based on acceptance of financial responsibility by state and local leagues. This desirable goal was not to be reached for some years, however.

30. Carrie Chapman Catt prepared a Tenth Anniversary statement released on August 24, 1930. It provided a characteristically astringent summary of ten years of suffrage. She wrote: "The truth is that the most painful experience the machine politician ever endured has been through his contact with women voters. He has not been willing to share his game or teach its subtleties . . . he manages to preserve his ancient rights pretty well. When a woman goes to a convention, it is through his 'advice and consent!' . . . Yet this great mass of women voters . . . sitting in the grandstand with their eyes open, studying party handbooks, listening to party speeches . . . asking questions and occasionally performing the unexpected . . . are doing something to politics that no one decade can diagnose correctly."

31. Founded as an organ of the American Woman Suffrage Association, the *Woman's Journal* had served initially as a medium for the most articulate women and men in New England reform circles. It became the official organ of the suffrage movement in 1910 (though NAWSA did not always have sufficient funds to provide the promised subsidy). In 1917 the journal was purchased by the Leslie Woman Suffrage Commission, and its name was changed to the *Woman Citizen* following its merger with two other suffragist publications; ten years later it reverted to its original title. See Harper, *History of Woman Suffrage* 5: 337, 528; Peck, *Carrie Chapman Catt*, 273–74 and 274n; and Fowler, *Carrie Catt*, 116–17.

10

The Tennessee Valley Authority

In 1934, the final year of Belle Sherwin's administration, the League's "Explanation of the Program" posed a question made ever more urgent in the aftermath of the Great Depression:

> How much or how little should government be asked to protect or regulate economic activities? Where should the dividing line be between private enterprise and public concern? . . . These are primarily questions of policy. . . . Wise consideration of them requires knowledge and information. But still more does it require a broad interest in the general economic welfare and a freedom from narrow economic partisanship.[1]

It was in marking the "dividing line . . . between private enterprise and public concern" that the League scored its greatest achievement in the Sherwin administration: its role in the creation of the Tennessee Valley Authority.

The story of how the League became involved in the controversy over the future of Muscle Shoals on the Tennessee River underlies the truth of Marguerite Wells's observation that much of what the League learned in the economic field came "not from separate shafts sunk down called 'study,' " but had "adhered to some root at which the League was tugging and come up with it."[2] Under the prodding of a Huntsville, Alabama, delegate, the 1921 convention passed a resolution supporting the conversion of facilities developed by the government at Muscle Shoals during World War I to produce nitrates (required for explosives) to the peacetime production of fertilizers. The following year, the Baltimore convention went further by proposing that if Congress felt unable to continue public operation of the installations, "the government be urged to accept the offer which best safeguards this great asset still owned by the people"[3]—a resolution reflecting the stir caused by a dramatic offer from Henry Ford, the Detroit automobile magnate, to lease the facilities and an unfinished hydroelectric dam nearby for one hundred years for the production of electric power and fertilizers.[4]

The Muscle Shoals presented a forbidding barrier on the Tennessee River as it passed through northern Alabama, a thirty-seven-mile stretch marked by rapids and jagged rocks as the river dropped 134 feet. Despite attempts after the 1820s to bypass the shoals with canals, the rapids continued to deny the great river to transportation, and the area had remained impoverished and underdeveloped. A pioneer in the hydroelectric power industry had early perceived the possibilities the shoals presented; a franchise granted by Congress in 1899 to erect a power plant lapsed, however, when the federal and state governments failed to agree over dividing the fees to be charged for the concession. Subsequent attempts to revive the franchise in 1903 and 1908 were vetoed by President Theodore Roosevelt on the grounds that the government should not dispose of valuable natural resources that might be developed at public expense for public use.[5] So the wandering and inconstant river, draining an area of forty thousand square miles ranging across seven states, was spared to become the center of one of the most important political debates of the postwar era.

In 1916, in an effort to end American dependence on overseas supplies of nitrates at a time of uncertainty over possible involvement in the European war, Congress had included provision in the National Defense Act enabling the president to initiate measures to ascertain feasible methods of producing synthetic nitrogen. Two plants were established in the Tennessee River Valley to experiment with nitrogen fixation—extracting nitrogen from the air. One of these utilized a method requiring substantial electric power; it was therefore sighted near Muscle Shoals, and what was to become the Wilson Dam was commenced in February 1918. While capable of producing forty thousand tons of nitrogen annually, this plant only began operations as the war ended, and had to be placed on standby.[6]

The 1916 act had explicitly allowed the nitrogen facilities to be converted to peacetime fertilizer production. When the War Department was unable to interest the chemical industry in the Muscle Shoals enterprise, the Wadsworth-Kahn bill was introduced in Congress in November 1919 to set up a public corporation to produce nitrogen for defense and farming needs, and to sell fertilizer and any surplus power from the neighboring dam on a wholesale basis. By March 1921, conservative opposition in the House of Representatives had blocked both this and an additional appropriation to sustain work on the dam. The War Department was making further efforts to interest power companies in Muscle Shoals when, in July 1921, Ford launched his unexpected initiative. The publicity given to the possibilities of cheap fertilizer from Muscle Shoals enabled his plan to swiftly attract a powerful supporting coalition of farming organizations and Southern members of Congress. A counterscheme advanced by the Alabama Power Company, by contrast, stressed the advantages to the public of abundant hydroelectric power.[7] In July 1922, the Senate Agriculture and Forestry Committee turned down both offers, and also rejected a bill sponsored by its own chairman, Senator George Norris of Nebraska, creating a government corporation to manage both the dam and the fertilizer operation. However, the Muscle Shoals question was placed in a new framework by the idea of multipurpose river basin development.

The League's Committee on Living Costs, with Louise Baldwin as its chair, was growing increasingly interested in the Muscle Shoals issue. Its prior work on problems of postwar inflation had already led it to recognition of the significance of fertilizer in food price-and-supply equations. But the committee's attention was soon extended to include the question of electric power. The rapid and disorderly growth of the power industry after the turn of the century had been accompanied by efforts at the state level (beginning as early as 1901) to regulate the industry through public utility commissions as well as a substantial attempt at federal regulation with the 1920 Water Power Act. Yet often enough, the industry's development had appeared to take little account of the fact that electric power was a "public utility" visibly clothed with the public interest. The spreading network of transmission lines threatened to swallow many municipally owned power companies. While industrial users of power might have gained in this process of growth through lower costs, ordinary consumers had felt fewer benefits, and rural areas—a particular grievance—had been slow to receive electrification. Moreover, congressional Progressives like Norris were not alone in the conviction that the power industry was a natural monopoly tending toward the restraint of trade by undermining freely competitive markets.[8]

The Living Costs Committee saw the complex of problems raised by the concentration of economic power as a central issue in the disposition of Muscle Shoals. Not initially did the membership see the issue in so large a context. Their interest had been aroused by a more immediate consideration: protecting the taxpayers' equity in a potentially valuable property built with public funds under the provisions of the 1916 National Defense Act. Further, in the shifting contest involving an intricate interplay of interests among the competing industrial corporations as well as among more broadly defined political forces— the Southern congressional bloc, spokesmen for Eastern industrial interests, administration loyalists, agrarian Progressive Republicans from the West and Midwest—the League's sympathies naturally gravitated toward those who had been their allies on previous battlefields. A still more powerful motivation for involvement derived from the boundless possibilities wrapped up in the potential development of cheap electric power. Under Louise Baldwin's guidance, local study groups were organized in 1923 and 1924 to explore power facilities at the community level: Where did power come from? What did it cost domestic and industrial users? What were the charges in those localities with municipally owned power plants? How efficient and dependable were such plants? Communications with the heads of local league Living Costs committees stressed the almost unlimited potentialities of electric power, especially in revolutionizing home management; the real results of women's emancipation might come after electric power had driven a wedge between the homemaker and drudgery, giving millions of women disposable time for an expansion of their community concerns.

In early 1924 both congressional chambers prepared to take action on the Ford proposals. A bill facilitating acceptance of the package was passed by the House in March. In the Senate, extended hearings conducted by Norris's Agriculture and Forestry Committee revealed increasing opposition to the scheme, however, and in October, Ford abruptly withdrew his offer. The Senate committee had already approved a revised version of Norris's earlier bill, this time separating the fertilizer and power aspects of Muscle Shoals and providing for a public corporation to manage the latter with authority to sell power directly to consumers.[9] In January 1925, the Senate passed instead a rival bill sponsored by Senator Oscar Underwood of Alabama; this aimed at leasing the Muscle Shoals operations to a private firm. When a conference committee of House and Senate representatives proved necessary to agree on a compromise formula for the measure, Norris seized a timely opportunity to block it, first by a deft parliamentary maneuver and then by threat of a filibuster.

Such was the situation when Mrs. Baldwin's committee proposed moving Muscle Shoals from study to action at the 1925 Richmond convention, calling for "development of Muscle Shoals as a national asset which will provide wide and economical distribution of electric power, provide for the production of chemicals and fertilizers, and serve the people's interests and safeguard their perpetual rights."[10] The debate proved the most vigorous of the entire convention. While a majority of the Living Costs Committee felt the Norris bill most nearly embodied League principles regarding the conservation of natural resources as well as protecting the public's already established equity in Muscle Shoals, the redoubtable Lucy Miller of Pennsylvania declared herself unalterably opposed to publicly owned power facilities; a sprinkling of delegates from eastern industrial states echoed her views. Mary Morrisson sought to moderate the heat by proposing that a decision be delayed until the report of a commission of inquiry recently appointed by President Coolidge. Mabel Costigan maintained that supporting the Norris bill did not imply dogmatic support for public power, but was merely the best alternative now available. When Miller and her supporters sought to postpone action, Baldwin insisted on a vote to know where her committee stood. As a concession, a statement was added to the program denying that endorsement of the Norris measure involved a commitment in principle to public power. The final vote was heavily in favor of active support for the Norris bill. At that moment, it had only the barest chance of passage.

For convention delegates, this was their first big plunge in support of an economic policy choice involving a major national issue, and they sensed its importance. Unsure at first where the path was leading, they became increasingly certain in the next few years as successive crises enveloped the issue. On two points the view of the great majority never changed: Muscle Shoals belonged to the American taxpayer, and the development of natural resources involving large regions should be determined by national rather than private interests.

Over the following year, local leagues examined the various Muscle Shoals proposals in detail, and the 1926 convention strengthened the statement of support by calling for legislation "which provided for a continuation of government operation as required by the National Defense Act of 1916 through a non-political corporation to provide nitrates for defense; to experiment with production of cheap fertilizers; to insure the development of the Tennessee River system as one project for hydroelectric power production and flood control."[11] In March 1926, Belle Sherwin testified for the first time in favor of the Norris bill before the Senate Agriculture and Forestry Committee. Soon after, Sherwin, Baldwin, and Staff Secretary Margaret Hicks visited Muscle Shoals at their own expense to learn the facts about its present situation. Senator Norris joined them, and a picture of the entire group was given wide publicity through the senator's office.

As the League assumed an active commitment to the Norris bill, opponents quickly surfaced. Their old foes charged them both covertly and openly with being dupes of "socialistic interests."[12] The spider-web chart was resuscitated. Propaganda from various sources labeled supporters of the Norris bill as "bolsheviks." Leagues in some areas appeared singled out for attack; in Ohio, for example, local leagues throughout the state were subjected to a ruthless vendetta through news stories and press editorials; the material in these had emanated from the Ohio Chamber of Commerce, later shown to be a tool of the National Electric Light Association (NELA). Though stronger local leagues appeared to thrive on the challenge, many were severely shaken by the necessity to defend their right to an opinion on a public issue. The propaganda attacks in turn stimulated the League to countermeasures. Louise Baldwin, a tireless traveler and effective speaker, held forums and conferences in every part of the country, lectured at universities, attended state board meetings to strengthen the organizational effort, and stirred interest wherever she went. In Washington, D.C., the League mounted an ambitious forum to debate the utilization of hydroelectric power.[13]

More important than these public activities in winning member involvement was the nationwide domestic electric power survey conducted by local leagues, to acquaint as many members as possible with the practical facts of their power services. The detailed questionnaire covered such topics as the industrial character of the community, the sources of electric power, the manner in which rates were computed, the number of houses on members' extensions, the cost of heating houses of different sizes and construction, and the composition and role of state power regulatory commissions. It was this survey that alerted the League to the limited rate-making powers of many such bodies—as power facilities so frequently crossed state boundaries—and to the political nature of most.

The survey also sharpened awareness of the far-reaching tentacles of NELA, propaganda arm of the private power industry: "Bruce Barton" leaflets distributed with light bills, newspaper editorials and articles in women's magazines extolling the "virtues of Aladdin," even propaganda in their children's textbooks; surveys by NELA purporting to prove the high cost and inefficiency of municipally owned utilities used findings that ran counter to their own investigations. The detailed reports of local leagues to national headquarters reflected their reaction; no single discovery appeared to do so much to strengthen member commitment. The information was compiled by the League's national staff and fed back to local and state leagues as well as to Senator Norris and his supporters. Senator Thomas Walsh of Montana, a Norris ally, initiated an official investigation by the Federal Trade Commission of the utility holding companies and their public relations activities, including those of NELA. What the testimony disclosed made sensational news. Spending millions annually, NELA had subsidized the work of editors and journalists, high school superintendents, professors of economics and engineering, deans of business schools, politicians, state power commissions and public officials—even the president of a major women's organization—to disseminate propaganda favorable to the private power industry. The record established "that, measured by quantity, extent, and cost, this was probably the greatest peace-time propaganda campaign ever conducted by private interests in this country."[15]

The shabby revelations created waves of public interest which were soon felt in Congress. An amended bill sponsored by Norris and others passed in May 1928, only to be vetoed by President Coolidge.[16] It was reintroduced in the next Congress, and the League followed the ensuing debates with the closest attention, keeping its state officers informed regarding precisely what was needed when a call to action went out. Letters flew back and forth between the senator's office and League headquarters, which forwarded to Norris all pertinent information from congressional replies to members' letters as well as copies of all their correspondence and research materials. Norris in turn alerted them to parliamentary maneuvers as these developed, and to opportunities for League activity. On one occasion, Norris took time to write Belle Sherwin a note of thanks: "I assure you, I appreciate more than I can say the assistance you have given in the Muscle Shoals controversy. It seems to me you have always said the right thing and said it in very fine language."[17]

The Norris bill was passed again near the close of the Hoover administration, and again was vetoed. In April 1933, having visited the Tennessee Valley as president-elect with a party of members of Congress and power experts, Franklin Roosevelt requested that Congress establish a Tennessee Valley Authority—"a corporation clothed with the power of Government but possessed with the flexibility and initiative of a private enterprise"—to undertake both the conservation and the multipurpose development of the natural resources of the Tennessee River basin; in less than forty days, Congress had approved the necessary act. After the measure was signed into law, Norris sent a brief but personal note to Belle Sherwin: "I wish to pause long enough to thank you, and through you, the members of the League of Women Voters," he wrote, "for their untiring efforts on behalf of the Muscle Shoals legislation."[18]

A final note on Muscle Shoals may be recorded, one of those dramatic coincidences that enliven history. The constitutionality of the law establishing the TVA was three times challenged in federal courts by the private power industry before the battle was won.[19] The second of these, the "nineteen companies" case, was decided in the Federal Court of Appeals of the Sixth District in 1938—the decision later sustained by the Supreme Court. Chief of the attorneys representing the utility companies was Wendell Willkie, Republican presidential candidate in 1940. The presiding judge who wrote the court's judgment—that the "complainants had no immunity from lawful competition"— was a League pioneer, Florence Allen.[20]

The Muscle Shoals controversy was in fact to mark an epoch in League history; for those deeply involved, it undoubtedly represented a more educative experience than anything they had undergone hitherto. For the first time, the organization had concentrated its energies on a major national issue in the economic sphere grounded on a broader basis than women's "special responsibilities." The experience established permanently an economic dimension to League thinking as well as emphasizing the growing preeminence of national concerns over regional interests. While TVA's significance to the League as an experiment in multipurpose river basin development was less visible in 1933 than it would be in the 1950s—when interest would again turn to this subject— it was well understood that it embodied their concept of elevating public concern for the "general economic welfare" beyond the reach of "narrow economic partisanship."

The spring of 1933 marked a new era in American political history as well as in the life of the League. During the Harding, Coolidge, and Hoover administrations, the League had been continuously engaged in a politics of confrontation. The needs it voiced and the goals it sought were not shared by dominant political forces. The intellectual attitudes of the League's leading figures had been shaped in the heady days when Theodore Roosevelt was encouraging the oncoming generation to critical attitudes toward the relation between government and business, and between the federal government and the states. Their intellectual baggage contained the principles voiced by Roosevelt at Osawatomie in 1910 concerning combating social injustice and improving the lot of the disadvantaged with all the powers at the national government's disposal; thus their program and policies formed cables in the bridge between the two Roosevelts. Not the least of the League's contributions during these years had been the forceful identification of what it considered relevant and critical among political issues; even in defeat it had furnished a small but attentive and highly educable portion of the public with a socially oriented view of political realities as well as political problems. In the debates on the Sheppard-Towner Act and its renewal, the child labor amendment, the disposition of Muscle Shoals, and on other questions like the need for protection against the hazards of unemployment, the League helped thrust economic and social issues into public forums for debate.

Once president, Franklin Roosevelt acted swiftly to place economic and social reform at the head of the nation's political agenda. But the trail had already been blazed. Muscle Shoals soon became TVA; the lame-duck amendment was added to the Constitution; Sheppard-Towner and the child labor amendment were reincarnated in legislation with a broader base. In short, the League of Women Voters now found itself moving with the political main currents.

Ironically, Roosevelt had not been the favored candidate of many who were or had been League leaders, partly because he gave little hint during the 1932 election campaign of the bold steps he would take to arrest the depression, and partly because he seemed to some less forthright on the World Court than Hoover. But many of the emergency measures enacted in the early months of the New Deal were warmly approved by the League since they embodied principles it had long supported. Belle Sherwin was named a member of the Consumers' Advisory Board (created under the National Industrial Recovery Act). It did not matter that the board was soon shunted aside, and that the NIRA was struck down by the Supreme Court in 1935. By that time, more effective measures serving the same ends were in the offing.

In a provocative speech to the 1934 convention, Belle Sherwin asked the delegates to ponder the course the country was taking, and to relate the meaning of efforts at "private cooperation under public supervision" to their own philosophy. Behind the facade of the economic recovery measures, it was evident that old conflicts between labor and business were being modified, and that newer issues were crystallizing: "Consumers, workers, producers, managers, and owners [were all] competitors . . . with each other"; Had it not become clear that "the public interest [lay] in the fine balance of a multitude of interests," each making its rightful claims? Out of the clamor and confusion of rival interests would emerge a balance, in turn determining " 'the necessary social costs of production.' " Such a conception went beyond treating the public interest as merely "the negation of dominance by 'special interests,' " or viewing it as identified with the interests of a single group, however large. It rather directed attention to the necessity "to set their preferences side by side with the preferences of others and examine them all with the same disinterestedness." The League had pressed for many socially necessary reforms in seeking to safeguard the interests of women and children in industrial and public life. Now "economic laissez faire [had] gone; political laissez faire [was] passing." Never were their purposes as League members challenged more compellingly than at present. Had not the opportunity presented itself, " 'to merge [their] individual interests and concerns in the wider and deeper currents of the society' " that was developing around them?[21]

NOTES

1. Quoted in LWV, *A History of the League Program*, by Kathryn H. Stone (Washington, D.C., 1949), 23.

2. LWV, *A Portrait of the League of Women Voters at the Age of Eighteen*, quoted in LWV, *History of the League Program*, 10.

3. See LWV, *Forty Years of a Great Idea*, 21.

4. For details of the Ford proposal, see Preston J. Hubbard, *Origins of the TVA: The Muscle Shoals Controversy, 1920–1932* (Nashville: Vanderbilt University Press, 1961), 28–29.

5. Herman Finer, *The T.V.A.: Lessons for International Application* (New York: Da Capo Press, 1972), 7–8.

6. Hubbard, *Origins of the TVA*, 1–4; and Finer, *The T.V.A.*, 10–11.

7. The Ford plan was vulnerable on this point, as Ford had always made it clear that all the power generated by the Wilson Dam would be utilized for his own projects.

8. At this stage in the debate over Muscle Shoals, most Alabama members of Congress, the state governor, and leaders of many Alabama civic and business groups were strong Ford partisans, and echoed similar suspicions of the "power trust"; see Hubbard, *Origins of the TVA*, 55–56, 57–60, 94.

9. The new Norris bill also empowered the secretary of war to survey the Tennessee River and build further dams for hydroelectric power, flood control, and improved navigation. See Hubbard, *Origins of the TVA*, 124n, 150–51.

10. Proceedings, Richmond Convention, April 16–21, 1925. LWV Papers, Minutes and Related Records, LC.

11. Proceedings, St. Louis Convention, April 14–21, 1926. LWV Papers, LC.

12. Committee on Living Costs, "Muscle Shoals," LWV Papers, Ser. 2, Boxes 104 and 105, LC.

13. The forum had as a second focus the tariff question (a major concern of the Living Costs Committee since Mrs. Baldwin became its head). Among those speaking were Frank W. Taussig, professor of economics at Harvard University; Benjamin Anderson, an economist with Chase National Bank; Morris Cooke, consulting engineer for a comprehensive survey of Pennsylvania's energy resources that Governor Gifford Pinchot had initiated in 1923; and Robert Bruere, editor of *Survey Graphic*. The Committee on Living Costs was also active in preparing the first of what became a valuable series of reports on Muscle Shoals: *Facts about Muscle Shoals* (Washington, D.C., 1927); *Muscle Shoals and the Public Welfare*, by Marguerite Owen (Washington, D.C., 1929); and *Muscle Shoals as a Yardstick*, by Louise G. Baldwin (Washington, D.C., 1934).

14. In the mid-1920s, NELA had provided financial assistance to the General Federation of Women's Clubs to enable it to conduct surveys on the use of electric household appliances in American homes; this funding had also supported a follow-up media campaign by the GFWC to encourage the spread of such appliances. See Hubbard, *Origins of the TVA*, 253; and James, James, and Boyer, *Notable American Women* 3: 281.

15. U.S. Congress, Senate, *Utility Corporations: Summary Report of the Federal Trade Commission . . . on Efforts of Associations and Agencies of Electric and Gas Utilities to Influence Public Opinion*, 70th Cong., 1st sess., S. Doc. 92, pt. 71A (Washington, D.C.: U.S. Government Printing Office, 1930), x–xi; quoted in Judson King, *The Conservation Fight*

from *Theodore Roosevelt to the Tennessee Valley Authority* (Washington, D.C.: Public Affairs Press, 1959), 207. See also Hubbard, *Origins of the TVA*, 219–21, 239–40, 252–54, 256.

16. The 1928 bill emerged as a compromise with a measure introduced in the House of Representatives by Congressman John Morin for the secretary of agriculture, and focused on the fertilizer and hydroelectric power aspects of Muscle Shoals; Norris omitted concern for the overall development of the Tennessee River system from this version of his proposals. Hubbard, *Origins of the TVA*, 210–11, 221–36.

17. Committee on Living Costs, Correspondence, May 1928, LWV Papers, Ser. 2, Box 105, LC. At around the same time, Sherwin received a letter from Senator Arthur Vandenberg of Michigan, "anxious" that she should understand his reasons for not supporting an amendment intended to strengthen the Norris measure: "I very much dislike to disagree with the League of Women Voters. I am tremendously interested in your organization . . . think it is a wonderful thing that women should thus focus their active interest in public affairs. I am sure that nine times out of ten we shall find ourselves in agreement." Ibid.

18. Letter of May 30, 1933, George Norris Papers, Box 9, Manuscript Division, Library of Congress, Washington, D.C.

19. See Thomas K. McCraw, *TVA and the Power Fight, 1933–1939* (Philadelphia: J. B. Lippincott, 1971), chap. 6.

20. Allen's association with the last phase of the suffrage movement and with the League's early years made for warm ties throughout her life; she had been appointed to the federal bench by President Roosevelt. See Florence E. Allen, *To Do Justly* (Cleveland: Press of Western Reserve University, 1965).

21. Proceedings, Boston Convention. April 23–28, 1934, LWV Papers, LC. Sherwin's speech was published by the League as *The Hard Road* (Washington, D.C., April 1934).

11

The Deserving Public

The 1934 convention elected Marguerite Wells to succeed Belle Sherwin as president. Having worked harmoniously for a decade on the national board, they shared many views regarding the League's evolving purposes. They both recognized the need for active and effective direction from the center to evoke and harness the energies of the outlying parts, and overcome tendencies toward particularism. They likewise sought to avoid the "snare of preparation"—the danger of finding in study an escape from direct engagement in political life.[1]

Sherwin had led the League through its stressful childhood and years of growing self-assurance. As the country's mood shifted rapidly with the onset of the depression, she had held the League firmly on its course of political education, building a "university without walls" (with its boundaries protected by the stiffening of procedures carefully adhered to). She sustained the League in courageously facing the inevitable falling away of its early membership. Age had caught up with many; the depression had overrun others: in 1935 the membership reached an all-time low of forty-one thousand.

Sherwin's probing thoughts in her valedictory—concerning new applications of old democratic principles under the Roosevelt administration—prepared the ground for the convention's climax in Wells's provocative call for an escape from the bog of a top-heavy program onto the firm ground where action took place.[2] Of the thirty-eight items in the adopted program, she pointed to two that ultimately affected the others. The first was civil service reform, and the second, reform of the tax system to provide both adequate revenue and an equitable distribution of the tax burden. The first of these was the heart of the matter. Why not concentrate energies on securing a career service for government personnel appointed on the basis of merit, without discrimination or partisan consideration? Relieving the parties of patronage would also help restore party responsibility. Why not make a national, coordinated attack on political patronage? The League should study the way patronage worked, and how its practice related to popular democratic government, from policy formation to legislative enactment and execution. A campaign by local leagues to professionalize the civil service could serve as "an excursion into American political life." The convention accepted her challenge.

Like Carrie Chapman Catt, Wells was a superb organizer for action. Decisive in judgment and confident of her own intellectual powers, she had the ability to associate her fellow workers with her decisions, and draw out their best energies. She also had a span of League experience unmatched by other leaders at the time. Like her predecessors, she spoke strongly in the accents of liberal progressivism; she had an even stronger conviction than they of political patronage as a serious malady of American politics. Her speeches dwelt on the "meaninglessness of the political game." A major aim of the League should be "to preserve and purify the parties." It was precisely the fresh courage and "unworn determination" of women voters that was needed to "find a way out of the dilemma over which good men were shaking their heads in despair."[3]

In a period of doubt and discouragement, the League was choosing a change of course without fully comprehending its own motives, as had happened before and would happen again. Exhilaration over the success of the Muscle Shoals project had been drained off by imminent defeat of the proposed American participation in the World Court. Other hopeful developments in international cooperation—not least the League of Nations—had been blunted. At home the New Deal promised to take some of the League's primary concerns off its shoulders, but with the passing of Julia Lathrop and Florence Kelley, it had lost two of its best friends and counsellors in this sphere. Something energizing, unifying was sorely needed.

The civil service and the progressive spread of the merit system had been in the League's program but had not engaged its energies for several years. The Hoover administration had extended merit coverage within the federal service, but after the late 1920s discrimination against women in public employment had, at many levels, been rapidly increasing.[4] This constituted a genuine grievance. However, the overriding concern was still the extensive system of patronage over which the parties presided. Political spoils guaranteed waste and incompetence, and, to the League, corrupted the parties themselves by encouraging loyalty to men rather than principles. Its persistence challenged the League's conviction that the educational system should produce individuals qualified to receive the jobs society had to offer. Still more deeply grooved was the recognition that it worked to exclude women from party, elective, and many public service posts except on the parties' own terms.[5] Nor was the League alone in thinking that a professionalized civil service would both provide institutional opportunities for an emergent social group and serve the best interests of the nation. The League's attitudes toward public administration reflected the then conventional wisdom, which drew a sharp distinction between those who won elections and formulated policy and those who implemented it. The context of the League's thinking was thus shaped by the intellectual modes of the period and reinforced by factors drawn from its own experience.

The effort to fix public attention on the civil service and merit systems opened a path to community involvement exceeding that of any prior attempt at political education, and was not matched again until the campaign for the United Nations in 1945.[6] The national board named Edna Gellhorn to head the Personnel Campaign; Mrs. Katharine Greenough of Indiana, national chair of the Department of Government and Its Operation, was in charge of field activities. A pamphlet on the campaign was soon ready, as a guide for the "excursion into political life."[7] The campaign committee discussed its approach with Leonard White, Harold Lasswell, and other political scientists, who made useful suggestions, including the need for an effective slogan. A nationwide contest soon produced: "Find the man for the job—not the job for the man," a phrase still echoing down the corridors of time.

The League also initiated an extensive survey of existing conditions within the public service.[8] Local study groups were briefed on election laws and practices, the history and uses of patronage, and the structure of political machines as well as the findings of voting research on popular attitudes toward elections, machines, and patronage. After League interrogators were briefed and trained, they questioned numerous local party officials (from county down to precinct levels) to discover their own attitudes and practices. These interviews were supplemented by local league analyses of local government positions in their own communities and the relationship between control of patronage and the outcome of elections, bond issues, and local ordinances.

These explorations threw a beam of light into many dark corners, and unexpectedly revealed fewer undeserved rewards than deficiencies in recognition, pay, and working conditions experienced by many humble individuals engaged in the people's business.[9] Moreover, the modest number of states and localities with civil service systems stemming from the Progressive reform era revealed large patches of gray in their workings.[10] A public service was only as good as its machinery for recruitment, job classification, and proficiency examinations, its scale of salaries, its pension provisions, tenure and in-service promotion arrangements, and the criteria for dismissal. Moreover, since a sound system in such respects was fairly expensive, the necessity for organized public support was continuously urgent. New York and New Jersey, for example, had operated with professionalized state civil services for three decades, with optional systems at the local level. Yet the League investigators found that there was little prestige attached to public service, that methods of testing were haphazard, and that rewards were uncertain at best; nor could local governments afford a competitive pay scale, provision for tenure and promotion, or retirement pensions. As one observer noted, "In no modern country has political indifference so handicapped the government in its administrative duties."[11]

The League's efforts continued unceasingly from 1934 to the early 1940s, with results soon becoming apparent. As the campaign acquired momentum, various cooperating groups were gathered in. Some twelve hundred organizational meetings were addressed by League members; twenty-five states reported six hundred general meetings on the merit system. State leagues sought legislation either establishing state merit systems or improving those already existing. A discussion petition was drawn up: "Can the Parties Live without Patronage?" Some 250,000 signatures were obtained. A Public Personnel Day mounted by the League in January 1936 involved a nationwide radio hookup to carry speeches by Mayor Fiorello La Guardia of New York City, Governor Frank Fitzgerald of Michigan, and U.S. Secretary of Commerce Daniel Roper; representing the three levels of government as well as three partisan viewpoints, the speakers echoed the League's call for a civil service based on the merit system.[12]

Both parties saw the wisdom of including a civil service plank in their 1936 platforms. Even Congress showed signs of feeling the heat, and the married woman's clause in the 1932 Economy Act was repealed. President Roosevelt was not only sympathetic to the public interest in efficient administration, but had been facing pressure from business and industrial groups to improve executive management. In early 1937 he sent a reorganization bill to Congress which, along with measures to strengthen his presidential office and establish two new cabinet-level departments, also extended the merit system to cover virtually all nonpolicy posts and placed various independent agencies under departmental control.

When the reorganization bill finally surfaced for congressional debate in February 1938, the opposition was fierce. The American Legion opposed surrendering the independent status of the Veterans' Bureau; organized teachers demanded exemption for the Office of Education; the League itself opposed the absorption of the Women's Bureau into the Wage and Hour Division of the Department of Labor; so it went with other independent agencies. The executive branch was accused of aggrandizement; in the wake of the unsuccessful attempt at Supreme Court reform, charges of "dictator" were hurled at Roosevelt. The bill failed to pass.

In June 1938, Roosevelt placed another hundred thousand jobs under civil service coverage by executive order; at the same time, Congressman Robert Ramspeck, chair of the House Civil Service Committee, introduced a bill empowering the president to extend such coverage to all federal agencies now exempt. The politics of the civil service legislative battle were intricate; and the League appeared to be at the center of the conflict every step of the way. The Ramspeck bill soon collided with the Hatch bill prohibiting political activities on the part of federal employees and limiting the size of campaign gifts. The first Ramspeck bill died with the close of the congressional session, but it was reintroduced in 1940. Though its foes sought to encumber it with amendments designed to arouse opposition, the measure survived to become law in November 1940.[13]

The League's national board was keenly aware, however, that the passage of the legislation was only the beginning of its task. A recent Gallup poll had reported that 88 percent of the public supported the merit system. But the League's own surveys had pointed to the exacting requirements of adequate arrangements: statutory provision for merit standards, strong executive will, clear public support for adequate appropriations, and, not least, competent administration of civil service recruiting machinery. A major session at the 1938 League convention was devoted to formulating a firm League policy on the merit system, with Professor Charles Merriam making a vigorous plea that local leagues explore the problems and build the necessary grass-roots support. A long and scholarly pamphlet, *The Awkward Age in Civil Service*,[14] with an accompanying questionnaire, was prepared for use by local study groups, and earnest efforts were made to keep alive the public interest aroused by the campaign.[15] Unfortunately, the onset of World War II shunted aside further concern for the merit system. The quality of the educational materials prepared and the importance of the problem deserved a better fate.

NOTES

1. Wells's *A Portrait of the League of Women Voters at the Age of Eighteen* underlines what priority this concern had in her own thinking. For Wells's background, see *supra*, Chap. 3, n. 20, and Sicherman et al., *Notable American Women*, 723–25.

2. Proceedings, Boston Convention, April 23–28, 1934. LWV Papers, Minutes and Related Records, LC. Wells's initiative came at the end of a debate on program realignment that had resulted in a reduction of the League's national structure of two departments and six standing committees to a framework of six departments, with the Women in Industry and Living Costs committees being grouped together (as the Department of Government and Economic Welfare) and the Social Hygiene Committee disappearing.

3. "Reminiscences," Marguerite M. Wells Papers, Arthur and Elizabeth Schlesinger Library on the History of Women in America, Radcliffe College.

4. With the onset of the depression, recruitment barriers to keep married women from competing with men for the available jobs were common at municipal and state levels (as well as among private firms). In 1932 Congress itself had passed the Economy Act, which included a clause effectively preventing more than one member of a family household from holding federal employment. See Nancy E. McGlen and Karen O'Conner, *Women's Rights: The Struggle for Equality in the Nineteenth and Twentieth Centuries* (New York: Praeger, 1983), 161; and LWV, *The Program Explained*, ed. Louise L. Wright (Washington, D.C., 1936), 2–3 and 3n.

5. How corrosively this sense of exclusion had worked into the minds of politically oriented women is amply revealed in the autobiographic writings of Eleanor Roosevelt, Frances Perkins, and Mary Dewson.

6. See Personnel Campaign, 1935–40, LWV Papers, LC.

7. LWV, *A Handbook for the Personnel Campaign: What, Why, How, Who, When, Where*, comp. Julia R. King (Washington, D.C., October 1935). With her gift for expressive phrasing, Wells struck the keynote: "In respect to appointment to office there are no 'deserving Democrats' nor are there any 'deserving Republicans.' There is only

the deserving public and it deserves that its affairs be run by men and women chosen for ability and devotion."

8. The results were to appear in LWV, *The Patronage System: A Guide to an Excursion into Political Life in the United States* (Washington, D.C., 1937).

9. Thus the results of the Indiana survey may have surprised the investigators about the actual workings of patronage. County and ward chairmen denied ever naming applicants for technical posts; moreover, it was the precinct committeeman's endorsement that appeared essential in patronage matters. See Indiana League of Women Voters, "Patronage Survey Summary," March 1938, LWV Papers, LC.

10. As a 1936 League publication noted: "Nine states and about 450 cities have civil service laws, although they are not always sympathetically carried out. It is estimated that about one-third of the employees of state governments, and one-half of those of municipalities, and less than 15 per cent of the employees of counties, townships, and districts are employed under merit systems." LWV, *The Program Explained*, 2.

11. Quoted in *The Awkward Age in Civil Service*, by Betsy Knapp, LWV (Washington, D.C., 1940).

12. The publicity was immense, and nine hundred press editorials commended the League.

13. See *News Letter*, 14 February 1940, and 23 April 1941, LWV Papers, LC.

14. See note 11.

15. Betsy Knapp, interview with author, May 1970.

12

The Search for Peace

Surveying the League's concerns with world problems during its first two decades provides ample reminder that social history must concern itself less with what happened than with how people viewed events as they were happening. World War I had been reluctantly accepted by a nation unprepared to understand the character of its position in the world community. The peace negotiations had been disillusioning, and the rejection of the League of Nations had occurred in an atmosphere poisoned by rancor. Everyone wanted peace; many wanted peace without obligations, wanted simply to be left alone. The League of Women Voters and a handful of other women's groups strove to channel the deep-rooted sentiment against war into a positive crusade for international understanding and cooperation, outside the framework of the League of Nations.[1] During the twenties, they largely followed international developments as spectators rather than activists, except for the passion spent on the World Court; during the thirties, there was less detachment and considerably more action, as the unfolding plot of external rivalries and conflicts drew America ineluctably onto the world stage.

At its 1920 Convention, the League had passed a resolution endorsing American membership in the League of Nations, but in 1921, with the League of Nations now the focus of a bitter partisan battle, convention delegates proved unwilling to support entry. The 1922 convention refused to go further than give tentative approval to the proposal to transform Elizabeth Hauser's Special Committee on the Reduction of Armaments into a permanent Committee on International Cooperation to Prevent War. The widely noted campaign she had organized the previous year to support passage of the Borah amendment, strengthened by the achievements of the 1921 Washington Disarmament Conference, had underlined the desirability of a permanent League organ to deal

This League campaign from the interwar era underlined the range of major commitments the League assumed even in this early period. The display supporting the World Court dates from 1925; the one backing civil service reform about a decade later.

with foreign policy concerns.[2] Yet the delegates shrank from a commitment that might involve them in the partisan divisiveness of the League of Nations fight; in establishing the special committee, a decision was postponed regarding its purposes until it presented its first program.

Following the Baltimore convention, the national board named Ruth Morgan of New York to head the new committee. A neighbor and friend of the Franklin Roosevelts, she possessed an internationalistic background, substantial means, and wide contacts. At the 1923 convention, when her committee was retitled the Department of International Cooperation to Prevent War, she proposed to delegates that its aims should include support for "measures for developing a code of international procedures by which war can be outlawed" and cooperation "for peace through world federation." The department quickly assumed a privileged position; developing an understanding of the ingredients of an international civil order was seized upon as the most exalted of the League's purposes.[3] Morgan established an independent office in New York, and by 1924 could report local officers in all organized states and most local leagues. Veering away from further tests of anti–League of Nations sentiment, she directed members' attention to existing American foreign policy concerns. Her department soon outstripped all others in the range of subjects examined. Dozens of local groups busied themselves with the opposing issues of disarmament and military preparedness. Also under their scrutiny were the terms of the Versailles Treaty and the machinery of the League of Nations; allied war debts and their entanglement in the German reparations question; the origins and evolution of the Monroe Doctrine; and the troubling legacies of the Spanish-American War. All subjects were studied dispassionately in an atmosphere quite removed from preparation for action, provoking some criticism that study appeared an end in itself. The department's only declared position at that time was a demand for Philippine independence, reflecting the influence of women in the foreign mission movement.

League members needed little study to perceive contradictions between historic principles of American foreign policy, as embodied in the Monroe Doctrine, and the current practice of precautionary intervention to protect American business interests and U.S. hegemony in the Caribbean. Armed with forthright educational materials, the study groups examined successive instances of such intervention; acting for the League, Morgan sent a strongly disapproving note to President Coolidge when the U.S. Marines intervened in Nicaragua in 1927.[4] But the issues of imperialism and "dollar diplomacy" offered less opportunity for expanding the intellectual horizons of League members than other, more encouraging developments in foreign policy—notably among these, the question of American membership in the World Court.

A generation of effort and negotiation at the international level had preceded the creation of the Permanent Court of International Justice in 1920 under League of Nations aegis. Secretary of State Charles Evans Hughes strongly favored America's joining; so did Commerce Secretary Herbert Hoover, who

The Personnel Campaign, though coinciding with a low ebb in League membership and funding, reached a wider public than probably any previous League undertaking.

made a persuasive plea at the League's 1923 convention, where the decision was taken to support the Court plan. President Harding had sent the membership protocol to the Senate for ratification in February 1923, adding four reservations to ensure that American rights before the Court were the same as those of League of Nations members. With Hughes leading a vigorous administration drive to secure early hearings by the Senate Foreign Relations Committee, the prospects for Senate approval seemed bright in the spring of 1924.

Maud Wood Park, retiring from the League presidency, became chair of the World Court subcommittee of the WJCC, with a roster of fourteen women's organizations. The most experienced and successful woman lobbyist of her time, Park mobilized considerable pressure on the Foreign Relations Committee concurrent with administration efforts. Broad public support was demonstrable; both parties carried a World Court plank in their 1924 platforms. In January 1926 the Foreign Relations Committee finally reported out its agreement to ratify—though with additional conditions, and particularly a fifth reservation enabling the United States to bar the Court from rendering "advisory opinions" where these might conflict with American national interests; the same month the Senate confirmed this action.[5] At its St. Louis convention that year, the League felt a glow of triumph.

Exhilaration soon vanished. The impression had been conveyed that the reservations were uncontroversial. But other signatory states balked at the fifth. Several foreign governments requested that it be reconsidered, but with the arrogant obtuseness that marked much American international conduct in the decade, President Coolidge, who originally proposed the reservation, declined to ask Congress to do so.[6]

League leaders were stunned when they realized Coolidge's intentions. The national board debated its options. Ruth Morgan and Marguerite Wells wanted vigorous protests and a nationwide campaign for Senate action. But Park, who had poured her energies into the ratification drive, was well familiar with the narrow dimensions of senatorial thinking, and counseled caution. The League might accomplish nothing at this stage, and could seriously embarrass the rest of its program. Though Morgan remained unreconciled, it was agreed to continue prodding Coolidge at every opportunity, and to keep the issue prominent among League membership concerns.

And League study groups did attentively follow such hopeful developments as the 1925 Locarno Pact and the negotiations leading to the Kellogg-Briand Pact in 1928.[7] In copious letters to her state chairs, Morgan showed herself a skilled interpreter of trends toward collective understanding.[8] She was an observer at the 1927 Geneva Conference, which sought unsuccessfully to define naval parity. In 1930, when the London Naval Treaty was drafted, she joined representatives of international women's organizations in offering thirty thousand petitions calling for disarmament (eleven thousand from the United States). She was present again at the tragically futile World Disarmament Conference convened in 1932 by the League of Nations (when more than a million women's petitions were delivered).

Working alongside the League's Department of International Cooperation in these years was Carrie Chapman Catt's independent Committee on the Cause and Cure of War, the idea for which originated at the League's 1924 Buffalo convention, when Wisconsin League leader Jessie Hooper and Catt collaborated in mounting a luncheon "on peace." Out of this grew plans for an ad hoc organizing committee of representatives from interested women's groups, chaired by Catt and with Josephine Schain as secretary.[9] Annual conferences would be held to "make a serious, bold and impartial study of the causes of war and to delve deep in quest of a cure." Catt's aim in this characteristically intellectualized effort was to propel the peace debate out of the realm of "cloudy idealism" and ideological bickering into that of informed and realistic discussion.[10] Catt's assumption that League state officers would enlist under the Conference Committee's banner, and furnish a sizable block of delegates as well as proportionate share of the funding, was accepted as an inescapable responsibility by the League board; at the same time, running through the correspondence between Belle Sherwin, Park, and Morgan in 1924 were expressions of mild alarm over potentially overlapping jurisdictions between the group Catt proposed to assemble and the state chairs of Morgan's department.

In the event, between 1925 and 1940 the successive Conferences on the Cause and Cure of War—and the attendant Marathon Round Tables—were to place a capstone on Catt's splendid career,[11] and greatly extended the influence of the League and other participating organizations through their association with the internationally minded scholars and writers who were preparing America between the wars to ultimately assume its international responsibilities.[12]

In the 1928 presidential campaign, Herbert Hoover gave firm backing for American participation in the World Court—the chief lure enticing many League leaders into overt support for his candidacy. And once elected, Hoover acted promptly to resume the negotiations broken off by Coolidge, raising high once more the hopes of the Court's advocates. A group of international jurists, including the eighty-four-year-old Elihu Root, drafted a new protocol (hinging on the so-called Root Formula) designed to meet Senate objections.[13]

Root's passionate desire to win American adherence to the World Court led him to cooperation with an old opponent, Carrie Chapman Catt. James McDonald of the Foreign Policy Association, with other Court advocates, had pointed out the role of the Cause and Cure of War Conferences in arousing popular support for the recently signed Kellogg-Briand Pact. Accordingly, Root, once a bitter antisuffragist, invited Catt, Ruth Morgan, and others to his home. Seating them around a dining room table "like a board of directors," he proceeded to hand down "his observations as if they were the opinions of the Supreme Court." Nonetheless, his eagerness to win their help was sincere and undisguised; and Catt was impressed by his responsiveness to their views and his agility in finding common ground between conflicting viewpoints. The two old warriors worked together henceforth in complete harmony.[14]

Word finally emerged from the Senate Foreign Relations Committee that the revised protocol would not be considered until other nations had ratified it, a tactic arousing understandable resentment abroad and exasperation among American World Court advocates. Mary Morrisson asked President Hoover how further the League might help. He admitted he lacked the votes to force action, especially since Senator Arthur Vandenberg of Michigan had defected to the "anti" forces. Dorothy Judd, president of the Michigan League, exerted all possible pressure to shift him back; everything failed. The WJCC's World Court subcommittee polled the Senate to discover that only thirty-one senators now declared themselves in favor of American membership in the Court.

By 1930 Hoover had far more pressing concerns than the fate of the World Court, and in the Senate the Foreign Relations Committee, at successive stages, found means to delay action. The Hearst press, outraged at the default by America's World War I allies on their war debts, had swung against the Court. Nonetheless, the League of Women Voters remained faithful, continued to study and discuss, and at their 1932 convention voted by a large majority not only to continue advocacy of the Court but also to demand American membership in the League of Nations (after eleven years of indecision on the issue). The vote expressed a despairing refusal to give up hope. Soon after, a final effort to secure Senate action failed, ending possibilities of breaking the deadlock before the 1932 elections.

With Roosevelt's victory, the League prepared itself to carry on the fight. But the new president, preoccupied with the massive problems of the depression, appeared in no hurry to bring pressure on the Foreign Relations Committee (now under a Democratic chair).[15] As 1933 merged into 1934, Marguerite Wells's impatience over the presidential foot-dragging found caustic expression in a League newsletter: "The real reason for the postponement was that the President was trading votes on the World Court for support of his domestic program.[16] Before the year ended, however, the Foreign Relations Committee did hold a final hearing on the Court; and Catt testified on behalf of all the organizations represented on the Cause and Cure of War Committee, voicing an impressive appeal for ratification. In January 1935, the League mustered a final effort to ensure victory; word went out to state presidents to reach every senator. The thirteen women's groups still active on the WJCC's World Court subcommittee were similarly mobilized. A few days later the Senate voted; the result fell seven votes short of the two-thirds required for ratification.[17] It had been a weary journey through twelve years of struggle, only to meet defeat at the end. Even the frustration over the failure to secure ratification of the child labor amendment did not match the disappointment now. More members had been intensely involved, and more significance attached to the Court, than in any other effort in the search for peace.

The national board resolved to hold a postmortem on the Court's defeat, a course of action never tried before. Several Senators opened their files to League staff to ascertain the source of the attacks on the Court. The similarly worded letters and telegrams opposing the Court—outnumbering those in favor by ten to one—underscored the formidable campaign of opposition in recent months, particularly by the influential radio priest Father Charles Coughlin and the Hearst press. The massive outburst of isolationist sentiment revealed the treacherous undertow of fear and distrust created by the depression at home and the gathering war clouds abroad.

As the world sank into recession and skies darkened over Europe and Asia, League opinion had begun to clarify on other issues, notably war debts and foreign trade. The debt question had been a subject of study since 1923, with interest confined mainly to Eastern leagues; they found little scope for action in this thorny thicket, though membership sentiment for downward revision of the debts (or even their outright cancellation) grew steadily. When the economic crisis forced Hoover to propose a one-year moratorium on the repayment of war debts in June 1931, Morgan sent him a warmly approving letter on the League's behalf. The Hawley-Smoot Tariff Act of 1930, however, had greatly magnified the debt problem as well as provoked retaliatory protectionism by European states; the barriers to commerce weakened the ability of European countries (and the political will of their governments) to make debt repayments. Morgan had denounced the act as "economic isolationism," and directed the attention of her state chairs to the complex interrelationships between tariff policies and the worsening debt crisis. At the 1932 convention, Morgan and Louise Baldwin, chair of the Living Costs Committee, deftly joined the Eastern concern with war debts and the Midwestern interest in the tariff issue into a national concern for a liberalized trade policy that would recognize the economic interdependence of nations. As heads of the two most active departments, they proposed a joint study of "economic factors involved in perpetuating the depression."

The League's two-year study of the international economic setting resulted in a consensus on the necessity for a downward revision of the tariffs; but events had moved faster than the League could. The Roosevelt administration had pushed through the first Reciprocal Trade Agreements Act in 1934 before the League had convention authorization to support it; in a preconvention press release, the board could only note "with satisfaction" that Congress had recognized in effect that America's economic well-being was linked to the economic health of its debtors. Two years later, the Cincinnati convention adopted, by a nearly unanimous vote, a strong statement of support for reciprocal trade agreements. At the 1937 General Council, twenty-nine state leagues reported having made the act's renewal that year their major program concern. Baldwin could testify at a hearing before the House Ways and Means Committee that the League viewed the tariff not only as an indirect tax on American consumers but a palpable cause of the present world plight; the League wanted the 1934 act not only renewed but strengthened by extending the president's negotiating powers. When the act faced its second renewal in 1940, there was fierce congressional opposition. War had broken out in Europe, and at home the isolationist tide had reached its crest. All local leagues were urged to hold public meetings to relate the trade question to the fearful tangle of foreign policy issues that were threatening to close the options of the American people.

In September 1931 the Japanese army had defied the civilian regime in Tokyo and seized Manchuria, providing the world with the first major test of its peace machinery. Formally, the United States was bound by the 1922 Nine-Power Treaty to join in putting down this aggression against China; but neither this nor the Kellogg-Briand Pact—nor the League of Nations—proved instruments by which an effective international response could be mounted. In January 1932, Secretary of State Henry Stimson warned Japan that the United States could not accept the legality of any situation impairing its existing treaty rights in China. But since no major power felt able to enforce sanctions, the so-called Hoover-Stimson Doctrine had little effect.

As the crisis unfolded, Belle Sherwin had sent two letters of support to Stimson. Both were released to the press; but no legislation was pending, and there appeared no opportunity for further action. Nevertheless, the national board faced rising pressure from state and local leagues for stronger efforts to head off foreseeable disaster. To the protesters, Ruth Morgan replied that economic sanctions could probably not be enforced with Congress in its present mood; the best course was to lend Hoover and Stimson their moral support. The national board was itself divided on the question, with Morgan and Sherwin, representing the older generation, leaning toward a cautious approach. Sceptical doubts about the value of consultative pacts (like the Nine-Power Treaty) had already arisen. Board members perceived that agreement to consult carried an implicit obligation to accept whatever decisions were made, and a few felt apprehensive that this concealed the possibility of undesired involvements.[18]

Signs of division within the board permitted new and vigorous voices to be heard, calling on the League to be more aggressive in shaping public opinion on critical issues rather than merely reacting to policies already formulated. One of these rising leaders was Louise Wright, Illinois state chair for Morgan's department. In 1931 she wrote Morgan calling for the League to declare its support of the League of Nations: "Either the League believed in international cooperation, or it did not." This was not the first voice asking for another measuring of sentiment on the issue. Marguerite Wells had sought this in 1925; in 1928 the New Jersey League had urged convention discussion and a test vote. Each time Morgan had hung back; those in the vanguard on this problem had to wait for the slower ones to catch up. The 1932 convention took matters into its own hands with a two-thirds vote calling for support for American membership in the League of Nations; and forced the issue onto the program for action. Louise Wright had stepped forward as the major influence on foreign policy, and succeeded Morgan as chair of the renamed Department of Government and International Cooperation in 1934.

If Manchuria had laid bare the limitations of postwar efforts to create machinery ensuring international stability, it also contributed domestically to a resurgent isolationism that was to culminate in the public exposures of the munitions industry, and in the 1935 Neutrality Act destined to leave a tragic imprint on American history. Internationally minded liberals shared with isolationists a tendency to see in economic motives the prime cause of modern wars. Sentiment grew that the profits must be taken out of war. The arms trade thus assumed a moral tinge. Public attitudes were complicated by reaction to the complex foreign debt crisis as well as the role of financial markets in the speculative boom leading to the 1929 stock market crash. Everything appeared to fit a theory of conspiracy on the part of international bankers and munitions makers. This onrushing tide of opinion swept onto the public stage the investigation of the armaments industry conducted between 1934 and 1936 by a special Senate committee headed by Gerald Nye. As the hearings proceeded, the disclosures stimulated sensational news coverage; there was little pretense to objectivity.[19] The League had supported the setting up of the Nye investigation. A pamphlet on the munitions industry carefully compiled the findings of fact which the committee had produced, concluding that there should be strict government control. Two hundred local leagues studied the question and reached a consensus on the need for government supervision, if not for nationalization of the munitions industry.

The first Neutrality Act swept to passage in 1935 on the wave of emotion generation by the Nye committee findings, and required the president to declare an embargo on exports of arms and munitions (and their shipment by American transporters) to countries at war. Though the administration had originally proposed the measure, Roosevelt had sought discretion to differentiate between aggressors and victims of aggression; Congress insisted, however, that all belligerents be treated alike. The 1936 League convention discussed the act soon after Congress renewed it for another fifteen months. The international situation was gloomier than ever. Despite a strong and persuasive stand by Louise Wright and others in support of Roosevelt's position, the convention voted for a somewhat diluted statement supporting a "foreign policy . . . as a non-belligerent which will not restrict the efforts of other nations to achieve peace."

The strength of isolationist sentiment in the late thirties was also underlined by the near-passage of the war referendum amendment, which would have limited the power of Congress to declare war until a war resolution had been approved by popular referendum. The proposed amendment had been introduced by Congressman Louis Ludlow, a Democrat from Indiana, in February 1937, and had lain quietly in the House Judiciary Committee's pidgeonhole while he sought signatures for a discharge petition. Months of effort had brought little support, but fate played into his hands. On December 12, 1937, Japanese planes sank the American gunboat *Panay* and three Standard Oil tankers on the Yangtze River near Nanking. There was great public outcry—not for reprisals but for keeping American shipping out of dangerous waters. Within two days Ludlow had the required 218 signatures to discharge his bill and force a vote, which was set for January 10, 1938. The League board had already considered the Ludlow resolution before the sudden need for action; a majority felt that the amendment should be opposed not only as an invasion of the constitutional powers of the presidency and Congress, but also as patently unworkable. The League's quick and courageous work in alerting its members and focusing public attention on the amendment helped bring about a large response. Even so, and despite strong administration opposition, the measure only narrowly lost.

The League's work on the Ludlow amendment, against the background of a deteriorating world situation, acted as a catalyst to clarify League opinion on the necessity for amendment or even repeal of the Neutrality Act. The League's 1938 convention gave clear endorsement to the need to change the act to permit presidential discretion in the imposition of arms embargoes. In 1939 the national board issued a statement that the League "had measured the dangers and decided that the victims of lawless aggression should be aided by the United States." By that time the long smouldering tinder in Europe had burst into flames. Years of search for peace had brought the membership to a realization of the truth of Secretary of State Cordell Hull's statement that "the threat of hostilities any-where . . . was a threat to the interests—political, economic, legal, social—of all nations." They had finally arrived at a realistic understanding of their own oft-stated belief in the "interdependence of all nations," but the path had not been straight.

NOTES

1. On the contributions of women's organizations to the peace movement after World War I, see Merle E. Curti, *Peace or War: The American Struggle, 1636–1936* (New York: W. W. Norton, 1936), Chap. 9.

2. From the Washington Conference, which the Borah amendment had helped to bring about, had emerged, in February 1922, seven treaties limiting major powers' con-struction of capital ships, denouncing chemical weapons and submarine warfare against merchant shipping, and seeking to sustain the power balance in the Far East.

3. Early League officers, and many members, had a mind-set toward such goals so pervasive that they were scarcely aware of it themselves. Extensive links had existed between the suffrage leadership and the foreign missions movement as well as the in-ternational feminist and peace organizations.

4. Department of International Cooperation, 1927, LWV Papers, Minutes and Re-lated Records, LC.

5. Richard W. Leopold, *The Growth of American Foreign Policy: A History* (New York: Alfred A. Knopf, 1962), 455–56.

6. League leaders were aware that John Bassett Moore, a sitting judge on the Court, had advised the Foreign Relations Committee on its response to the Court protocol. They had also had reliable reports that he opposed American membership, and had assisted in drafting the unacceptable fifth reservation. They were reluctant, though, to believe that the public was being deliberately misled. See the League's World Court

records and the Catt correspondence relating to the Cause and Cure of War conferences, LWV Papers, LC.

7. The first of these entailed agreement by key European states to submit disputes to arbitration, and paved the way for Germany's admission to the League of Nations. Under the second, fifteen major states renounced war as an instrument of policy toward one another.

8. Department of International Cooperation to Prevent War, Morgan Letters, 1927–30, LWV Papers, Ser. 2, Box 50, LC.

9. Conference Committee on the Cause and Cure of War, Catt-Hooper Correspondence, LWV Papers, Ser. 2, Box 113, LC.

10. Initially nine groups joined the organizing committee, with three more being added later; Peck, *Carrie Chapman Catt*, 410n. None was formally part of the peace movement, for Catt was seeking to reach a women's constituency not already committed to such goals. Selig Adler describes Catt's group as a secessionist faction from the Women's International League for Peace and Freedom, of which Jane Addams was president; see *The Uncertain Giant, 1921–1941: American Foreign Policy between the Wars* (New York: Macmillan, 1965), 41. There was in fact no connection between the two, and Catt did not "break" with Addams.

11. With one interruption, the conferences occurred annually. The Marathon Round Tables, reportedly twelve thousand in number, were extension courses held to disseminate the ideas generated by the conferences among the public. Catt continued to chair the Conference Committee until 1932, when Ruth Morgan succeeded her.

12. Among them James T. Shotwell, Edward M. Earle, Carlton J. H. Hayes, Manley Hudson, James G. McDonald, and Philip Jessup.

13. Having served in turn as secretary of war, secretary of state, and U.S. senator between 1899 and 1915, Root was also a noted constitutional lawyer who had helped create the World Court in 1920; then, as now, he had acted in a private rather than an official capacity.

14. Peck, *Carrie Chapman Catt*, 439–41.

15. Despite preelection suggestions of support for the Court to Ruth Morgan and other members of the Cause and Cure of War Committee.

16. *Congressional Newsletter*, 1934, LWV Papers, LC.

17. President Wells released a characteristic statement to the press: "Fear—the fear of something unknown . . . is responsible for the defeat of the Court. Senators who understood the Court too well to fear it themselves apparently voted unfavorably out of deference to the fears aroused in the minds of their uninformed constituents." Quoted in Betty G. Lall, "The Foreign Policy Program of the League of Women Voters of the United States: Methods of Influencing Government Action, Effects on Public Opinion and Evaluation of Results" (Ph.D. diss., University of Minnesota, 1964), 162.

18. Sherwin insisted that the "Explanation of the Program" in 1930 and again in 1932 should state clearly that consultative pacts involved both responsibility and obligation, and must be understood as a "new principle" in American experience.

19. See Dorothy Detzer, *Appointment on the Hill* (New York: Henry Holt, 1948), chaps. 11 and 12, for a lively and detailed account of the pressures exerted by the peace lobby to secure the Nye investigation.

13

Two Endings and a Beginning

The 1940 convention was held in New York City.[1] The League had not forgotten Carrie Chapman Catt's suggestion that the anniversary of its birth should be celebrated decennially, to review past achievements and mark out future goals. The first such anniversary in 1930 had been a low point in the League's history, and a troubled year for the nation. The second commemorative observance in 1940 found the League sturdier in health, though not less troubled about the plight of the world. Membership had climbed slowly from the low point in 1935, and a new generation of leaders had moved forward to replace the founders, especially in state and local leagues. The convention banquet was dedicated to remembrance of things past, with Eleanor Roosevelt, the League's star member, as the evening's key speaker. Seated on the dais were Carrie Chapman Catt, Maud Wood Park, Belle Sherwin, and Marguerite Wells. It was the last time all the early leaders would be present at a League convention.

The commemorative banquet was the convention's only festive hour. Hitler's attack on Norway and Denmark three weeks earlier had marked the end of the phoney war that succeeded the conquest of Poland. The convention reaffirmed a demand for a policy of nonbelligerence that permitted the United States to discriminate against aggressors and aid countries under attack; they also maintained their opposition to further threats of war referendum legislation. Looking to the future, support was given to international efforts to establish "an effective system for collective peace," while delegates gave voice to their sense that the times were critical by calling for "the preservation of the greatest degree of civil liberty consistent with national safety."

Within seven weeks of the convention, France, the Netherlands and Belgium had all fallen. In a letter to state presidents, Marguerite Wells declared that the American people were finally united in defense against a possible external enemy;

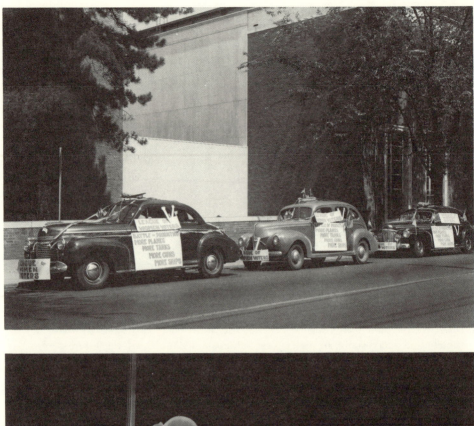

The ambitious "Battle of Production" Campaign—shown here, *above*, in Portland, Oregon, and, *below*, Houston, Texas—was begun six months before the Japanese assault on Pearl Harbor, and sought to increase public acceptance of America's role as an arsenal for other democracies under threat of attack. (Portland: Photo-Art Studios; Houston: Bob Bailey)

but she saw a terrible warning in the fifth columns in European democracies, as the penalty exacted from those who had "shirked the responsibility of citizenship."[2] Meeting in June 1940, the national board voted unanimously to commence an education campaign stressing the importance of an international organization with effective power to invoke both economic and military sanctions against aggressors.[3] They were aware that Secretary of State Cordell Hull shared their conviction that America's failure to join the League of Nations had been primarily the result of a lack of public understanding of the nation's responsibilities. The League was indicating its readiness to shoulder its share of the burden of preparing the public this time. If little could be done to broaden certain senatorial horizons, much might be accomplished in adding new dimensions to the thinking of senatorial constituents.[4]

The education campaign that Wells contemplated might be difficult to undertake in the atmosphere of official restraints on freedom of speech and press now likely to arise. The program included authorization for measures to protect civil liberties, and this concern was pursued through a series of letters to state presidents reflecting an individualistic spirit drawn from Wells's pioneer background. She warned that one of the League's functions at a time of disruption must be to display the civic courage to defend individual rights. She remembered the hysteria directed against hyphenated Americans during World War I; and how readily ugly nativist impulses found public channels in allegations of disloyalty against those who sought to exercise freedom of speech. State leagues were encouraged to oppose a rash of state legislation requiring loyalty oaths of teachers and mandatory saluting of the flag; the protection of academic freedom particularly concerned the board. Members were urged to hold discussion groups to examine their own thinking on freedom of inquiry and association.

In December 1940, Wells raised the question with state presidents as to whether the country's safety did not call for pledging everything possible to the victims of aggressions; murmurs of dissent were heard from Quaker elements in some quarters of the League, but the question quickly became rhetorical. A month later Roosevelt proposed the lend-lease program. The League announced its support on January 24, 1941; letters flew from Wells to state presidents, and in turn from local leagues to their members of Congress, though the response to the urgent calls for action reminded League officers that many citizens, including many women, still misunderstood the risks involved in continued isolationism. With the policy of all-out aid to Britain gaining congressional sanction by March, the next problem was how to enable the country to mobilize its productive capacity rapidly enough. This effort, Wells realized, would require social and economic planning and controls on a scale undreamed of before in the United States. In May, the General Council agreed to undertake a two-month effort to interpret to the nation the necessity of, and requirements for, comprehensive planning to win the "battle of production."

With her instinct for timing, Wells took advantage of the state of public alarm to plan a campaign to be carried out by unaccustomed methods. Her program of activities called for mass rallies and street corner speeches backed by impact appeals through slogans and arresting fliers; she contrived novel ways to catch the totally uninformed and the totally indifferent (for she had long felt that this was an audience the League must learn to reach). Wells was entirely right that the general public had little conception of the defense program on which the government had already embarked, or of what it would entail for their own lives. She saw the League as containing thousands of women "prepared to be a steadying and enlightened influence upon public opinion during these months of crisis"; yet League members as well as other citizens needed a broader understanding of the relation of defense policies to everyday patterns of living. As Wells and the board had anticipated, the sudden expansion of defense-related industrial activity under the Office of Production Management, and the consequent increase in administrative activity, did create confusion and mis-understanding. Wells saw no end of problems, all calling for study and analysis of ways to create an enlightened nucleus to serve the larger public. Her imaginative and ambitious "Battle of Production" project had great potential value when it was launched in June 1941.[5] None could foresee that Pearl Harbor was less than six months away.

For Marguerite Wells, the crisis had an almost apocalyptic urgency. America's democratic institutions were all too easily threatened by anarchy. "The rigid provisions of our Constitution with its separation of powers makes it unbelievably difficult to speak and act as a nation." The founders had believed that "only the people can put together the powers of government the Constitution has separated." But the expectation that the people would unite and harmonize the separate functions had not been realized; the founders could not have foreseen the difficulties of "uniting the opinions of 135 millions in forty-eight states." The voice of the people was inaudible unless articulated by the leaders, whose task was precisely to understand the issues and express an opinion on policies. The choices the average citizen had to make could and should be reduced to simple terms. The political parties were supposed to do this, but had abdicated such functions in order to concentrate on winning elections. Neither, she felt, had the president provided the necessary leadership in this deeply troubled period. Thus, the responsibility came back to them—the fifty thousand women in the League. Throughout her long career, Wells's steady purpose had been to develop in League members a general capacity to understand and analyze public issues—thereby to create an active, self-directing nucleus in the electorate consciously exercising its power to influence others by virtue of its superior knowledge and trained judgement.[6]

Wells had always objected to the League's stress on program specialists, and the resulting fragmentation of the membership into groups devoting themselves to particular areas of concern. The committees and departments with their inward-turning preoccupations made the League "a little bundle of pressure blocs." Despite her continuous efforts to concentrate program activities in a few areas, the League was still operating under the system established in its earliest years, with committees and departments developing the program under the guidance of the national board; and conventions adopting it.[7] The most visible result of such fragmentation was the program's length and the range of subjects it covered. The 1938–40 program, at the high point of Wells's career, contained seventeen items listed as "federal," eleven as "state," and thirteen as "federal-state." Individual items did not define an area for exploration and study, or declare support for a specific policy, but briefly stated a position regarding a desirable policy within an area—for example, "downward revision of war debts," or "statutory guarantees of rights to bargain collectively."[8] It was customary for the national board to select two federal measures for active study by state and local leagues: in effect, their homework. Wells put her characteristic stamp on this procedure by stating that "the program does not propose to cover [fully] any one field entered upon nor to enter every field." The program, she wrote, was "representative of the opinions of a membership with varying political and economic views," united principally in their purpose to promote government in the public interest. Consensus, as the League knows it today, was not present.

Immediately after Pearl Harbor, Wells summoned the national board to Washington to seek approval for her decision to call an extraordinary council of state presidents in Indianapolis early in 1942 (rather than awaiting the biennial convention due in April). With board approval, the council was convened. Those state presidents able to attend agreed with Wells that the moment had come for the League membership to draw upon its experience and knowledge of government to carry the issues at stake to a wider public. She eloquently defined the key areas where public understanding was crucial: for example, the need for higher taxes to finance the war effort, and for rationing and price controls, the importance of guarding against threats to civil liberties, and the necessity—once the war ended—for both a worldwide reconstruction program and an international organization to preserve the peace. It was her hope that every local League member could be recruited for this "Wartime Service for Carrying Information about Government to the Public." The national board would undertake to furnish the material for a members' canvass of their neighborhoods and communities. In her own report on the Indianapolis meeting, Wells declared that the League had "proceeded to make history for itself" in choosing to become a "single purpose organization," though it was "only by a hair's breadth" that it had "escaped doing nothing" but offering pious hope. It can be inferred that the state presidents were caught somewhat unprepared for such a sudden shift in method and attitude. Nonetheless, the scheme was accepted, and the national board was authorized to draw up a master plan to be adapted by state boards for each local league.

The 1942 convention confirmed the decision to pool the League's energies in a massive educational program, and adopted an active list of ten items covering the League's position on the issues dealt with in the "Wartime Service" project.[9] The national board and staff lost no time in turning out a series of brightly colored one-page fliers—"Cues" and "Broadsides"—each devoted to a single issue. Some contained small but pertinent scraps of information about steps the government was taking to meet particular needs: information intended to be morale-building. Others furnished details about wartime agencies in Washington about which there was risk of misinformation, or outlined government plans for financing the war, and urged citizens to buy bonds and shoulder heavier taxation. All the material was accurate, informative, and often presented with evocative symbols and slogans designed to reach a mass audience. By August 1942, Wells could report that half a million copies had gone out, but she was not satisfied. "Either there is no need to awaken the citizens of a democracy to a lively sense of their responsibility, or the League of Women Voters is not adapted to meet the need, or it has not yet found the way." In a sharp letter to state presidents, she noted that "50,000 women now await instructions and 600 presidents of local leagues are responsible for their success or failure."[10] Yet League members were accustomed to slower processes of shaping opinion, relying on the power of facts to persuade reasonable people. The sudden shift to buttonholing neighbors, even strangers, to engage in a dialogue on current issues found many members unwilling.

The autumn of 1942 and spring of 1943 had proved a trying period. Roosevelt had been having difficulty getting wartime tax measures through Congress, not to mention the wage and price control legislation; debate over the renewal of the Reciprocal Trade Agreements Act revealed signs of resurgent isolationism. Alarmed, Wells decided on a single massive attack on the "great American myth" that the nation ever was, or could be, independent of other nations. In mid-1943 she sent a memorandum to the national board outlining a plan to "stop isolationism now" by a campaign to reach at least three million individuals face-to-face "with a few simple truths about foreign policy." The reasons for assuming leadership in such a campaign were compelling. Yet the plan was not immediately approved. Some thought the summer an unpromising time for a crash program on this scale. Others cited a Gallup poll indicating that 70 percent of the public was now "safe" on the subject of a postwar international order to secure peace—though Wells had no confidence in such flimsy evidence, as she subsequently made clear in a letter to state presidents.[11] In the end the broadside "Am I an Isolationist?" was prepared. The state presidents were reminded that "in the last resort, success or failure in each League will depend upon the conviction of its leaders."

The situation within the League became steadily more exacerbated as the person-to-person program seemed to fail in its purpose. The tendency of so many leagues, in Wells's view, to cling to "the set pattern of meetings," now almost impossible because of the wartime disruptions of normal existence, was an added difficulty. Such fixed habits, she felt, were beneath the level of performance now required. The League's seeming inability to reach outward toward the community was a symptom of an "ingrowth" she saw as a positive danger. Her sense of frustration was quickened by an aggrieved sense that the state boards retained a significant potential for stifling the League's capacity for action by standing between the national board and the local membership. When state presidents were slow to act, or uncooperative, they effectively blunted convention decisions entrusted to the national board for execution. Wells had sought actively to counter these organizational problems throughout her administration. Sherwin had perceived the same structural faults, and had tried to get around them by procedural means. It was characteristic of Wells that she would try to remove the obstacles themselves.

To her associates, Wells had often expressed the view that institutions bore within themselves the seeds of their own decay. The structure of an organization should "facilitate constant and direct interpretation of [its core] purpose. Leaders should be chosen for their ability to interpret and promote it." But an organization of long standing might find that the original methods of implementing its founding goals no longer applied. It was essential then to reexamine these goals as well as its bylaws and structure. As the price of survival it had to refit itself to the time and occasion.[12]

Late in 1942 Wells and the national board resolved on a sweeping revision of the bylaws to bring League members directly within the embrace of the national leadership. The departments with their tedious procedures and tight control of the program would be eliminated, and the program would instead be made by the membership at annual conventions composed of delegates from local leagues; the state organizations might be eliminated altogether as an unnecessary layer of authority. The League nationally would become a closely knit, unitary organization of local leagues.

The proposed revisions were drawn up without direct consultation with the state presidents—though not in secrecy; some board members had close ties with state leagues. Since Wells was retiring, a slate of candidates supporting the reforms was chosen for the posts of president, treasurer, and secretary. In 1943 a national staff member toured the states to explain the changes in standing committee and study group organization designed to realize the "single purpose" goal accepted at Indianapolis.[13] The essential step was to discard the departmental structure at the state level so that the national board could convey information and requests for action more quickly to local leagues, a change in turn having the implication of greatly altering the composition and functions of state league boards, if not eliminating them altogether—as was so understood by several state boards. The issues were ones of principle, not personalities. As skillfully as Wells had done her work, a number prepared to organize the defeat of the reforms, also drawing up a substitute slate of candidates to be nominated from the floor of the 1944 convention.

Marguerite Wells presided over this, her last convention, with her accustomed parliamentary skill and courtesy. Nothing in her long career became her more than her self-control and judicious moderation in allowing the deliberations to take their course, however great her disappointment must have been. There was tact and delicacy of spirit displayed on both sides. An inexperienced participant would scarcely have known what was happening until it was over.[14]

Wells was informed in advance of the substitute slate; and at a signal, it was introduced, to be voted on the following day.

Lucia McBride of Cleveland nominated Anna Lord Strauss for the presidency on the substitute slate. A more appropriate symbol of the enduring psychological ties binding the League to its heritage could hardly have been found. As the great-granddaughter of Lucretia Mott, Strauss represented the very source of League tradition; equally she represented the postsuffrage generation of League leaders. The substitute slate of three officers, as well as the rest of the regularly nominated slate, was elected by a large majority.[15] The program presented by the outgoing administration was debated and adopted; along with other reforms, the League transformed itself from a federation of state leagues to an organization based on its individual members.[16] A change in direction had been effected by time-honored democratic methods; and the League turned its face to the future.

The first three presidents of the League were women of unusual intellectual and personal capacity who put an ineffaceable stamp on the organization they collectively created. Each had come out of the suffrage movement, and had been deeply influenced by its ideology. Each attracted into her orbit strong and like-minded individuals who helped make it possible that her contribution would be permanent. The first president was actually the youngest, both in years and spirit, having led the suffrage youth movement. The second and third presidents were past middle age when they assumed the presidency, and spoke strongly in the accents of the liberal reform movement that preceded World War I, voicing especially its confidence that "the will of the people" was an ascertainable force only needing to be freed from constraints. Collectively they confirm the aphorism that an institution is but the lengthened shadow of an individual—in this case successive individuals, and their examples, initiatives, and decisions. The human element, at all times luminously visible, furnished the causal nexus between events. This is most directly perceived, of course, in the period that already belongs to history. Most of the great actors have departed, and the atmosphere in which they worked is now imbued with a sense of the past. Since 1944, the record of events belongs to the ongoing present.

NOTES

1. Proceedings, New York Convention, April 30–May 3, 1940, LWV Papers, Minutes and Related Records, LC.

2. Marguerite Wells, letter to state presidents, June 1940, LWV Papers, LC.

3. Minutes, national board meeting, June 1940, LWV Papers, LC.

4. The national board continued to give consideration to the organization they hoped might emerge as a postwar successor to the League of Nations. Thus, shortly before Pearl Harbor, the board sent a memorial to Hull suggesting that there should be a security council within the proposed body composed of the most powerful nations, with no requirement of unanimity in taking decisions, and with no single state having a veto power.

5. "The Battle of Production," LWV Papers, Ser. 2, Boxes 438 and 440, LC.

6. Wells's view of the League as a "feminine civic elite" came into focus in the critical years between 1939 and 1942. She had always held a deep conviction that leadership in a democracy consisted in the personal exercise of persuasive influence by the firm articulation of profoundly held beliefs. Just as political education as a "continuous reconstruction of experience" had been the controlling concept in Sherwin's thinking, the concept of leadership exercised through the power of ideas shaped the views of Wells. The passages cited are drawn from her speeches and letters to state league presidents which were brought together and published by friends; see Marguerite M. Wells, *Leadership in a Democracy: A Portrait in Action* (New Haven: Printing Office of Yale University Press, 1944).

7. There had frequently been vigorous minority dissent over the program; but the ablest and most powerful of the chronic dissenters, Pennsylvania, had sacrificed its opportunity to exercise the power it might have had by refusing to implement the committee and department structure, thereby foregoing the chance to express its views at the point where the program was being formulated.

8. LWV, "Historical Review of the Evolution of Program as Shown by Printed Programs since 1938–40" (Washington, D.C., April 1966, Mimeographed), 1.

9. Proceedings, Chicago Convention, April 28–May 1, 1942, LWV Papers, Ser. 2, Boxes 446 and 465, LC. The expectation was that the League work on the program and the information project could be dovetailed.

10. Marguerite M. Wells, letter to state presidents, August 20, 1942, LWV Papers, LC.

11. Marguerite M. Wells, letter to state presidents, August 1943, LWV Papers, LC.

12. Wells, *Leadership in a Democracy*; and also Marguerite M. Wells, "The Enfranchisement of Women and the League of Women Voters, 1919–1944," Marguerite M. Wells Papers, Arthur and Elizabeth Schlesinger Library on the History of Women in America, Radcliffe College.

13. For a view of the "experimental plan" from a state angle, see Virginia C. Abbott, *The History of Women Suffrage and the League of Women Voters of Cuyahoga County, 1911–1945* (Cleveland, 1949).

14. As the author can testify, having attended the convention as a delegate from the Delaware County (Pennsylvania) League.

15. The two vice-presidents as well as two directors subsequently resigned, their successors being appointed to the national board after the convention. LWV, *Forty Years of a Great Idea*, 35–36.

16. "The Convention was determined to vest the power structurally where in fact it had always been—in the members. The [official] slate was no less determined to achieve the same purpose, but some of those named . . . wanted to do away with the state Leagues entirely. Delegates did not want to go *that* far." Ibid., 35 (emphasis in the original).

Anna Lord Strauss—first of the postsuffrage League presidents, 1944-50. (Anna Lord Strauss: Glogau, Washington, D.C.)

nations . . . offering mutual guarantees of political independence and territorial integrity to great and small nations alike." This proposal to encourage the initiative of local leagues was the first trial of the formula for direct communication between the national league and the local league presidents; its success was extraordinary. The State Department was soon inundated with a thousand letters a day, 90 percent of them from League members.[1] The Dumbarton Oaks Conference (to consider American draft plans for what was to become the United Nations) had opened in August, and officials were pleased that public interest was so manifest. They were still more pleased when a pamphlet prepared by the League's research staff on the conference sold more than a hundred thousand copies in a few weeks.[2]

In the autumn of 1944, five thousand League members were trained for a nationwide "Take It to the People" campaign, designed to reach small and large groups wherever people could be assembled. In the most successful community-based contribution to public understanding of a major issue in which the League had ever engaged, over a million pieces of literature were distributed. The reciprocal flow of communications between Washington and local leagues generated a dynamism that soon reinvigorated the organization.

The San Francisco Conference—convened to formally draft the United Nations Charter—was opened in April 1945, less than two weeks after Roosevelt's sudden death and as the Nazi Reich veered toward collapse. Not permitting momentum to be lost, the board sent Anne Hartwell Johnstone, a foreign-policy expert, as League representative to join those of forty-one other nongovernmental organizations appointed by the State Department to play a consultative role at San Francisco. Monitoring proceedings from beginning to end, she reported back to the board on the successive crises in wresting agreement over the Charter.[3] The official United States delegation sought the views of these nongovernmental representatives at many points, and she presented the League's ideas on several key issues, arguing for a more flexible amending procedure, for example, and strongly supporting the U.S. position on the question of subordinating regional peace machinery to the United Nations. Johnstone was asked by the U.S. delegation to assume leadership in helping resolve the question of creating a Commission on the Status of Women as a specialized UN agency— a step ardently sought by women from other countries (many still unenfranchised) as well as by other American women's groups. Though the League had no official position in support of such a body, she accepted the task, and the commission was established. The first American representative was Judge Dorothy Kenyon, a specialist in international law and former officer of the New York League.

The League's 1945 General Council was held in Washington during the San Francisco Conference. From all regions came positive reports on the UN campaign. The council took official note that the League clearly accomplished most when it concentrated nationally on narrowly focused objectives; and voiced a

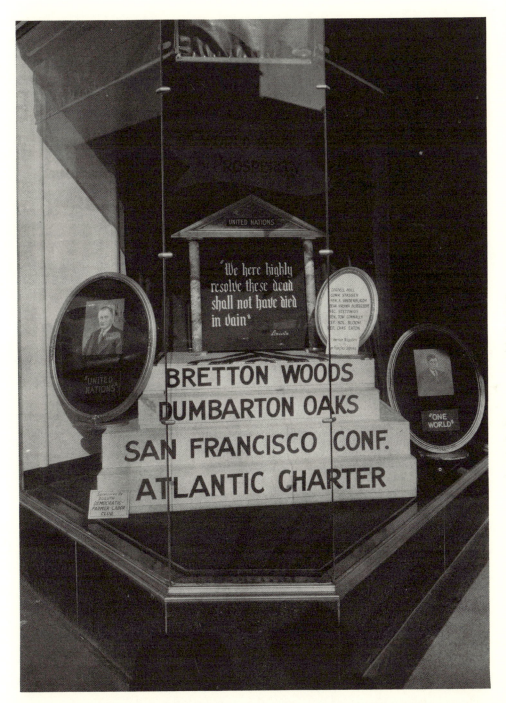

Concerned to avoid a resurgence of isolationism, the League gave the United Nations vigorous support during its formation in 1944-45. Besides window displays (like this one in Duluth, Minn.), speakers addressed thousands of local meetings; over a million pieces of literature were distributed.

14

The Atomic Age

The League of Women Voters entered its second quarter-century with a forward-looking president and a national board that assumed its responsibilities in a manner both energetic and conciliatory. While preserving the best of the tradition bequeathed to it, the organization was ready for unsparing self-analysis preparatory to redefining its role and redesigning its structure, partly along lines that Marguerite Wells herself had desired. Anna Lord Strauss brought to her task personal qualities of integrity, tact, human warmth, and a most disarming modesty, as well as administrative skills fashioned from extensive League and business experience. Imposing order on the internal disorganization resulting from the decisions of the 1944 convention required that she reconstitute the administrative and research staffs, appoint and galvanize a committee to revise the bylaws, and deal with immediate program concerns almost simultaneously. Since convention action had abolished the standing committees, changes in program-making procedures and publications policies had to be improvised under current bylaws, pending their revision.

The 1944 convention had adopted the program formulated by the outgoing board, the change of administration making no difference to League attitudes on major economic and foreign policy issues. Since 1940 the League had looked toward a "post-war organization for peace." Marguerite Wells, during her last months in office, had drafted plans for a campaign to win public support for such an organization.

Soon after the convention, Anna Lord Strauss suggested that the League seize the initiative by asking local leagues to spell out the principles that should guide the drafting of a charter for a democratic international organization; she herself phrased a few simply stated ideas drawn from Franklin Roosevelt's Four Freedoms and Woodrow Wilson's Fourteen Points, in calling for "a general association of desire for a selective national program to which the entire League would apply its efforts.

Once the Charter was ratified by the Senate on July 28, 1945, the national board saw its responsibility as constant oversight of future developments.[4] In late May Strauss had written local league presidents asking that they assume a continuing commitment to ensuring that the new organization was thoroughly understood and widely supported.[5] The 1946 convention took a firm position calling for "acceptance by the United States of its full share of responsibility for strengthening the United Nations." This vigilant concern has never wavered.

Nine days after Senate ratification of the UN Charter, the nuclear era was inaugurated with the devastation of Hiroshima. It was immediately clear that a bodeful element had entered the international arena. Strict control and responsible stewardship by the nation possessing a weapon of such deadly power was widely accepted. But control by whom? And to what ends? The introduction of the atomic bomb into the life of the League was so sudden that the board could not wait for the 1946 convention, and took action instead under existing League principles of support for "domestic policies which will facilitate the solution of international problems" and the "fullest use of resources."[6] On November 1, 1945, Strauss sent letters to President Harry Truman, Secretary of State James Byrnes, and the chairs of relevant congressional committees asking for rapid formulation of a national policy and urging control of nuclear power for peaceful purposes. The dramatic impact of events on the 1946 convention was reflected in the decision to give top priority to a current agenda item calling for both "international control of atomic energy through the United Nations" and "domestic control under a civilian agency to ensure full development in the public interest."[7]

Controversy, in fact, had quickly developed over whether control of the new technology should be vested in civilian or military authorities. Senator Brien McMahon, chair of a joint congressional committee to draft legislation, argued for civilian control; Senator Arthur Vandenberg and a committee majority favored either military control or capacity to veto civilian policies. McMahon won the support of President Truman, the scientists who had developed the bomb, women's organizations, and educational and religious leaders. In waging its own campaign to build public understanding on this issue, the League drew on long-established attitudes toward the subordination of the military to civilian control and toward the threat of a concentration of economic power. The almost illimitable possibilities of this new source of power—capable, if unleashed, of destroying humanity itself—tended to make all forms of bigness take on new dimensions, creating an apprehensive feeling that found reflection in the League program over the next decade. The legislative battle culminated in the passage in August 1946 of the Douglas-McMahon bill creating the Atomic Energy Commission.[8]

As the war neared its end, the specter of economic maladjustment resulting from demobilization and industrial reconversion made economic stability an issue of highest priority, in turn producing the setting for the legislation that eventuated in the 1946 Employment Act, after years of inconclusive debate regarding public responsibility for maintaining a stable economy, Congress had finally acted to create machinery for a continuous oversight of the nation's economic health. Despite the League's own deep concern for securing a stable economy, and authorization to take action, it was unable to support the Employment Act. In the board's view, there was too little time to master the complexities of the issue involved, and instead it threw the League's support to such austerity measures as continued wage and price controls and high taxes. The 1948 program, however, declared the League's intention to approach these issues by analyzing "federal taxes and expenditures in order to understand and support such fiscal policies as make for a stable domestic economy." The League had long favored an "equitable and coordinated tax system." Now the League elected to bite off a chunk of a far larger problem, and break that down into assimilable elements before attempting the major task. The "Explanation of the Program" noted that while the government's taxing power and other instruments like debt management, monetary policy, and credit controls were key tools for maintaining economic stability, League members required an understanding of the nature and role of the federal budget before they possessed an adequate basis for judging federal fiscal policy.

The League had also been actively committed over this period to a fundamental recasting of its own structures and procedures. The Bylaws Committee created in the 1944 convention's wake had begun its task by appealing to state and local leagues for comments and suggestions.[9] The response was both copious and instructive, as state and local presidents seized the opportunity to appraise their own leagues' experience. Facts came to light regarding the disarray on many state boards, traceable partly to wartime conditions but even more to an emergent divide between local and state league leaders; at the grass-roots level the torch was passing to a new generation. Recommendations were preponderantly in favor of closer ties between local leagues and the national board; increased national guidance and improved coordination of work on national program items; and direct representation of local leagues at national conventions along with increased status in the organizational structure. The constitutional debate became, in effect, an absorbing process of self-appraisal carried on over a period of two years. The 1946 convention adopted the revised bylaws by a large majority after extensive review at all levels.[10]

The National League of Women Voters was reconstituted as the League of Women Voters of the United States.[11] Its primary objective, as rephrased, was to promote "political responsibility through informed and active participation of citizens in government." The former emphasis on political education was seen now as unnecessary—perhaps too optimistically—for a generation no longer representing an emergent group needing politicization; also eliminated was the injunction that every woman should enroll as a registered voter and party member. The policy of nonpartisanship remained unaltered.

The change in aims and policy brought to fulfillment evolutionary trends set in motion during the Sherwin era toward a concept of individual responsibility. Article III made this explicit: "The League of Women Voters shall be composed of the individual members of the several affiliated Leagues of Women Voters." These latter were not the state leagues as formerly, but the local leagues, recognized by the national board after meeting the affiliation standards formulated by the board and approved by the national convention. The main communication channel was to be between the national and the local leagues, instead of through the state leadership (which Wells had found so frustrating). The local league emerged as the organization's core, and the local president would hold a key position. Theoretically the League had become what Maud Wood Park had dreamed of: "an every woman's organization," drawing vitality in substantial measure from the participation by the individual member in her own community. With remarkable speed and smoothness, the League structure at the state and local level was dismantled and put together again on a new basis.[12]

The shift of initiative for program making from the standing committee specialists to local boards and members required new procedures for broadening member participation; previously local leagues had been fractured into groups with special program interests. The neighborhood unit—growing out of the wartime experience with gasoline rationing—was adopted in 1948, and was to be an admirable structural device for developing member involvement through small discussion groups. The local league president and her board in turn would serve as the coordinators and chief strategists for the League's work in the community, and would be responsible for integrating the three program levels—local, state, and national—within a working schedule in which all neighborhood units would deal with the same aspect of the program at approximately the same time.

Self-appraisal after 1944 necessarily involved a review of the League's Voters Service. The involvement in such activities had been somewhat diluted during the late thirties and the war years. Yet the sharpened stress on the local league carried with it a challenge to increased participation in the political life of the community through the Voters Service. Anna Lord Strauss seized the opportunity provided by the turbulent 1948 elections to rouse the League to greater emphasis on political action.[13] The board reviewed and rephrased the Voters Service Guidelines regarding candidates' questionnaires, candidates' meetings, and nonpartisanship. A complete Voters Service plan for the local league was drawn up with activities running throughout the year. Probably few leagues would have found time to do everything specified, but the range of suggested services was instructive; members were reminded that Voters Service was the key to recruiting new members, securing local funding, meeting editors, broadcasters and public officials, and winning the interest and support of community business leaders.

By 1948 the reorganization of the League was complete, except for the state of Pennsylvania where trouble had arisen over the resistance to the reforms shown by the powerful Allegheny County League (covering the Pittsburgh area). The county leadership was concerned that the changes being introduced, while enlarging the scope for participation by local leagues in the affairs of the national league, exposed them at the same time to far more direct pressures to become involved in active support for the national program objectives. The Pennsylvania delegation at the 1946 convention had been headed by Eliza Kennedy Smith, for nearly a quarter-century president of the Allegheny County League and sister of Lucy Kennedy Miller, the Pennsylvania League's founding president. Following the report of the Bylaws Committee, Smith had been the first to raise a question: Would the existing leagues have to reincorporate and change their names? She was assured that they would. During the next two years, the Pennsylvania League as well as local leagues elsewhere in the state were reorganized to bring themselves into conformity with the new national bylaws, but though the Allegheny County League obtained new articles of incorporation from the state, it declined to take further action. In January 1948, the national board called its attention to this neglect. In May the Allegheny County League voted to refuse to conform to the new bylaws, and informed the national board that since its original incorporation papers antedated those of the national League it had no intention of surrendering its valuable name. That November the rebellious league was disaffiliated, at the formal request of the reconstituted Pennsylvania state league.[14] Two difficult but necessary steps followed. More than a hundred members withdrew from the disaffiliated group and organized an alternative League of Women Voters of Pittsburgh. In addition, the national league, on the advice of its attorneys, brought suit in the federal district court to prevent the Allegheny County organization from using the name League of Women Voters; the case was dismissed for lack of jurisdiction (since the issue in controversy had a monetary value of under $3,000).

Thus ended the long controversy between the national board and the Allegheny County leadership. Courts of equity lack adequate measures for intangible values. The differences went to the heart of the League's purpose and function as conceived by its early leaders, and still more to the fundamental principles governing organizational life. The real issue between them had been debated earlier, between 1921 and 1923. When Lucy Miller was outvoted in her attempt to become architect of the League's structure and purpose, she might have withdrawn to go her own way, with her faithful constituency; the parapolitical organization she envisioned might well have become a factor in the politics of western Pennsylvania, and analysts of women's political behavior would have had an additional clinical specimen. For its part, the national board might have sought to excise the Allegheny County League at several points before 1946 for nonconformity with bylaws provisions; but voluntary associations are naturally reluctant to use such exclusionary tactics.

Over the years the Allegheny County League had tended to dominate the state league because of its size, resources, and the sustained personal leadership of Lucy Miller and her sister. The state presidency had been held intermittently in the east, but always drifted back to the Miller-Smith fiefdom. On state issues like constitutional revision, tax and election laws, and schools, the state league often did effective work despite the deep ideological differences over national issues. As the conservative views of the two sisters grew increasingly out of harmony with those of League members elsewhere in Pennsylvania, many once flourishing leagues in the eastern and central parts of the state declined; indeed the polarization was disastrous for the state league. Since the disaffiliation of Allegheny County, the Pennsylvania League has had a remarkable revitalization under excellent leadership in all parts of the state.[15]

It soon became apparent that the era into which the world had stumbled with the explosion of the first atomic bomb would bear little resemblance to any benign vision of a confederation of nations united for collective security. Rather, the postwar age was dominated by a bitter global rivalry between East and West.

Despite the darkening shadow of the cold war, the League's 1946 convention in Kansas City, Missouri, committed the members to work for continued adherence to strengthening the principles of international security through the UN. But the relation between critical external events requiring immediate American response and broad policies resting on the principle of collective security created dilemmas for the League not easily resolved. In March 1947, Truman asked Congress for $400 million for military assistance to Greece and Turkey, declaring his intention to "support free peoples who are resisting attempted subjugation" as the price of America's own freedom. The Truman Doctrine, soon to become the policy of "containment" of Soviet expansion, came as a dismaying surprise to the League, appearing an abandonment of the UN almost before it had met its first trials.

Though the national board was unable to take a formal stand on the Truman Doctrine (since the League had not yet had opportunity to discuss the complex issues involved), it did assert in firmest tones the wisdom of continuing to identify America's national security with the principle of collective security.[16] The program adopted by the 1948 convention called for strengthening the UN by bolstering its security functions and supporting the development of its specialized agencies; the League recognized that the United States might find it necessary to enter into regional security arrangements (permitted under Article 51 of the UN Charter), but urged nonetheless that these be made subordinate to the goal of a universal security system anchored to the UN. The convention also pledged a major effort over the next two years to develop a clear understanding of the UN and its role among its own members as well as the public.

Soon after the 1948 convention, the Soviet blockade of Berlin precipitated the first major postwar crisis. As the differences with the Soviet bloc sharpened, the League's perplexity mounted. League members were extremely reluctant to surrender their high hopes for the UN and their faith in the principle of collective security; and they could well see the dangers inherent in the widening gap between East and West. Yet before the blockade had ended, the League had moved toward acknowledging that the UN machinery was not yet strong enough to protect Europe in its present weakened condition, and declared its support for the North Atlantic Treaty signed in April 1949. Though League leaders had not been alone in finding fault with the Truman Doctrine and the containment of communism by regional alliances, in such a threatening context the vital necessity of preventing the Soviet Union from dominating all of Europe was decisive even among those who still clung to a messianic hope that the international organization was the only road toward the peaceful development of all nations. As far as the League was concerned, the die was cast. The program adopted at the 1950 convention called both for strengthening the UN and for supporting the position taken in 1949 regarding the North Atlantic Treaty, though a small but vehement minority pressed the convention to abandon this support.

While considerations of security always point to the future, they are anchored in the experience of the immediate past. The most relevant experience of the oncoming generation of League members had been the years of economic depression and war. Political and cultural affinities had played a large part in that experience. It seemed increasingly clear that it was an unavoidable commitment for the United States to resist the encroachments of the Soviet adversary, so lately its ally, and that America's institutions depended for their preservation on protecting those nations from whom America drew its cultural inheritance.

The year 1948 marked the hundredth anniversary of the Seneca Falls convention which called into being the movement for woman suffrage by its Declaration of Sentiments. One of the prime movers of the Seneca Falls meeting had been Lucretia Mott, then at the height of her career: a leader in the abolition and temperance movements, the Hicksite Reform movement (within the Society of Friends), and the embryonic feminist movement. One hundred years later, Anna Lord Strauss, Mott's great-granddaughter, presided over an organization that had grown from the seeds planted there. The year 1948, like 1848, was one marked by a general crisis in Europe and by an unsettled domestic political scene. The League convention, caught up in the flurry of world developments, devoted only a single dinner meeting to a commemoration of Seneca Falls. "This is the only period," Strauss said in her introductory remarks, "at which we will glance back over the road over which women have come. The rest of the Convention will be devoted to deciding how we can contribute to the progress of the future." It was characteristic of Anna Lord Strauss that she would deem their time better spent on the present and future than in sentimentalizing over the past.

NOTES

1. "Dumbarton Oaks Conference," LWV Papers, Minutes and Related Records, LC.
2. LWV, *The Story of Dumbarton Oaks* (Washington, D.C., 1945); this was the first

in what became a long series of League publications on the United Nations and its agencies.

3. "San Francisco Conference," LWV Papers, Ser. 2, Box 474C, LC. See also the *Voter* (May–June 1970) for a retrospective account of the drafting of the Charter.

4. The Charter was accepted without change, with only two opposing votes and five abstentions—a dramatic contrast to the Senate's response to the Versailles Treaty and the League of Nations in 1919–20. Anna Lord Strauss was among those who testified at the five days of hearings held by the Senate Foreign Relations Committee.

5. She also wrote President Truman and members of the Senate Foreign Relations Committee pledging full support by the League in building public understanding.

6. LWV, *A History of the League Program*, 44.

7. Ibid., 47.

8. Three weeks before the bill's passage, the joint committee's staff had reported that local leagues furnished much of the effective pressure. "Rarely has the League had so accurate an index of the extent of its support of a measure." Ibid., 44. The League also backed actively the Bartuch Plan for international control of nuclear energy, blocked by Soviet opposition at the UN.

9. This committee was an experienced group headed by future president Percy Maxim Lee.

10. See Revised Bylaws, LWV Papers, LC.

11. Minutes, General Council, May 1945, LWV Papers, LC. The change of name had stemmed largely from Strauss's feeling that the League at that stage was not properly a "national" organization, having affiliates in only thirty-five states in 1944. By the mid-1950s, it had regained organizations in all states; indeed, the number of local leagues had doubled and the membership trebled.

12. Under these changes, program making assumed a more open if more complex pattern, entailing an extended series of interchanges between the national board and local leagues. League members at the local level were to begin discussing possible issues for inclusion in the national program the October prior to the biennial national convention (occurring in late April of each even-numbered year). After the national board had considered the recommendations submitted by local leagues, a proposed program would be drafted in January, followed by a second round of discussion at the local level (with responses being sent to the national board). The board would then revise the proposed program, as necessary, before submitting it to the convention. Though no new subject could be added to the program by the convention, any concern initially recommended for inclusion but not incorporated into the proposed program could be raised there; a two-thirds vote (subsequently a majority) sufficed to have it considered, and a two-thirds vote to have it adopted. See LWV, *Forty Years of a Great Idea*, 45–47; and *History of the League Program*, 2–3. In 1970, the national convention decided upon changes to this formula which had the effect of telescoping national program discussions into a single round; see LWV, *National Board Report* (Washington, D.C., June 1971).

13. In this she was aided by Vice-President Kathryn Stone, keenly interested in practical politics and destined to have a successful career in the Virginia state legislature after leaving the League's national board.

14. Material drawn from formal statements presented by the national board to the 1948 convention, and from personal knowledge; the author had been active in the Pennsylvania League. See also League of Women Voters of Pennsylvania, *Fifty Years Old and Proud of It* (Philadelphia, 1970), 41–43; and Allegheny County League of Women

Voters, *A History of Allegheny County League of Women Voters—Sixty Years of Achievement*, by Mrs. Lester K. Wolf and Mrs. Carmen R. Capone (Pittsburgh, 1980), 13.

15. Despite its disaffiliation, the Allegheny County League of Women Voters also continued to be active, Eliza Kennedy Smith remaining as president until 1965. See *A History of Allegheny County League of Women Voters*.

16. LWV, *History of the League Program*, 49–50.

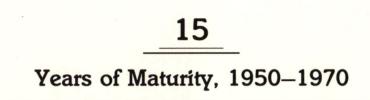

15

Years of Maturity, 1950–1970

The League by 1950 had reached organizational maturity. In its first three decades, a set of procedures had been fashioned for the direction and focusing of its efforts. A sturdy institutional fabric had been woven, joining the national, state, and local leagues and able to withstand the stresses of the often emotionally charged and at times divisive issues of the 1950s and 1960s.

Contradicting the "iron law of oligarchy" which Robert Michels perceived as inherent in all organizations, the League had developed as a fundamentally grass-roots organization.[1] Its vitality lay in the action of its approximately twelve hundred local Leagues, organized in all fifty states. In contrast to most national political-action organizations, whose decisions were made by a small cadre of officers and board members, League positions bubbled up from below. Its program was adopted by the biennial conventions after a prolonged process of solicitation of local suggestions and review of proposals. The League's voice on a given issue had to be rooted in an organizational consensus, procedurally crafted to ensure that it represented a preponderance of membership opinion.[2]

In this process lay one of the keys to its organizational vitality. The active study and discussion of the major issues, facilitated by high-quality informational materials assembled by the national office, ensured that League participation was a continuous process of political education for its members, whose numbers fluctuated between 120,000 and more than 150,000 during the two decades after 1950. The sense of purposive participation and internal democracy sustained by this ongoing process of action-oriented study of public issues underpinned the commitment and enthusiasm of the membership in a daily enactment of citizenship, a continuous reaffirmation of the initial purposes of the League.

The League was a grass-roots organization par excellence in another sense. Its action was not confined to national questions, but also extended to state

League presidents during the testing quarter-century after 1950. *Above left*, Percy Maxim Lee, 1950-58; *above right*, Ruth Phillips, 1958-64; *below left*, Julia Stuart, 1964-68; and *below right*, Lucy Benson, 1968-74. (Percy Maxim Lee, Ruth Phillips: Bradford Bachrach)

and local concerns. Within the broad framework of its principles and operational code, state and local leagues developed their own programs for issues arising at these levels. Indeed, much of the most influential action of the League occurred at the community level, above all in the smaller cities and suburban jurisdictions, where League organization was strongest in these decades.

The postwar years brought some significant organizational refinements. In 1947, the Carrie Chapman Catt Memorial Fund (later the Overseas Education Fund International) was established to encourage and assist "the development of citizen initiative, participation and action" within the cultural framework of other countries. In 1957, the League strengthened and expanded its capacity to apply its skills to the function of mediating between citizens and government by creating the League of Women Voters Education Fund as a separate legal entity to develop and promote educational programs with financial support from foundations, corporations, government agencies, and individuals—whose financial support would not otherwise have been available because of the League's nondeductible tax status as a political advocacy organization.

Although these innovations opened opportunities for more extensive political education and outreach projects, the League remained essentially a volunteer organization. Its national office had only a relatively small complement of salaried staff, to provide a basic administrative infrastructure and field services and manage its crucial educational outreach publication program. National officers and board members continued to be unpaid, as were their counterparts in the state and local leagues. At the time of its fiftieth birthday, the League of Women Voters expenditures were a skeletal $3.5 million, of which only 12 percent was national office outlay. Among other things, the League was a model of frugality.[3]

The League's civic action across the country poised upon a slender resource base reflected the volunteer, personal engagement that has always been a bedrock principle of the League. The counterpart was the high commitment demanded of members, and especially board members and officers at all levels. League participation involved more than a few stray moments of leisure time; its levy upon the hours and energy of individual women was substantial. So also were the satisfactions; a University of Michigan Survey Research Center study of League membership in 1957 found that "psychologically the members and leaders have a high regard for the League as an organization" and "a favorable feeling of identification and support for the League."[4]

The commitment corollary to League membership suggested a profile for the typical participant that was confirmed by data collected in a League self-study just after its fiftieth birthday. She was a woman in her most active years: in 1972, 54 percent were from thirty to forty-nine years old, and another 21 percent were in their fifties. She was well educated: 68 percent had a college education, and nearly 40 percent had pursued some graduate training. She was married: 85 percent; only 2 percent were divorced or separated, and 5 percent had never

A League delegation with President Dwight D. Eisenhower in 1957, in the White House Rose Garden, where he was presented with a document by President Percy Lee outlining League views on foreign policy. Eisenhower responded with a major speech on foreign aid. (Wide World Photos)

married. Her husband was generally a professional of some description. Only 25 percent held a full-time job.[5]

A high level of engagement in League activities was documented by the finding that 35 percent of the members described themselves as spending at least "a fair amount of time" on them. One may doubt whether any other national political advocacy organization could have come close to matching that figure. At the same time, the implicit obligation to participate lodged in the organizational culture of the League brought some social self-selection in the ranks of its membership. The obligations of full-time employment were not easy to balance with active League involvement. The self-supporting woman, especially if her income was meager, found this even more difficult. This active League membership was above all drawn from the middle and upper-middle sectors of society.

The changing sociological profile of American society as a whole had important implications for the League. The rapid entry of women into the labor market in the postwar years suggested a challenge in sustaining levels of membership and vigor of activity. Through the golden anniversary year, this challenge was being more than met. In the 1950s and 1960s, membership slightly increased, and there was no sign of diminished dynamism. Turnover, however, was significant; for example, in 1972—a typical year—an attrition of 19 percent of the membership was balanced by recruitment of an equivalent number of new members.[6]

The shifting composition of large city populations affected urban leagues, as large elements of the middle class migrated to the suburbs in the postwar period. The life circumstances of poverty-stricken women militated against League involvement. The disproportionate numbers of minority group women falling in this category made it difficult for League action to attract members from these sectors of society. The center of gravity of the League in the 1950s and 1960s continued to be in smaller cities and suburbs.

There was also some regional concentration. The heaviest clustering of leagues was in the north-central region. Although the League was present in all corners of the country, its membership was sparsest in the South, Southwest, and Rocky Mountain region, which collectively accounted for less than 20 percent of local leagues.

During the 1950s and 1960s, the League had four presidents, Percy Lee (1950–58), Ruth Phillips (1958–64), Julia Stuart (1964–68), and Lucy Benson (1968–74). Each left the imprint of her own leadership style and priorities upon the organization. At the same time, each preserved the institutional stability which was a principal strength.

At the thirtieth anniversary convention in Atlantic City in 1950, Anna Lord Strauss, after six years in office, declined renomination. Percy Lee, elected as new president by the convention, represented the second generation of those who had been bred in the League tradition, and was well qualified to keep alive the sense of the living past symbolized by Anna Lord Strauss. Through her mother, Josephine Maxim, and through Katharine Ludington, Connecticut League founder and national league treasurer from 1922 to 1927, Percy Lee had close ties with both the suffrage movement and the early League. Her experience included six years on the national board following several years as president of the Connecticut League.

The eight years of the Lee administration furnished abundant opportunities for Percy Lee's qualities of leadership and initiative, grounded in her sense of the historic significance of the League's political role. Momentum had already been generated; her energy was directed to accelerating League activities at all levels of government. Her mandate spanned troubled years and a succession of crises: the Korean War and the ongoing international tensions associated with the cold war, the virulent attack on individual liberties by Senator Joseph McCarthy, and the beginning of school desegregation.

A characteristic of the Lee administration was a readiness to assume that innovation and change were necessarily aspects of organizational growth. President Lee quoted approvingly a comment of Belle Sherwin's that "stereotyped ways of doing things were to be avoided like a poison for which there is no antidote." Several "fresh looks at old ways" marked her leadership, from program-making and financial and administrative procedures to the Voters' Service and publication policies.[7] Scrutiny was directed first to the inherited program format. The one adopted in 1950 had consisted of a current agenda of broadly stated program goals,[8] a platform of thirty-eight specific legislative and policy commitments on matters to which the League had already "given sustained attention," and thirteen principles.

Percy Lee peered into this storehouse of the past and decided that, like all attics, it needed cleaning. A committee of experienced former board members was set up in 1952, and, assessing the platform item by item, concluded that the League was dragging its dead past behind it; "as a historical record the Platform was incomplete; as authority for action, misleading." The Platform Committee recommended to the 1954 convention a revised program format containing a current agenda and a platform consisting of a shortened list of eight continuing responsibilities and eighteen principles.[9] The exercise had sought to update the program and clarify the distinction between current agenda and continuing responsibilities. The dead wood had been trimmed away and a few items of finished business laid aside; the entire program could be neatly set forth on one page of the *National Voter*.

One of the items jettisoned in the League's programmatic housecleaning was its earlier opposition to the equal rights amendment. An instance of how "time dissolves the solid angularity of facts," few convention delegates in 1954 had any knowledge of the history of the amendment; still fewer had been involved in the controversy it had engendered in the 1920s. The original reasons for opposition had ceased to exist. Statutory discriminations in federal law had been all but erased. Inequities still remained in various state codes relating to family and civil law, and in the discriminatory treatment women received in the judicial process. But state and local leagues had been whittling away at the removal of such disabilities for thirty years, and were empowered to do so by the League principle calling for the "removal of legal and administrative discriminations against women." The quiet abandonment of opposition to an equal rights amendment was to pave the way for the vigorous support given to the ERA proposal subsequently passed by Congress in 1972.[10] The League was to become a major partner in the pro-ERA coalition, and an active participant in the intense campaign of female mobilization which echoed the suffrage struggle out of which the League had been born. This effort, which marshalled $2.5 million of resources and engaged the energies of League members across the country, was to be a dominant feature of League action in the 1970s.[11]

Another "fresh look at old ways of doing things" was undertaken by a committee of former board members who made a comprehensive study of the League's financial structure, publications policies, and tax problems. The committee started its investigations at the base of the pyramid by careful scrutiny of the methods used by state and local leagues in their finance drives. Although the tradition of low membership dues was to be retained, and though the League's handicap in failing to qualify for tax-deductible contributions (as a legislative action group) was recognized, the committee concluded that the greatest hindrance to generating adequate local financial resources lay in the reluctance of many League members to ask for them. This theme was repeated in successive treasurer's reports at conventions after 1952; at issue in fact was the disposition of many League members to undervalue their own contribution.

The sector of society from which the majority of League members came—married women in their child-bearing years—had disposable time but little freely available money. Educated, politically oriented, and often professionally experienced, they furnished the League with incalculable resources of voluntary service. Since they were unaccustomed to placing a price tag on services voluntarily rendered, they tended to be exceedingly modest about asking others to do so. Lee's successors in the presidency felt even more strongly that the community's willingness to support the disinterested civic services which the League rendered was a mirror in which the members saw a reflection of their own, too modest valuation of what they did. Focusing attention on money as a tool, therefore, was a means of augmenting their self-esteem by evaluating their own estimate of the size and importance of their undertakings.[12]

As part of the overhaul of publications policies, the *National Voter* was established in 1951, finally fulfilling a dream of preceding presidents and providing a major medium for developing the high degree of internal cohesiveness that characterizes the League. After support for the *Woman's Journal* had been reluctantly abandoned in 1930, the League had relied on newsletters and bulletins to state and local officers as devices for binding together the organization. The need for a communication channel that would reach every member had been deeply felt, but funds had simply been lacking. The revised structure, with its stress upon individual membership, made imperative such a channel for program guidance as well as implementation.

The *National Voter*, originally austere in design, was always well edited and substantively nourishing. Over the years, its design was made more attractive, its size increased, and its content became more stimulating. Both the subject matter and its treatment were determined by the national board in close co-ordination with program planning for other educational materials.

Percy Lee ended her presidency in 1958 with a valedictory address calling imperatively for fresh initiatives in interpreting the League's involvement in political life. She urged the delegates to join the vanguard challenging the American people—seemingly "unsure and unconvinced of their birthright"—to reach "new dimensions in their own space rather than outer space," and to break out of "psychological grooves" and restate their foreign policy goals, encourage governmental reforms to meet the needs of metropolitan areas, and satisfy the educational demands of the oncoming generation, especially those disadvantaged by race or poverty. Toward these goals the League was a "tool"—to be kept sharp by "flexibility, initiative, and involvement." The familiar words "informed and active participation in government" would remain dry words, indeed, "until we invest them with the power of thought and passion."[13]

Lee's exceptional gifts of leadership perhaps found their most eloquent expression in the League's role in defense of civil liberties placed at risk by the wave of near-hysteria triggered by the demagoguery of Senator Joseph McCarthy in the early fifties. In her cool-headed, courageous, and principled stance, Lee provided inspired guidance to the League in the face of malicious attacks by the American Legion and extreme right-wing organs. League action in the civil liberties sphere will be considered in more detail later in this chapter; suffice it to note here that Lee played a major part in one of the League's finest hours.

The convention delegates turned back to the Middle West for the League's sixth president, electing Ruth Phillips of St. Charles, Illinois. Phillips brought to the presidency a distillation of experience gained from almost three decades of active association with the Illinois League of Women Voters, including twelve years on the state board and four years as state president. Like her predecessors, she left an indelible stamp on the organization. The breadth of her League experience had yielded a pragmatic sense of the realities of grass-roots political life and the consequent points of access available to the League. Skill in inter-personal relationships and self-assurance—masked by a quiet manner—enabled her to countenance and encourage bold ideas, especially in Voters Service, public relations, and community-action techniques. She carried further the modernization of organizational and program-making procedures initiated by Percy Lee, further updated and professionalized the internal administration, and developed fruitful channels for horizontal communication among leagues. Not least of her achievements was the overcoming of psychological barriers to a more aggressive approach by local leagues toward securing adequate financial support for greatly expanded community activities. The keynote of her administration was community action.

The Phillips presidency bridged some major alterations in program emphasis. The 1950s agenda concern with civil liberties, a product of the excesses of the McCarthy period, was broadened into a wider involvement with civil rights. The social agenda expanded to take in the war on poverty and the urban crisis. A long-standing interest in water resources began to evolve into a more broad-gauged concern with environmental protection. The commitment to a liberal foreign economic policy was broadened in scope and given new impetus. A crisis of confidence in the United Nations spurred a major restudy of this body's problems, culminating in a restatement of the League's strong support for the UN system.

The Phillips administration came to an end at the memorable 1964 convention in Pittsburgh. The meeting drew unprecedented media attention—in itself emblematic of the coming-of-age of women's political participation. National Educational Television covered the proceedings over two days, while the American Broadcasting Company recorded a day and a half for documentaries. The United States Information Service filmed the entire convention for use overseas as a commentary on women in American politics.

President Lyndon B. Johnson and First Lady Ladybird Johnson paid an unanticipated visit to the convention. This surprise event marked the first time a president of the United States had appeared at a national League convention, although President Wilson had helped assure his reelection by addressing the 1916 convention of NAWSA, the League's forerunner organization. President Johnson "dropped in" ostensibly to declare September 13–20 Women Voters' Week (following up a suggestion put to him by Ruth Phillips for recognition of the role of women in the electoral process). He also used the occasion to urge League support for his War on Poverty—a priority already recognized, as the convention had adopted a call to "evaluate government policies and programs . . . to provide for all persons equality of opportunity for education and employment."

The League presidency moved west of the Mississippi River for the first time when the delegates elected Julia Stuart. A native of Missouri but now resident in Spokane, Washington, Julia Stuart had joined the Spokane League in 1950 "to have someone to talk to," and found herself president of the local league a year later. The Spokane League was beset with problems common to small leagues in politically conservative regions: "no money, no public confidence, a shifting membership, and witch hunters behind doors at every public and private meeting." These exacting conditions tested the mettle of the president and uncovered capacities for organization and leadership that moved her rapidly to the state presidency in 1954, and to the national board in 1960. Her adaptive capacity and navigational skills in the roiled social and political waters of the mid-1960s permitted her to keep the League on an even keel in the face of the complex problems buffeting the organization. She herself likened the period of her national presidency to a "cultural shock front," a time when the challenge to leadership was to employ the League's strengths while recognizing its limits in a crisis atmosphere where the irresistible urge of many members was to "do something about every crucial problem which plagues our society."[14]

As the League neared its golden anniversary, the 1968 convention elevated Lucy W. Benson of Amherst, Massachusetts, to the national presidency. Benson's election as the League's eighth president was a recognition of her personal achievement in the Massachusetts League and on the national board, on which she had served as a member (1965–66) and as second vice-president (1966–68). Her experience and qualifications well prepared her to sustain the League's role as a broadly active agent in national politics. Her favorite mode of action during her six-year term as president was political, especially the pursuit of the consensus coalition politics vital in the turbulent context of the revolutionary social and political change that marked the late sixties and early seventies.

Programmatic developments in the fifties and sixties reflected the organizational maturing and deepening which characterized these years. The major areas of action built upon League concerns dating back to its creation: a peaceful and secure international order, good government and citizen rights, the well-being of the least-protected members of society, and resource conservation. However, each of these program categories experienced major transformation, expanding its focus and adapting its content to meet the challenges of the profoundly altered postwar world. League internationalism directed its energies to the United Nations, the plight of developing countries, and promoting freer trade. Citizen rights and governmental reform enlarged to take in issues of civil rights and reapportionment. The League's preoccupation during its founding years with protective social legislation for women and children broadened into a commitment to the struggle to eradicate conditions of deprivation among all disadvantaged social groups. An early interest in water issues became by metamorphosis a broad-front program of environmental protection. In this process, the agenda of the Progressive reform movement of the early years of the century, which had so influenced (and been influenced by) the founding mothers of the League, grew into a program tailored to the challenges of the welfare state thrust out of isolation into world responsibilities.

Organizational maturity, then, was an adaptive capacity rooted in a striking continuity of the overarching principles guiding League policies, joined to a constant process of modification to meet changing needs. The League proceedings of these years attest to a simultaneous self-questioning and a sturdy self-confidence in the validity of the organization's time-tested procedures in selecting issues and developing consensus. The commitment to extensive member involvement and careful study at all levels in program development and consensus building had its costs in the volatile and turbulent world of the fifties and sixties, whose crises were now instantly projected into every living room by the potent media of the electronic age. The League could not be an "ambulance-chasing" organization, whose spokespersons were positioned for immediate comment and dramatic pronouncements on each new trauma rocking the nation. Its abiding strength lay precisely in the careful crafting of its positions, and the longer perspective born of its sustained attention to questions chosen for agenda action.

Throughout the postwar period, the internationalist heritage of the League was reflected in its consistent support for the United Nations. The League was haunted by the failure of the League of Nations to fulfill the hopes vested in it as a vehicle for the preservation of world peace; both the failure of the United States to participate and the passivity of the League of Nations in the face of Japanese aggression in Manchuria in the 1930s seemed exemplary lessons of the past, to be heeded through strong League commitment to the United Nations. The intensification of the cold war generally, and the particular crisis triggered by the North Korean invasion of South Korea within weeks of Percy Lee's assumption of the presidency, sorely tested this engagement. It was the fact that it proved possible to use the UN as the framework for a collective response to aggression, through the "Uniting for Peace" resolution, that ensured strong League support for American involvement. The national office swiftly issued a background document, "The UN and Aggression," and state and local leagues undertook an intensive campaign of workshops, public meetings, and forums to explain the UN's role.

Public disappointment in the effectiveness of the UN was quick to form, and a hostile undercurrent persisted, ranging from the McCarthyites raising a hue and cry over alleged Communist employees at the UN to world federalists and neo-isolationists, who wanted a very different body or none at all. President Lee set the tone for League backing for the UN, urging state and local leagues to make clear to their communities the perils of the revisions of the UN Charter being proposed by the UN's various opponents. An official League observer, Zelia Ruebhausen, was appointed to cover and report on the meetings and activities of the United Nations and its agencies. As a member of the national board (1951–58), she was destined to play a major role in carrying on the extensive educational campaigns designed to preserve a solid bastion of understanding and confidence in the UN at the community level.[15]

Doubts about the UN continued in the public mind, reinforced by its changing nature as dozens of newly independent third world countries were added to its membership rolls, and as both superpowers sought to manipulate its machinery for foreign policy advantage. Though uncertainties about the United Nations inevitably seeped into the ranks of the League membership, the national board pressed local and state leagues to arouse citizen support for the emergency bond issue which the UN resolved upon in December 1961 to avert imminent bankruptcy. However, misgivings were sufficiently widespread to return the UN system to the current agenda adopted by the 1962 convention, for special study and appraisal.

The groundwork for the reappraisal had been laid by a steady flow of articles in the *National Voter* from the League UN observer. In 1959, Ruebhausen contributed an incisive evaluation, "The United Nations: A Candid Appraisal," a widely distributed report whose cool objectivity served as a useful starting place for League members. The League subsequently undertook a two-year study, whose results were announced by the national board in January 1964 and provided the basis for a strong reaffirmation of support for the UN. Scrutinizing its "strengths and weaknesses" with "a friendly but critical eye," the League was "heartened by the United Nations' success in peace-keeping and in contributing to creation of basic conditions for a peaceful and stable world through its specialized agencies and their economic, educational, and social programs." Although peacekeeping procedures needed strengthening, the UN "presence" had cooled many threatened conflicts. It had provided a forum for discussion of the control of nuclear armaments, and prepared the way for international control of outer space and the world's seabeds. It had sped decolonization and eased the first steps into independence for many countries. The League upheld the principle of collective financial responsibility for peacekeeping, administration, and development, with contributions commensurate with member states' ability to pay. The controversial one-nation, one-vote procedure used in the General Assembly won continuing support, and emphatic backing was expressed for the World Court. Although recognizing the limitations of the UN system, the League reaffirmed its "unswerving support," and pledged to deepen public understanding of the United Nations as potentially "a dynamic instrument of governments" for acting on the common concerns of mankind.[16]

League internationalism also found expression in consistent and thoughtful support for foreign economic assistance. This found its initial statement in the 1950 current agenda, formulated during the legislative debate over President Harry Truman's dramatic proposals for "bold new programs" in foreign policy, whose Point Four called for making available "benefits of our scientific . . . and industrial progress" for "improvement and growth of underdeveloped areas."[17] Hastening the development of less-developed nations, he argued, would create conditions favoring expansion of mutually beneficial commerce and the development of mutual goodwill, assuring us a decisive voice in shaping a world democratic order.

The League had already supported the Marshall Plan in 1948, but Point Four touched deeper chords of humane concern and psychological motivation among League members because of the elements that differed from the Marshall Plan. Long-term economic and technical assistance to stimulate economic growth in developing countries held out the promise of diminishing the social and economic distance between America and emergent nations, and of developing friendly contacts manifesting mutual confidence and the acceptance of common ends. It would thus help realize the vision of an international civil society presented by the United Nations Charter.

Development assistance found a valuable ally over the years in the League. Foreign aid never enjoyed robust domestic backing, lacked interested constituencies, and was susceptible to misuse as a cloak for military assistance, or as financial reward to regimes whose sole merit was vocal support for American global policy objectives. Unintended testimony to the League's impact came from Congressman Otto Passman, a Louisiana Democrat who long headed the Subcommittee on Appropriations for Foreign Aid. A cantankerous and relentless foe of development assistance, Passman took the floor of the House of Representatives to denounce the League for pressuring Congress on foreign aid legislation. In the patronizing vein of old-fashioned sexism, Passman sneered, "They're a fine bunch of ladies, but they don't know anything about the program . . . [and] would be better advised to concentrate on matters they are more qualified to handle, like child-rearing."[18]

The support for foreign aid was joined in League foreign economic policy positions to steady backing for liberalized trade policies. The League was one of fifteen national organizations invited to appear by the bipartisan Commission on Foreign Economic Policy, chaired by Inland Steel Company president Clarence Randall, which was created in 1953 by joint presidential-congressional action.[19] Percy Lee's statement to the commission not only reiterated the League's long-held belief in reciprocal trade agreements, but went beyond it to argue that the key to expanding world trade lay in a positive encouragement of imports to correct trade imbalances, with government and private-sector assistance to adversely affected industries to facilitate adjustments.

Soon thereafter President Lee seized the initiative in proposing a nationwide grass-roots trade survey to make local communities better understand their own stake in foreign trade. By directly involving local leagues in the survey, she intended to galvanize them to go beyond long-standing acceptance of liberal trade policies to investigate the actual impact of foreign trade on their own communities. Some thirty-five-hundred women conducted over eleven-thousand interviews in 186 counties and over five hundred communities, using a questionnaire and sample designed with the help of economists drawn from universities, the twelve Federal Reserve banks, and trade associations. The results provided a rich storehouse of data useful in communicating with Congress, and illuminating both to League members participating in the survey and, often enough, to those whom they interviewed. Among the surprises was the discovery that few business people fully recognized their own personal stake in world trade. Rigidly protectionist attitudes were uncovered in Boise, Idaho; yet half the manufacturers in that city were in the export business and hardly anyone could show negative impact from competitive imports. Manufacturers in Louisville, Kentucky, were surprised to learn that they sold more goods to foreign customers than all the local department stores combined sold to Louisville residents. In city after city, those interrogated were unaware of the community's aggregate stake in world trade. Although few of those interviewed held extreme protectionist views—far fewer than Congress appeared to assume—many communities and even whole regions had a mind-set mirroring the economy of an earlier time, their basic attitudes determined by "old, rigid or moribund industries" rather than the industries actually dominating the economic life of the areas.

Ailing industries, often controlled by old established families, appeared to color the attitudes of many members of congress, while new industries on the upsurge either lacked commanding spokesmen or were too busy to be concerned; obsolete views won by default. Farmers as a class were not only most favorable to liberal trade, but also best-informed on government policies, reflecting both the interests of agriculture as an exporting sector and the results of a half-century of educational efforts by farm organizations.[20]

A year after the survey was completed, the House Foreign Affairs Committee held hearings in six different regions to conduct its own test of public sentiment on trade and aid, the first time this committee had ever gone to the country to sample opinion. League members testified in all six regions, drawing heavily on the harvest of facts. One congressman remarked with apparent surprise that people were better informed than he had expected.[21]

During the fifties and sixties, League work on the trade issue, in terms of congressional lobbying and orchestrating member pressures on their representatives, reached peaks of intensity in 1954, 1958, and 1962, when renewals of major trade legislation were before Congress. An influential academic study of the politics of trade legislation concluded that the League had "been by several orders of magnitude the most active group . . . on either side of the controversy" surrounding the 1954 renewal of the Reciprocal Trade Agreements Act.[22] Walt W. Rostow, then a White House aide for President John F. Kennedy, told the 1962 convention that the League's nationwide campaign on behalf of the trade expansion bill that year "is already a legend in Washington."[23] President Kennedy added a telegram of thanks and appreciation for the "admirable educative program" the League had conducted on behalf of the new trade program.

The cold war pitting the United States and other Western democracies against the Communist bloc led by the Soviet Union was at its peak of intensity during the fifties and sixties, posing many troublesome issues for the League. The failure of international collective security machinery to halt aggression in the 1930s was a vivid recollection for League members. Yet the League heritage of internationalism precluded policy responses limited to military strength and muscular containment.

The UN commitment provided one beacon for navigating the perilous shoals of the cold war. The use of UN machinery for responding to North Korean aggression had provided a key basis for League support. In the case of the Vietnam War, the unilateral nature of the American intervention, outside the UN framework, meant that the League never boarded the bandwagon of supporters of official policy at the time of the 1965 Tonkin Gulf Resolution. The inability of the United Nations to deal effectively with the Vietnam issue forced recognition of the practical limits of its power, while also dramatizing the dilemmas the League faced when confronted by an international crisis for which its established policy principles supplied no clear guidelines. A session of the League National Council in 1967 was devoted to a full discussion of what the League could do, but no agreement on possible League alternatives emerged; the issue of Vietnam offered no handle by which the League could seize it.

However obliquely, the stalemate over Vietnam gave impetus to a developing League initiative on America's China policy. The powerful emotional currents of fear and hostility toward the Communist regime that had seized power in 1949 were a major underlying factor in the costly American intervention in Vietnam. By the 1960s, the China policy enunciated by former Secretary of State John F. Dulles—"moral disapproval, diplomatic isolation and economic pressure"—seemed increasingly irrelevant.[24] From 1960 on, League UN observer Betty Little regularly noted the annual General Assembly debate on seating the People's Republic of China, and the declining credibility of the fiction enforced by the United States that Nationalist China (Taiwan) was the "real" China. By 1965, as member concern deepened over American Asian policy generally, the national board proposed that a study of Sino-American relations be added to the national program, a proposal confirmed by the 1966 convention. "Although it was not clear whether the new ferment over U.S. relations with Mainland China would actually result in any meaningful changes," reported the national board, the League recognized that any forward-looking alterations in U.S. policies would require the backing of an informed and enlightened public.

The China question generated intense interest in local leagues. By January 1967, a League background pamphlet, *The China Puzzle: An Introductory Sketch*, was issued. Meetings were organized across the country, drawing on such resources as academic specialists and Canadian and European journalists with recent China assignments. The intense passions surrounding the China question, and the recriminations over who "lost" China which had characterized the fifties, still persisted in some corners of the country. In certain communities emotionalism ran so high that the effort to disseminate information or create a setting for discussion was nearly impossible.

A consensus on the multi-faceted China issue took time to achieve. Although some leagues were eager for action at the 1968 convention, the majority favored further evaluative study. However, a target date was set for early 1969. This consensus, announced in April 1969, was overwhelmingly in favor of the United States taking the initiative in "normalizing" relations with China by seeking formal cultural, trade, and diplomatic relations with Beijing, and ceasing opposition to China's assumption of the UN seat still held by Taiwan. "Present U.S. policies of isolation and containment of China are invalid," the League concluded.[25]

Few League positions evoked more favorable press comment than the organization's call to the newly inaugurated Nixon administration to take the first steps on the long and difficult road to friendly relations with the People's Republic. Ironically, the League study and consensus formation coincided with a period of paralysis in Chinese foreign policy, a result of the near-anarchy unleashed by the catastrophic Great Proletarian Cultural Revolution (1966–69), but came, propitiously, at the point when China began to extricate itself from this moment of chaos. The League position served as a barometer signaling a significant shift in the climate of public opinion which was to make possible the dramatic visit by President Nixon to Beijing in 1972, cementing the rapprochement with China.

Against the background of evolving international concerns, it is worth noting the League's severance of formal membership in organizations of international feminism. As the leading offspring of the suffrage movement, the League had inherited a membership in the International Council of Women, founded by Susan B. Anthony and others in 1888, and in the more active International Woman Suffrage Alliance, which Carrie Chapman Catt had helped launch in 1904. By the period following World War I, the International Council had become a mere clearinghouse for the exchange of information; formal League ties were dropped early. But the League remained a member of the IWSA, renamed after World War II the International Woman's Alliance. In 1950, as part of President Lee's program refocusing, the board regretfully but somewhat abruptly dropped its membership, concluding that the organization lacked the time and resources for such external concerns. In retrospect, the decision was a reflection of the degree to which the League had outgrown the separatist view that set women apart as a special class—a vital aspect of the feminist heritage. The postwar generation of League leaders saw themselves as having fashioned an authentic political role for women which had assimilated the earlier feminist heritage.

The resolute internationalism of the League was not always reflective of dominant moods in collective opinion. The deepening intensity of the cold war in the late forties set the stage for the frenzy of anti-Communist phobia catalyzed by Senator McCarthy. The poisoning of national life for a time by paranoic fears of external subversion brought the defense of individual civil liberties onto center stage of the League national program in the fifties. Revelations after World War II that some public servants with Communist affiliations had served the Soviet espionage apparatus led, in the climate of fear and uncertainty associated with the onset of the cold war, to widespread apprehensions that the federal government was riddled with "subversives." These fears were exploited by demagogues of the McCarthy stripe, creating for a time at the beginning of the fifties a veritable national hysteria.

While a sprinkling of delegates to the 1948 and 1950 conventions had expressed concern over the rapidly emerging threat to civil liberties, the majority were not yet ready to act. Early in Eisenhower's first term, and with a growing public disquiet over the conduct of loyalty-security investigations by both the executive and Congress, former League president Anna Strauss devised a strategy for constructive response to the situation by promoting the idea of a "freedom agenda" under the sponsorship of the Carrie Chapman Catt Memorial Fund (CCCMF).[26] Intended as a nationwide discussion program with no immediate goal of action, the Freedom Agenda was to involve as many organizations as might wish to participate. Its purpose was to remind Americans of the enduring meaning of individual liberties, as enshrined in the Constitution, by applying such principles to concrete human situations, personalizing and dramatizing them.

CCCMF president Anna Lord Strauss announced funding for the Freedom Agenda project at the 1954 League convention in Denver after the delegates had formally adopted a program item calling for the "development of understanding of the relationship between individual liberty and the public interest."[27] In late 1954, a Freedom Agenda Committee was formed under Strauss's leadership, with a distinguished national board of public figures. A leading constitutional specialist, Professor Alfred Kelly, was enlisted to bring together a group of fellow scholars to prepare authoritative pamphlets on the philosophic and historical background of the Bill of Rights, the evolution of freedom of speech, congressional investigations and their relation to the Constitution, and the various loyalty-security programs of the federal government.[28] More than a hundred organizations were invited to participate on a community basis; a total of 800,000 pamphlets were printed. Ultimately, leagues in 797 communities in forty-eight states organized local Freedom Agenda projects.[29] Energetic League mobilization on this issue occurred from top to bottom of the organization, and well illustrated its remarkable capacity for grass-roots action. Although by the mid-fifties the most virulent phase of McCarthyite fever had begun to subside, the League found itself under attack from a suburban New York American Legion committee for attempting "to further the delusion that the danger of communism was nonexistent." Other Legion sources alleged that the authors of some of the pamphlets had "Communist front records."[30]

President Lee chose Indianapolis, seat of the national headquarters of the American Legion, as the appropriate place to take public note of these attacks. In an October 1955 speech, she firmly refused to countenance Legion demands that the League repudiate the Freedom Agenda program. "This, of course, we will never do," she declared. "We will indeed work all the harder to secure thoughtful and free discussion of our constitutional liberties." The Legion allegations, like their predecessor of the 1920s, the spider-web chart, traveled in underground channels and turned up in such extreme right-wing organs as *The Freeman* and *Human Events*.[31] Undaunted, however, the 1956 League convention resolved upon a study of the balance needed between national security and protection of individual liberties, and members reached a consensus in 1958 calling for a major overhaul of federal loyalty-security programs.[32]

A consistent and crucial dimension of League action has revolved around good government and citizen rights. A program item on "strengthening governmental procedures to improve the legislative process and relationship between Congress and the Executive" dates from 1944. This provided the basis for active League support for the 1946 Legislative Reorganization Act. In 1954, after study and consensus formation, the League called for "coordination and simplification of congressional budgetary procedures." In 1970, a comprehensive study of

Congress was added to the League program. In the late sixties, growing public concern over presidential powers and their possible abuse entered the list of League policy preoccupations, leading subsequently to a 1974 program item. Enfranchisement of the voteless citizens of the District of Columbia was the longest-lived item on the national program, dating from 1924.[33] In 1969, the League General Council initiated a national campaign to petition Congress against the denial of the "citizen's inalienable right—a voice and a vote" in the nation's capital. A million and a half signatures were affixed to petitions presented by delegates to the 1970-Fiftieth Anniversary Convention to their senior senators.[34]

To much of the public at large, the most visible part of League activity has been its service to voters through making known to the citizenry the issue positions of the candidates. Most dramatic have been the televised presidential candidate debates in 1976, 1980 and 1984, which were sponsored by the League. These had their precursor in the audacious strategy conceived by the planners of the 1952 League convention, who invited presidential aspirants to take part in a "Citizen's View of '52" forum; the National Broadcasting Company and *Life* magazine cooperated in assuring nationwide media coverage.[35] Although less dramatic, the local league candidate questionnaires, eliciting written responses on key community issues and widely distributed to the public, have been an invaluable contribution to an informed electorate over the years.

The League commitment to citizen voting rights was well demonstrated in the key role played in securing more equitable electoral apportionment. Since the early 1920s, the problem of malapportioned state legislatures, many of them scandalously overrepresenting rural areas, had been a major League concern. Not only did malapportionment represent serious inequalities for individual citizens; it had also proved a chronic obstacle to League-supported legislative proposals reflecting urban needs in the fields of education, welfare, and taxation. When the issue first reached the Supreme Court in 1946—in a suit brought by Illinois citizens under the due process clause—the Court declined, in an oft-quoted opinion, "to enter this political thicket," on the grounds that such questions were "too political to be justiciable."

But state leagues did indeed enter the "political thicket" in large numbers, seeking through the political process to persuade rural-dominated legislatures to accept fairer representation. For the most part, they were unsuccessful, and from the late 1950s the litigation route was again pursued.[36] The landmark *Baker v. Carr* case in 1962—which brought reversal of the 1946 decision—originated in Tennessee, where the state league spearheaded a citizen's movement in the five underrepresented urban counties. Following a statewide league educational campaign in 1957 to stir public interest in the existing disenfranchisement of urban dwellers, a legislative proposal to reapportion the state was defeated in 1959, establishing deliberate neglect by the state legislature. Suit was brought by citizens in the five urban counties, with the support of the state league, alleging that inequitable apportionment deprived them of equal protection of the laws by the "debasement of their vote." When a federal district court declined to provide a remedy, one of the two citizens chosen to appeal the case to the Supreme Court was state league leader Mrs. James Todd.

The Supreme Court, in *Baker v. Carr*, declared that dilution of the citizen's right to representation might violate the equal protection clause, and was clearly subject to federal court adjudication. However, the decision offered no guidance as to the specifics of an "appropriate remedy"; efforts to settle these questions, in the words of two constitutional scholars, "produced something like a volcanic eruption of new apportionment litigation."[37] In two of the critical cases spelling out the *Baker v. Carr* implications, state leagues played a pivotal role.

Until 1962, the small Alabama League had been the only organization in the state actively pressing for reapportionment by the classical route of wide dissemination of its careful study of the gross distortions in the existing legislative district boundaries, unaltered since 1901. On the heels of *Baker v. Carr*, a federal court moved swiftly to place the Alabama legislature under a three-month deadline for redistricting. In 1964, in *Reynolds v. Sims*, this dispute reached the Supreme Court, which enunciated the doctrine that equal protection of the laws demanded "no less than equal state representation for all citizens, of all places as well as all races."[38]

In Colorado, the reapportionment battle involved highly complex issues climaxing in two rival plans for reapportionment by initiative petition: one drawn up and supported by a coalition of the League of Women Voters, the Colorado Education Association, and organized labor, the other by agricultural, mining, and ranching interests. The latter petition won at the polls, but the losers brought suit in the federal district court. The issue reached the Supreme Court, which in *Lucas v. Colorado* (1964) held that "an individual's constitutionally protected right to cast an equal weighted ballot cannot be denied even by a majority of the state's electorate."[39]

Senator Everett Dirksen, Illinois Republican, led a forceful congressional effort to nullify the reapportionment decision; simultaneously, a movement to summon a constitutional convention for the same purpose surfaced in many state legislatures, at one point coming within one state of the requisite two-thirds to invoke this unprecedented constitutional amendment procedure. In defining a national strategy in the face of this threat to roll back the clock, the League found itself in a procedural quandary. More than thirty state leagues had reapportionment on their current agendas; several were involved in litigation on this issue. Yet there was no formal national consensus. A majority of state leagues pressed for the submission of an emergency study item to the 1965 National Council. Though no precedent existed for alteration of the national program by the council, the crisis was immediate. The council, on board recommendation, agreed unanimously to an immediate study and early consensus on the reapportionment question.[40]

Despite these procedural difficulties, the reapportionment issue well illustrated the capacity of the League for effective action on an issue mobilizing the near-unanimous consensus of its membership. The struggle was dispersed, taking place both on the national level and on the scattered battlefields of the numerous state legislatures involved. The vitality of the League at its lower levels uniquely qualified the organization for a coordinated yet decentralized impact. President Stuart read to delegates at the 1966 League convention a telegram from Illinois Democratic senator Paul Douglas, leader of the Senate opposition to the Dirksen amendment, who credited the League's work with being "decisive in turning back the attempt to overrule the Supreme Court's defense of the basic right of equality of citizenship . . . and would go down in history as the crucial public support for this principle at a moment of great danger."[41] A legal scholar, William Boyd, declared that "the League of Women Voters deserves more credit than virtually any individual or group" for the reapportionment reforms, suggesting that "we would doubtless be embroiled in a national constitutional convention were it not for these hardworking persuasive women."[42]

The broader issue of civil rights had surged to the forefront of the nation's agenda with the unanimous Supreme Court decision in May 1954 striking down school segregation in *Brown v. Board of Education of Topeka*. Percy Lee quickly convened a gathering of the presidents of eleven southern state leagues in Atlanta in July.[43] In her opening address, Lee sharply stated the dilemma: fidelity to principle versus organizational well-being. "Every effort must be exerted to protect the integrity of the League and its usefulness and at the same time promote the principles in which it believes. The League must find a way to exert a calm, unemotional, and wise leadership in the search for solutions."[44]

The Southern leagues represented only 15 percent of the total national membership and were not as strongly rooted as those in some other regions of the country. Their black membership was exceedingly slender; only six of the eleven state leagues represented at Atlanta had any black participation, and black membership appears to have been less than a hundred for the entire region, many drawn from black colleges. None of the Southern leagues felt strong enough to challenge frontally the pervasive racial attitudes in their communities, even if their individual members had been so inclined. Some leagues reacted constructively by accelerating voters-service activities and providing channels for moderate elements to temper extreme expressions of opinion; but all sought to avoid internal disruption by maintaining an official position of neutrality on the school integration issue.

In her last presidential address in 1958, Percy Lee felt impelled to elaborate on national League policy concerning school integration.[45] She defended the neutral policy of the Southern leagues as "the only tenable course" where the pressures were greatest. Over the years they had worked "unobtrusively and undramatically to better conditions"; but League history offered substantial evidence that "under certain circumstances an indirect approach in seeking solutions may be more effective than a direct attack." She acknowledged the "crisis quality" of the situation, but concluded "that activity . . . would handicap, possibly destroy the League's ability" to help toward a constructive solution. "It is impossible to ignore the problem of integration; it would be disastrous ... to become involved in it." She was defining what she saw as the limits of effective action for a voluntary association whose strength lay in its community base and internal cohesion.

By the early 1960s, it was apparent that civil rights were a national, not a Southern issue, and that a more active League commitment was imperative. President Phillips in 1963 sent a memorandum to local presidents, urging initiation of local efforts. "We have no Current Agenda item; we have no national consensus," she wrote, "but we need not sit with folded hands. . . . The crisis is national; the problem is local. . . . In every League some sort of effort is needed."[46] Even most Southern leagues responded favorably, reflecting a change in the social climate induced by a mounting sense of urgency; by that time many local leagues throughout the country were already deeply involved in local antidiscrimination measures in such fields as housing. The 1964 convention authorized a study of equal access to education and employment, in collective realization that it was a "glaring omission"—as one League put it—that a domestic issue of such moment was not already on the League's national program, especially since it was already on many state and local programs. A consensus for support of government programs promoting equal opportunity for all in education and employment was reached in 1966, with housing added in 1968 at a convention whose tone was set by the shock waves of the Martin Luther King assassination and the resulting widespread urban unrest which had occurred on the eve of the meeting.

The civil rights issue in the 1960s became intertwined with the question of social welfare. The latter, central to the League's interests in its early years, had tended to fade into the background after many initial policy proposals, especially concerning women and children, were enacted into law. The reawakened preoccupation with social groups who had failed to share in the overall prosperity of the fifties and sixties, many of them minorities locked into ghettoes in the large northern cities, emerged against a background shaped by the civil rights struggle, the widespread urban riots in the sixties, and the War on Poverty launched by President Lyndon Johnson. Yet, as with most of its program choices, the League's shift of emphasis represented a convergence of forces from both inside and outside the League that had been at work for several years.

Leagues in the major urban centers, once a backbone of the organization, had found themselves drained of membership by the suburban flight of the middle class, and in search of a mission to restore their vitality.[47] A conference of urban leagues, which had been held in 1960 after several from northern industrial cities had appealed to the national board for help, led to an initial proposal for a project aimed at identifying and training "natural leaders" from inner city areas to establish two-way communications between the urban core and the suburban rim. Ruth Phillips, then national president but with lengthy experience in the Illinois League and a long-standing interest in inner city problems, presented the proposal to the national board in March 1961. Board opinion, though, was divided and nothing happened until the summer of 1963, when the long-gathering civil rights storm burst over North and South alike, clearing the way for the League to reconsider its priorities.[48]

The Economic Opportunity Act of August 1964 rapidly became the focus of League interest, particularly its provision for community action agencies authorized to exercise local initiative in mobilizing resources drawn from public and private sources for projects designed to increase human capabilities, improve employment opportunities, compensate for unfavorable environmental conditions, and elicit the maximum feasible participation of the poverty groups themselves. Once the 1966 consensus had been reached, League members moved aggressively to participate in such programs, becoming involved in Head Start and Upward Bound projects, day care, family planning, medical and recreation centers, and school lunch and adult education programs. Members served on community action boards and worked as volunteers on project staffs. The challenge to equalize opportunity through the development of human resources, specifically reflecting its inherent concern for the primary needs of people, gave a new dimension to League thinking.[49]

The League also plunged into the legislative struggle over renewal of the Equal Opportunity Act in 1966, a battle that focused on the provisions for community-action agencies. When the act was finally renewed in December 1967, it contained only a two-year authorization, a barebones appropriation, and the controversial Green amendment requiring that a third of community-action agency boards be composed of local officials. Nonetheless, League support helped to assure a reprieve for this major experiment in social legislation. Officials of the Office of Economic Opportunity considered "the League to have been the most effective of their supporters."[50]

The manner in which conservation and development of water resources became a major program concern in 1956 and gradually broadened in scope until it included the protection and enhancement of the total environment is illustrative of the League's program-making methods as well as its fundamental orientation. League involvement with water issues dated from the 1920s, when it entered the Muscle Shoals controversy discussed earlier; however, with the launching of the Tennessee Valley Authority the issue faded. When water returned to the agenda in 1950, it was no longer a question of harnessing electric power to the public interest; the stress instead was on reforming the complex network of conflicting authority and competing agencies involved in water resource management. Indeed the accumulated League experience and expertise in areas of governmental organization, and its capacity to operate at all levels of the jumble of local, state, and national authorities sharing (often disputing) water responsibilities, well qualified the organization to play a constructive role. A number of organized groups were vocal and active on water issues: conservationists, wildlife protection organizations, sportsmen's and recreational associations, western farm interests, thirsty municipalities. The special contribution of the League lay in its keen knowledge of the institutional passageways where problems became translated into policies, and its examination of the issues from a more global perspective of the public interest than was true of the other action groups concerned with water questions. Yet communications from state and local leagues in the early 1950s amply underlined the diversity of viewpoints within the League itself. Leagues in the northeast wanted flood control and pollution abatement; those in the southwest simply yearned for water to drink. Leagues in the Mississippi watershed wanted support for the proposed Missouri Valley Authority; those in the Pacific Northwest were concerned with the issue of private versus public river basin development.

Despite these early stirrings, the 1950 program item did not bring immediate action, though the subject was retained in the 1952–54 program as evidence that the League had not abandoned interest. In 1955 nature stepped in dramatically to furnish opportunity, with some regions suffering disastrous floods and others severe droughts. At the insistent call of several hundred local leagues and twenty state boards, the issue returned to the current agenda in 1956. Reflecting the diversity of regional problems and desires, the mandate for exploration was given an expansive focus, with attention to be given to "interrelationships of federal, state and local agencies whose responsibilities interlocked and sometimes overlapped," as these were framed within the "broad scope of national interest." As the League now plunged actively into the water resource issue, its many ramifications became apparent: conservation, pollution, flood control, irrigation policies, riparian rights, jurisdictional problems in river basins embracing several states in their drainage areas, statutory conflicts between the twenty-five federal agencies in five departments with a role in this sphere, constitutional tensions in state-federal relationships, disputes arising over multiple uses, and the problems of balancing cost-benefit ratios against the intangibles of the social accounting ledger. Like a stream from a distant source that eventually flows into the sea, the concern for water resources gradually broadened until it encompassed the quality of the total environment.

By late 1950s the League reached consensus on water resources. This comprehensive position, which served as basic authorization for all subsequent League work on water policy and legislation, called for comprehensive, long-range developmental planning, water management on a river-basin or regional basis, federal financing with cost-sharing by state and local governments and private users, improved coordination between agencies and departments, acquisition of adequate data for intelligent decisions, and citizen participation in water resource decisions.[51] As an organizational innovation to facilitate effective League action on this issue, procedures were developed for inter-League collaboration in studying river-basin problems, arriving at a consensus, and taking action, under national board supervision.[52]

To soften the impact of his veto in 1960 of the amended Water Pollution Control Act, on the grounds that pollution was a "uniquely local blight" and hence must be solved by state and local governments, President Eisenhower announced a three-day Clean Water Conference to "help local taxpayers and business concerns realize their obligations to prevent and control pollution."[53] Suvia Whittemore, the League's national board water resources chairman, was named to the Steering Committee, and was influential in formulating the conference agenda; President Phillips and ten other League representatives participated, playing a significant role in shaping the conference findings that "users did NOT have an inherent right to pollute water, and DO have a responsibility to return it after use in a reasonably good state." However, the conference also revealed all too plainly the strength of forces opposing federal water pollution control action, and the magnitude of the educational task that lay ahead.

What Eisenhower had denied in his 1960 veto message the League had come to see as the heart of the matter: the necessity for a much enhanced federal role, especially in sharing the costs of major water resource projects; and when the new Kennedy administration (with conservation-minded Stewart Udall as secretary of the interior) reintroduced the water pollution control bill, local leagues worked with special ardor to help secure its passage in May 1961. Nonetheless, much League activity in this area had state and local levels as its focus. More than a dozen instances of successful local league action on serious water problems were collected and published as *The Big Water Fight*.[54] Illustrative of League techniques in opinion formation and its persistence was League involvement in the Salt Lake City water pollution crisis. In the 1940s, Salt Lake City water was so impure that railroads and airlines threatened to bypass the city; the U.S. Public Health Service declared the water unfit for use on interstate carriers. The League enlisted the cooperation of the Utah Medical Association and the Utah Engineering Council for an education campaign, but twelve years of ceaseless pressure were to be required before Salt Lake City had water fit to drink. Since the city, under the Utah Constitution, had no power to levy taxes or issue bonds for sewage facilities, it was necessary to arouse local citizens sufficiently to wrest the required enabling legislation from the state legislature and then win a bond issue referendum before any water purification program could occur.

The fact that the League, by the mid-1960s, had carved for itself a wide slice of influence in the field of water resources was reflected in various forms of institutional recognition. League water resource specialist Janeth Rosenblum was named to the Federal Water Pollution Control Advisory Board in 1963, and many League members were named to state and local planning commissions. As civic entrepreneurs, League members at all levels had a broad range of opportunities for political action, given the unusual complexity of governmental interrelationships in the water field. In the process, the conviction deepened that an integrated approach was required weighing both economic costs and social requirements, and involving federal coordination and leadership. Pollution increasingly became the central concern.

By the late 1960s, the principle of a federal role was no longer at issue, but the costs and their allocation clearly were. Heavily polluting industries, such as steel, chemicals, and paper, asked for tax relief to cover "nonproductive" investment in pollution-abatement equipment. With a major role being played by Ruth Clusen, the League sought to address the cost-allocation question.[55] In January 1967, a consensus was reached that the "immense costs involved" required acknowledgment, albeit reluctant, that "limited financial incentives" to industry were necessary, with due regard for the individual company's actual financial need, economic position in the community, and the complexity of its pollution problem. Clusen, in a letter to the fourteen senators and fifty-five congressmen who had introduced pollution tax-credit bills, clearly stated these limits; while recognizing "that some companies . . . face difficulties which seem insurmountable, . . . " she wrote, "League members are certain that companies supplying the greater part of U.S. productive capacity have the skill and will to bring their waste discharges into line with federal requirements . . . without federal assistance . . . [by] application of free enterprise strengths to increase efficiency and reduce costs."[56]

As League action with respect to water experienced successive transformation from power and the public interest, to integrated water resource development, to pollution abatement, the seamless web that joined it to the total environmental challenge of protecting air, land, and water became increasingly apparent. The Fiftieth Anniversary Convention in 1970 reformulated the program item to incorporate the "quality of the environment" as a whole, an integrated ecological perspective that has shaped League action since that time. From 1950 on, the organization's activities in the environmental field have constituted one of the longest, brightest chapters in its history. The effort to restore a balance between human society and its environment required the multifront, earnest, and unremitting struggle at national, state, and community levels to secure the necessary public support for the heavy social investment required. The nature and structure of the League uniquely suited it for such a role.

The League at half-century could take legitimate pride in its accomplishments. To be sure, precise measurement of its impact on the broad array of policy issues that the organization had confronted is impossible. The immense complexity of the policy process in American government, with its division of powers, federal structure, and vast scale, and the large number of groups and individuals clamoring for influence on any particular issue, defies any such effort. What can be concluded with confidence is that League of Women Voters in its first five decades had developed a remarkable capacity for political action. Its accomplishments were certainly not attributable to its financial resources—the national budget was a mere pittance. Nor were they explained by the numerical weight of its membership: the 150,000 women on its rolls in 1970 were a modest cohort, far less than the 2 million in the ranks of NAWSA, the predecessor suffrage association, at its peak.

Rather, the crucial strength of the League lay in the quality of its human resource base, and the mode of operation developed to deploy their energies. League members contributed to the organization the social commitment, high intelligence, and solid education of a talented pool of women. Many also offered substantial amounts of volunteer time; many of those whose active labors energized the League did not hold full-time employment. This activity was an invaluable training ground for leadership. Many of the swelling numbers of women winning electoral office from the sixties on, especially at state and local levels, received their political training in the local leagues.

Political education was the pivot around which the League turned. In the selection of issues for agenda action, and the development of a consensus, members first educated themselves through sustained study and extensive discussion. The political education process then was carried into the community at large, through the extraordinary range of devices crafted by the League over the years: appearances before public bodies, participation in action coalitions, publications, and forums, among others.

The compass guiding the League was the public interest. Of course, this notion is susceptible of differing interpretation, and on most major issues there was a spectrum of opinion among the membership as to the precise policy direction in which public interest pointed. But the very process of consensus formation yielded results that could be claimed as a fair approximation of public interest at any given juncture. In this sense, the League was a female organization but not an explicitly feminist one. Although it was born of the feminist struggle for suffrage, and included in its early years a special concern for measures protecting and benefiting women and children, its agenda was far broader than overcoming the disfiguring legacy of patriarchy.

In celebrating five decades of accomplishment at its 1970 convention, the League could at once take pride in its accomplishments, and recognize the magnitude of the challenges ahead. The changing nature of big city populations, and the difficulties a number of urban leagues had experienced in sustaining their organizational capacities, had revealed one set of challenges of adaptation. The massive entry of women into the work force, which accelerated in the sixties, raised some concerns as to whether the available pool of member talents and energies would constantly be replenished. The new phase of feminist consciousness, signaled by the publication of such widely read books as *The Feminine Mystique, Sexual Politics*, and *The Female Eunuch*, would be likely to direct some part of the female activism once available to the League into different channels.[57] In the wake of the resurgent feminism, new organizations such as the National Organization for Women (founded in 1966) emerged as voices for female aspirations. At the same time, the new levels of consciousness symbolized by the creation of women's studies programs in many universities might well enlarge the pool of the socially active, recalling the Kennedy aphorism, "a rising tide lifts all boats."

The demonstrated solidity and resilience of the League in its first fifty years, however, give every reason for confidence in its ability to rise to the demands of the future. Its enduring principles have stood the test of time. If past is prologue, it may be said with confidence that the League of Women Voters in its second half-century will be as vital and constructive a force in service of the public interest as it has been in the years described in this volume.

NOTES

1. Robert Michels, *Political Parties: A Sociological Study of the Oligarchical Tendencies of Modern Democracy*, trans. Eden and Cedar Paul (New York: Dover Publications, 1959).

2. The changes in program-making introduced in 1946 (and modified in 1970) are discussed *supra*, chap.14, n. 12. "Consensus" on any national policy is declared only after members have had ample time to study and reflect upon the issue at hand. The national board declares a "consensus" when "it is evident that there is a wide area of agreement among the membership." LWV, *Forty Years of a Great Idea*, 46.

3. In 1970, total League of Women Voters expenditures were $3,588,293. Of this, $2,319,731 was spent by local leagues, and $847,020 by state leagues. The expenditures of the separately financed League of Women Voters Education Fund (just over $1 million) and Overseas Education Fund are not included in these figures. Budget data are drawn from documentation distributed to the 1973 National Council.

4. Survey Research Center, University of Michigan, *A Study of the League of Women Voters of the United States*, Report IV, Organizational Phase, Part 1: "Factors in League Functioning" (Ann Arbor, August 1957), 66.

5. *The Report of the Findings of the League Self-Study* (Washington, D.C., 1974), 4–6.

6. Ibid., 12. Subsequently, there was a significant drop; membership in 1987 stood at 105,000.

7. President Lee was seeking to modernize and professionalize League management procedures not least because substantial membership growth was occurring, with a commensurate increase in headquarters work. It was in this context that the well-situated offices in historic Jackson Place had to be abandoned for larger quarters in one of Washington's modern office buildings.

8. The 1950 convention approved three such goals: (1) "the expansion of world trade and international economic development with maximum use of United Nations agencies"; (2) "a continued analysis of the federal budget, and support of such fiscal measures as make for a stable and expanding domestic economy"; and (3) "reorganization measures to improve administrative efficiency in the development and use of natural resources." "National Program 1950–1952," LWV, Minutes and Related Records, Ser. 2, Box 792, LC.

9. Items adopted for the current agenda related to issues with which the League was actively concerned—either because it was in the process of arriving at member consensus through study and discussion or because it was then seeking to influence public, legislative, or executive opinion. Items included under continuing responsibilities were matters to which the League had already given sustained attention—and in many cases seen its original objectives incorporated into public law or governmental practice—but on which it might want to take further action in future. Principles referred to "governmental principles supported by the League as a whole," and which in turn provided a source of authority for the adoption of national, state, and local current agendas. See LWV, "Historical Review of the Evolution of Program."

10. Strong support for the ERA campaign developed within the League during the

1960s, and reflected not only traditional League concerns with the legal status of women but also its growing involvement with the question of equal rights for all, in turn spurred by the development of strong League support for the civil rights struggle and efforts to deal with inner city poverty. See LWV, *Impact on Issues 1986–88: A Leader's Guide to the National Program* (Washington, D.C., 1986), 37–39.

11. In May 1972, the League national convention voted overwhelming support for the ERA. Particularly after 1974, when the ratification campaign began to stall, League commitment became intense. A special task force guided this struggle, and generated what by League standards were unusually large resources. In a postmortem on the League role in the ultimately unsuccessful ratification effort, Patricia Jensen, 1983–84 League ERA chair, noted that "if there's ever been an issue that the membership felt down to their toes, it's this one." LWV, Education Fund, *Changed Forever: The League of Women Voters and the Equal Rights Amendment* (Washington, D.C., 1988), 35.

12. See reports of the treasurer and board member in charge of organization in the years after 1950, proceedings of biennial conventions and minutes of meetings of the General (subsequently National) Council, LWV Papers, LC.

13. Proceedings, 1958 Convention, LWV Papers, LC.

14. The Stuart quotes are from interviews with the author.

15. Successive UN observers through the end of the 1960s were Zelia Ruebhausen, Betty Little, Anne White, and Ruth Hinerfeld, who later became national president (1978–82).

16. See LWV, *National Board Report* (January 1964).

17. President Truman made these proposals in January 1949, in the inaugural address commencing his second term.

18. Congressional debate cited in speech by Ruth Phillips, New York, February 1959.

19. Only two other women's organizations were among the fifteen, the American Association of University Women and the General Federation of Women's Clubs; both joined the League in urging a liberal trade policy.

20. LWV, *Facts and Attitudes on World Trade* (Washington, D.C., 1954). The League was a pioneer in organizing a study of this nature on such a scale at the local level.

21. "What Will It Be—Words or Action?" *National Voter*, 7 January 1955.

22. Raymond A. Bauer, Ithiel de Sola Pool, and Lewis A. Dexter, *American Business and Public Policy: The Politics of Foreign Trade* (New York: Atherton Press, 1963), 389. Their account of the League's role concludes, "The League must be credited with having done a remarkable job of producing united activity among a large number of dedicated and intelligent women." Ibid., 392.

23. LWV, Proceedings, 1962 Convention (Washington, D.C., 1962).

24. Link with Catton, *American Epoch*, 827; and Leopold, *The Growth of American Foreign Policy*, 751–54.

25. Press release, statement by Gail Bradley, League of Women Voters, April 1969.

26. The CCCMF had already published two pamphlets on the Constitution and civil liberties, designed to prompt League members to start thinking about the issues.

27. Proceedings, 1954 Convention, LWV Papers, LC.

28. Carrie Chapman Catt Memorial Fund, "Freedom Agenda, 1954–58," LWV Papers, LC. Writers of individual pamphlets included Alfred H. Kelly, T. V. Smith, Alan Westin, Zechariah Chaffee, Jr., Robert K. Carr, Richard A. Edwards, and Jack Peltason.

29. Martha Mills, LWV deputy executive director, personal communication.

30. "Freedom Agenda," 1955, LWV Papers, LC. See also the exchange of letters

between Lee R. Pennington, National Americanism Commission of the American Legion, and Percy Lee and Mrs. Orville Foreman (May–August 1955). The national board was forced to prepare and distribute materials to local leagues to help them counter the distortions of the American Legion attack. The *Christian Science Monitor*, 9 February 1956, reports on this episode.

31. Bettina Bien, "The League of Women Voters," and an editorial, "The Busy Termites," *The Freeman* (October 1955); and Russell Turner, "The Ladies Won't Knit," *Human Events*, 22 October 1955.

32. The League concluded that the government's security program should be reformed in order to limit coverage to sensitive positions, develop procedures to protect the rights of the individual, and institute more nearly uniform procedures among the five existing programs that imposed a requirement of security clearance for ten million persons (seven million in private industry). In 1955 Congress itself had set up a bipartisan Commission on Government Security to review the security system, and Percy Lee had been named a member of a Citizens' Advisory Committee to this body. The Supreme Court by this stage had also intervened—in *Cole v. Young (1956)*—to rule that summary suspension of government employees on security grounds applied only to those in sensitive posts; and when Congressman Francis Walter, chairman of the House Un-American Activities Committee, sponsored a bill to reverse the effects of this decision, the League was in a position to take a prominent role in mobilizing public opposition to the measure. The national board's report for May 1958 contains a summary of the legislative controversy over the Walter bill; for Congressman Walter's attack on the League's role, see the *Congressional Record*, 85th Cong., 2d sess., 1958, 104, pt. 4: 4561–62.

33. LWV, *Impact on Issues 1984–86: A Leader's Guide to National Program* (Washington, D.C., 1984), 4–8.

34. The League provided strong backing for the Twenty-Third Amendment to the Constitution, which was ratified in 1961 and extended voting rights to District residents in presidential elections, and for the subsequent introduction of a limited home-rule charter in 1974.

35. Five major candidates agreed to appear: Senators Estes Kafauver and Robert Kerr, Governors Harold Stassen and Earl Warren, and Ambassador Averell Harriman; General Dwight D. Eisenhower, still at his Paris NATO post, sent Paul Hoffman as his representative; Governor Adlai Stevenson had not yet declared his candidacy. On the League's role in the 1976 and 1980 debates—the first to occur since the famous Kennedy-Nixon presidential campaign debates in 1960—see Theodore H. White, *America in Search of Itself: The Making of the President, 1956–1980* (New York: Harper & Row, 1982), 401–3.

During the 1988 elections, the League sponsored several presidential primary debates in the spring. During the autumn campaign, however, it was forced to withdraw its sponsorship of a scheduled TV debate between the Republican and Democratic presidential candidates in protest over the restrictive conditions the rival campaign organizations were seeking to impose on the debate.

36. Of these campaigns, none was more dramatic and widely publicized than the battle waged in Washington state between 1954 and 1956, during Julia Stuart's presidency of the state league. Becoming the League's national president in 1964, she was to be deeply involved in the chain of events that began when the apportionment issue was catapulted into national politics in 1962. Stuart's own account of the Washington state league's adventure appeared in the *National Municipal Review* 46 (February 1957): 66–70; see also

Gordon E. Baker, *The Politics of Reapportionment in Washington State* (New York: Holt, Rinehart and Winston, 1960).

37. Alfred H. Kelly and Winfred A. Harbison, *The American Constitution: Its Origins and Development*, 3rd ed. (New York: W. W. Norton, 1963), 983.

38. "Alabama," in LWV, *Inventory of Work on Reapportionment by State Leagues of Women Voters*, rev. ed. (Washington, D.C., 1963). "Reynolds, Judge, et al. v. Sims et al." (1964), *United States Reports* 377: 533–632.

39. "Colorado," in LWV, *Inventory of Work on Reapportionment.* "Lucas et al. v. Forty-Fourth General Assembly of Colorado et al." (1964), *United States Reports* 377: 713–65.

40. Almost simultaneously, the League found itself without a position on which to base national legislative action on behalf of the Voting Rights Act of 1965. "Pressed by events and stung by its powerlessness to take action on such a significant issue," a League document records, "the 1970 convention adopted a bylaws amendment that enabled the League to act 'to protect the right to vote of every citizen' without the formality of adopting voting rights in its national program." See LWV, *Impact on Issues 1984–86*, 8.

41. LWV, Proceedings, 1966 Convention (Washington, D.C., 1966).

42. William J. D. Boyd, review of *Democratic Representation: Reapportionment in Law and Politics*, by Robert G. Dixon, Jr., *Journal of Public Law* (Emory University Law School) 18, no. 1 (1969): 226.

43. Those represented were Alabama, Arkansas, Florida, Georgia, Louisiana, Mississippi, North Carolina, South Carolina, Tennessee, Texas, and Virginia. Tensions over the race issue were not new to the League, and indeed had divided the suffrage movement in the Southern states. Although the League was from the outset an open-membership organization, in the early years the fragile Southern leagues found this a delicate issue in view of the rampant racial animosities of the dominant white population. At the 1921 Cleveland convention, delegates encountered a public challenge by Walter White, Mary Ovington, W.E.B. DuBois, and James Weldon Johnson, influential black leaders, to respond to the needs of black women for rights and justice. A Special Committee on Inter-Racial Problems was established under the leadership of Julia Lathrop, but its work was hampered by the difficulty found by Southern leagues in securing representatives.

44. Minutes, Meeting of Presidents of Southern States, Atlanta, Georgia, July 27–28, 1954, LWV Papers, LC.

45. Proceedings, 1958 Convention, LWV Papers, LC.

46. This memorandum was already in preparation when President Kennedy, on July 9, 1963, summoned three hundred women representing ninety-three organizations to the White House to rally support for the comprehensive civil rights legislation just submitted to Congress. Phillips and other League representatives attended this gathering.

47. Indeed in this context, the League's discovery of the gray face of the "other America" had actually come in advance of the public discovery of the problem of poverty after the mid-1950s. After leaving the League presidency in 1950, Anna Lord Strauss had initiated a study of impacted leagues in large industrial centers under the auspices of the Carrie Chapman Catt Memorial Fund. With Mrs. Errol Horner as director, an exploration was undertaken in several cities to observe how voluntary associations, including the League, were coping in the context of the centrifugal patterns of urban development evident after 1940; with the movement of the middle-class groups to the urban suburbs, there had been a slow paralysis of civic effort in the inner cities as well as an increase in urban problems unique in their complexity.

In addition to the published report, in April 1953 Horner presented the national board with a constructively critical memorandum directly applicable to the League's own role. Yet local leagues at the time were preoccupied with other concerns, and only the Cook County (Chicago) League responded actively to its proposals. See LWV, Metropolitan Area Project Committee, *The Big City: An Inquiry into Civic Participation*, Carrie Chapman Catt Memorial Fund Publication No. 4 (New York, 1953); and "Report of the Metropolitan Area Project Committee to the League of Women Voters of the United States" (Spring 1953).

48. With the 1964 elections in prospect, Ruth Phillips sought to revive earlier initiatives by proposing a program of political education for minority groups. The League's Education Fund drafted an imaginative project for civic leadership training in urban ghettos—its maiden effort in the inner cities—which received funding support from the Sears, Roebuck Foundation.

49. On the League's participation in the community-action programs, see "Current Reports" of the Human Resources Committee, LWV Papers, LC; and LWV, "1968 Convention Workbook" (Washington, D.C., 1968) pt. 2: 80–83.

50. William C. Selover, "The View from Capitol Hill: Harassment and Survival," in *On Fighting Poverty: Perspectives from Experience*, ed. James L. Sundquist (New York: Basic Books, 1969), 175.

51. LWV, *Study and Action: 1968–70 National Program* (Washington, D.C., 1969), 20.

52. By 1963, inter-League groups were at work studying the river-basin problems of the Potomac, Columbia, Susquehanna, Delaware, Ohio, Tennessee, Hudson, Red, upper Mississippi, and several smaller rivers; a number of their reports were published, and widely distributed to libraries and educational institutions with the help of the U.S. Army Corps of Engineers. This experience was to furnish a solid foundation for further inter-League cooperation on the problems of metropolitan areas that cross state boundaries.

53. "National Affairs," *Facts on File Yearbook*, 1960, 80B.

54. LWV, Education Fund, *The Big Water Fight: Trials and Triumphs in Citizen Action on Problems of Supply, Pollution, Floods, and Planning across the U.S.A.* (Brattleboro, Vt.: S. Greene Press, 1966), esp. chaps. 1 and 2.

55. Ruth Clusen subsequently served as League president from 1974 to 1978.

56. The League favored long-term, interest-free loans for companies facing special difficulties in adopting pollution control measures; only one bill among the spate introduced after the League announced its position met its criteria for support. For a statement of the League's views on federal financial assistance to industry to expedite pollution control, and a summary of the consensus, see the "1968 Convention Workbook," pt. 2: 110.

57. Betty Friedan, *The Feminine Mystique* (New York: W. W. Norton, 1963); Kate Millet, *Sexual Politics* (Garden City, N.Y.: Doubleday, 1970); and Germaine Greer, *The Female Eunuch* (New York: McGraw-Hill, 1971).

Lash, Joseph P. *Eleanor and Franklin: The Story of Their Relationship, Based on Eleanor Roosevelt's Private Papers*. New York: W. W. Norton, 1971.

League of Women Voters. *The Awkward Age in Civil Service*, by Betsy Knapp. Washington, D.C., 1940.

———. "Beyond 1984: A Long Range Plan for the League of Women Voters." Washington, D.C., March 1984.

———. *The China Puzzle: An Introductory Sketch*. Washington, D.C., 1967.

———. *The Convention and the Primary: Their Strength and Weakness*, by Charles E. Merriam. Rev. ed. Washington, D.C., September 1924.

———. *Facts and Attitudes on World Trade*. Washington, D.C., 1954.

———. *Five Questions?* Washington, D.C. [1921].

———. *Forty Years of a Great Idea*. Washington, D.C. [1960].

———. *A Handbook for the Personnel Campaign: What, Why, How, Who, When, Where*, comp. Julia R. King. Washington, D.C., October 1935.

———. *The Hard Road*, by Belle Sherwin. Washington, D.C., April 1934.

———. "Historical Review of the Evolution of Program as Shown by Printed Programs since 1938–40." Washington, D.C., April 1966. Mimeo.

———. *A History of the League Program*, by Kathryn H. Stone. Washington, D.C., 1949.

———. "How the League of Women Voters Reaches Consensus," by Ruth C. Clusen. Address to Society of American Foresters Assembly Meeting, Philadelphia, September 29, 1968. Mimeo.

———. *Impact on Issues 1984–86: A Leader's Guide to the National Program*. Washington, D.C., 1984.

———. *Impact on Issues 1986–88: A Leader's Guide to the National Program*. Washington, D.C., 1986.

———. *Inventory of Work on Reapportionment by State Leagues of Women Voters*. Rev. ed. Washington, D.C., 1963.

———. *National Board Report*. Washington, D.C., January 1964.

———. *National Board Report*. Washington, D.C., June 1971.

———. *National League of Women Voters*, by Nathaniel Peffer. Washington, D.C., January 1927. Reprinted from Nathaniel Peffer, *New Schools for Older Students*. New York: Macmillan, 1926.

———. *The National League of Women Voters: An Achievement in Citizen Participation in Government*. Washington, D.C., October 1936.

———. *The National League of Women Voters: What It Is, Why It Is, How It Works*. Washington, D.C. [1920].

———. *National Program, 1950–1952*. Washington, D.C., 1950.

———. "1968 Convention Workbook." Washington, D.C., 1968.

———. *The Patronage System: A Guide to an Excursion into Political Life in the United States*. Washington, D.C., 1937.

———. *A Portrait of the League of Women Voters at the Age of Eighteen*, by Marguerite M. Wells. Washington, D.C., 1938.

———. *Principles and Policy of the National League of Women Voters*. Washington, D.C. [1921].

———. Proceedings, 1962 Convention (Washington, D.C., 1962).

———. Proceedings, 1966 Convention (Washington, D.C., 1966).

———. *The Program Explained*, ed. Louise L. Wright. Washington, D.C., 1936.

———. *The Program Record.* Washington, D.C., 1955.

———. *A Record of Four Years in the National League of Women Voters, 1920–1924,* by Maud Wood Park. Washington, D.C., April 1924.

———. *The Report of the Findings of the League Self-Study.* Washington, D.C., 1974.

———. "The Report of a Special Committee of Nine to Present Recommendations for Activities of the League of Women Voters with Reference to the Approaching General Elections of 1928." Washington, D.C., 1927. Mimeo.

———. *The Story of Dumbarton Oaks.* Washington, D.C., 1945.

———. *Study and Action: 1968–70 National Program.* Washington, D.C., 1969.

———. *Ten Years of Growth,* by Belle Sherwin. Washington, D.C., 1930.

———. *25 Years of a Great Idea,* by Kathryn H. Stone. Washington, D.C., 1946.

———. *What Has Been Done in Conformity with the Program of the National League of Women Voters to Remove Legal Discriminations against Women and to Establish Equality of Rights under the Law, 1921–1922,* comp. Carina C. Warrington. Washington, D.C., n.d.

———. *A Woman's Platform Presented to the Political Parties.* Washington, D.C. [1920].

League of Women Voters, Carrie Chapman Catt Memorial Fund. *Freedom Agenda in the Community, 1954–1956.* New York, 1957.

League of Women Voters, Committee on the Legal Status of Women. *The Legal and Political Status of Women in the United States: A Summary of the Outstanding Facts in the Present Situation.* Washington, D.C., November 1927.

League of Women Voters, Committee on Living Costs. *Facts about Muscle Shoals.* Washington, D.C., 1927.

———. *Muscle Shoals and the Public Welfare,* by Marguerite Owen. Washington, D.C., 1929.

———. *Muscle Shoals as a Yardstick,* by Louise G. Baldwin. Washington, D.C., 1934.

League of Women Voters, Department of Efficiency in Government. *Changing the Constitution: A Study of the Amending Process,* by Dorothy Kenyon. Washington, D.C., 1926.

———. *A Handy Digest of Elections Laws,* by Gladys C. Blakey. Washington, D.C., 1928.

League of Women Voters, Education Fund. *The Big Water Fight: Trials and Triumphs in Citizen Action on Problems of Supply, Pollution, Floods and Planning across the U.S.A.* Brattleboro, Vt.: S. Greene Press, 1966.

———. *Changed Forever: The League of Women Voters and the Equal Rights Amendment.* Washington, D.C., 1988.

League of Women Voters, Metropolitan Area Project Committee. *The Big City: An Inquiry into Civic Participation.* Carrie Chapman Catt Memorial Fund, Publication No. 4. New York, 1953.

———. "Report of the Metropolitan Area Project Committee to the League of Women Voters of the United States." Washington, D.C., Spring 1953.

League of Women Voters of Minnesota. *The Enfranchisement of Women: An Opportunity,* by Marguerite M. Wells. Minneapolis, October 1924.

League of Women Voters of Pennsylvania. *Fifty Years Old and Proud of It.* Philadelphia, 1970.

Lemons, J. Stanley. "The Sheppard-Towner Act: Progressivism in the 1920s." *Journal of American History* 55 (March 1969): 776–86.

————. *The Woman Citizen: Social Feminism in the 1920s.* Urbana: University of Illinois Press, 1973.

Leopold, Richard W. *Elihu Root and the Conservative Tradition.* Boston: Little, Brown, 1954.

————. *The Growth of American Foreign Policy: A History.* New York: Alfred A. Knopf, 1962.

Lerner, Gerda. *The Grimké Sisters from South Carolina: Rebels against Slavery.* Boston: Houghton Mifflin, 1967.

Lief, Alfred. *Democracy's Norris: The Biography of a Lonely Crusade.* New York: Stackpole Sons, 1939.

Link, Arthur S. *Wilson.* 5 vols. Princeton: Princeton University Press, 1947–65.

Link, Arthur S., with William B. Catton. *American Epoch: A History of the United States since the 1890s.* 2d ed. New York: Alfred A. Knopf, 1963.

Linn, James W. *Jane Addams: A Biography.* New York: Appleton-Century, 1935.

Linton, Ralph. *The Study of Man. An Introduction.* New York: Appleton-Century, 1936.

Lutz, Alma. *Created Equal: A Biography of Elizabeth Cady Stanton, 1815–1902.* New York: John Day, 1940.

————. *Susan B. Anthony: Rebel, Crusader, Humanitarian.* Boston: Beacon Press, 1959.

McCraw, Thomas K. *TVA and the Power Fight, 1933–1939.* Philadelphia: J. B. Lippincott, 1971.

McGlen, Nancy E., and Karen O'Conner. *Women's Rights: The Struggle for Equality in the Nineteenth and Twentieth Centuries.* New York: Praeger, 1983.

Mann, Arthur. *Yankee Reformers in the Urban Age.* Cambridge, Mass.: Harvard University Press, Belknap Press, 1954.

Martineau, Harriet. *Society in America.* 3 vols. London: Saunders and Otley, 1837.

Merriam, Charles E. *The Making of Citizens: A Comparative Study of Methods of Civic Training.* Chicago: University of Chicago Press, 1931.

Merriam, Charles E., and Harold F. Gosnell. *Non-Voting: Causes and Methods of Control.* Chicago: University of Chicago Press, 1924.

Michels, Robert. *Political Parties: A Sociological Study of the Oligarchical Tendencies of Modern Democracy.* Translated by Eden and Cedar Paul. New York: Dover Publications, 1959.

Millet, Kate. *Sexual Politics.* Garden City, N.Y.: Doubleday, 1970.

Morgan, David. *Suffragists and Democrats: The Politics of Woman Suffrage in America.* East Lansing: Michigan State University Press, 1972.

Newcomer, Mabel. *A Century of Higher Education for American Women.* New York: Harper & Bros., 1959.

O'Neill, William L. *Everyone Was Brave: The Rise and Fall of Feminism in America.* Chicago: Quadrangle Books, 1969.

————, ed. *The Woman Movement: Feminism in the United States and England.* New York: Barnes & Noble, 1969.

Park, Maud Wood. *Front Door Lobby.* Edited by Edna L. Stantial. Boston: Beacon Press, 1960.

————. "Reminiscences." Maud Wood Park Papers, files 694–700. Arthur and Elizabeth Schlesinger Library on the History of Women in America, Radcliffe College.

Peck, Mary G. *Carrie Chapman Catt: A Biography.* New York: H. W. Wilson, 1944.

Perkins, A.J.G., and Theresa Wolfson. *Frances Wright, Free Enquirer: The Study of a Temperament.* New York: Harper & Bros., 1939.

Pope-Hennessy, Una. *Three English Women in America*. London: Ernest Benn, 1929.

Potter, David M. "American Women and American Character." In *History and American Society: Essays of David M. Potter*, edited by Don E. Fehrenbacher, 277–303. New York: Oxford University Press, 1973.

Robinson, Edward S. "Trends in the Voter's Mind." *Journal of Social Psychology* 4 (August 1933): 265–84.

Rogers, Agnes, comp. *I Remember Distinctly: A Family Album of the American People, 1918–1941*. New York: Harper & Bros., 1947.

Roosevelt, Eleanor. *If You Ask Me*. New York: Appleton-Century, 1946.

———. *It Seems to Me*. New York: W. W. Norton, 1954.

———. *On My Own*. New York: Harper & Bros., 1958.

———. *This I Remember*. New York: Harper & Bros., 1949.

———. *This Is My Story*. New York: Harper & Bros., 1937.

Roosevelt, Eleanor, and Lorena A. Hickok. *Ladies of Courage*. New York: G. P. Putnam's Sons, 1954.

Roosevelt, Theodore. *Theodore Roosevelt: An Autobiography*. New York: Macmillan, 1913.

Russell, Charles E. "Is Woman-Suffrage a Failure?" *Century Magazine* 107 (March 1924): 724–30.

Schlesinger, Arthur M. *The American as Reformer*. Cambridge, Mass.: Harvard University Press, 1950.

———. *New Viewpoints in American History*. New York: Macmillan, 1922.

———. *Paths to the Present*. Rev. ed. Boston: Houghton Mifflin, 1964.

———. *Political and Social History of the United States, 1829–1925*. New York: Macmillan, 1925.

Schlesinger, Arthur M., Jr. *The Age of Roosevelt*. 3 vols. Boston: Houghton Mifflin, 1956–60.

Scott, Anne Firor. *The American Woman: Who Was She?* Englewood Cliffs, N.J.: Prentice-Hall, 1971.

———. *Making the Invisible Woman Visible*. Urbana: University of Illinois Press, 1984.

———. *The Southern Lady: From Pedestal to Politics, 1830–1930*. Chicago: University of Chicago Press, 1970.

Scott, Anne F., and Andrew M. Scott, eds. *One Half the People: The Fight for Woman Suffrage*. Philadelphia: J. B. Lippincott, 1975.

Selover, William C. "The View from Capital Hill: Harassment and Survival." In *On Fighting Poverty: Perspectives from Experience*, edited by James L. Sundquist. New York: Basic Books, 1969.

Sicherman, Barbara, and Carol Hurd Green, with Ilene Kantrov and Henriette Walker, eds. *Notable American Women, the Modern Period: A Biographical Dictionary*. Cambridge, Mass.: Harvard University Press, Belknap Press, 1980.

Sinclair, Andrew. *The Better Half: The Emancipation of the American Woman*. New York: Harper & Row, 1965.

Stuart, Julia D. "Women Carry the Day." *National Municipal Review* 46 (February 1957): 66–70.

Sullivan, Mark. *Our Times: The United States, 1900–1925*. 6 vols. New York: Charles Scribner's Sons, 1928–35.

Survey Research Center, University of Michigan. *A Study of the League of Women Voters of the United States*. 5 parts. Ann Arbor, 1956–58.

Taylor, A. Elizabeth. *The Woman Suffrage Movement in Tennessee.* New York: Bookman Associates, 1957.

Tims, Margaret. *Jane Addams of Hull House, 1860–1935.* London: Macmillan, 1961.

Titmuss, Richard M. *Essays on "The Welfare State."* New Haven: Yale University Press, 1959.

Tobey, James A. *The Children's Bureau: Its History, Activities and Organization.* Brookings Institution, Institute for Government Research. Baltimore: Johns Hopkins Press, 1925.

Tocqueville, Alexis de. *Democracy in America.* Trans. G. Lawrence and ed. J. P. Mayer. New York: Doubleday, 1969.

Turner, Russell. "The Ladies Won't Knit." *Human Events,* 22 October 1955.

U.S. Congress. *Utility Corporations: Summary Report of the Federal Trade Commission . . . on Efforts of Associations and Agencies of Electric and Gas Utilities to Influence Public Opinion.* 70th Cong., 1st sess. S. Doc. 92, Part 71A. Washington, D.C.: U.S. Government Printing Office, 1930.

Upton, Harriet Taylor, "Random Recollections." Women's Archives, Arthur and Elizabeth Schlesinger Library on the History of Women in America, Radcliffe College.

Wells, Marguerite M. "The Enfranchisement of Women and the League of Women Voters, 1919–1944." Marguerite M. Wells Papers, Arthur and Elizabeth Schlesinger Library on the History of Women in America, Radcliffe College.

———. *Leadership in a Democracy: A Portrait in Action.* Privately Printed. New Haven: Printing Office of Yale University Press, 1944.

———. "Reminiscences." Marguerite M. Wells Papers, Arthur and Elizabeth Schlesinger Library on the History of Women in America, Radcliffe College.

White, Leonard D. "Public Administration." In *Encyclopedia of the Social Sciences,* edited by Edwin R. A. Seligman et al. Vol. 1, 440–50. New York: Macmillan, 1930.

White, Theodore H. *America in Search of Itself: The Making of the President, 1956–1980.* New York: Harper & Row, 1982.

White, William Allen, *The Autobiography of William Allen White.* New York: Macmillan, 1946.

Wilson, Howard E. *Mary McDowell, Neighbor.* Chicago: University of Chicago Press, 1928.

Wood, Mary I., *The History of the General Federation of Women's Cubs for the First Twenty-Two Years of the Organization.* New York: General Federation of Women's Clubs, 1912.

Woodward, William C. "The Sheppard-Towner Act: Its Proposed Extension and Proposed Repeal." *American Medical Association Bulletin* 21 (May 1926).

Wright (D'Arusmont), Frances. Views of Society and Manners in America, in a Series of Letters from That Country to a Friend in England, during the Years 1818, 1819, and 1820. New York: E. Bliss and E. White, 1821.

Young, Louise M. "American Women at Mid-Century: A Bibliographic Essay." *American Review* (European Center of American Studies, Johns Hopkins University, Bologna Center) 2 (December 1961).

———. "Women's Place in American Politics: The Historical Perspective." *Journal of Politics* 38 (August 1976): 295–335. Reprinted in *200 Years of the Republic in Retrospect,* edited by William C. Havard and Joseph L. Bernd. Charlottesville: University Press of Virginia, 1976.

————, ed. "Women's Opportunities and Responsibilities." *Annals of the American Academy of Political and Social Science* 251 (May 1947).

Young, Rose E. *The Record of the Leslie Woman Suffrage Commission, Inc., 1917–1929.* New York: Leslie Woman Suffrage Commission, 1929.

Index

About the Author

LOUISE M. YOUNG is a freelance writer and historian and Professor Emeritus of The American University. She played a major role in the deposition of the League's records in the Manuscript Division of the Library of Congress, negotiating the transfer of the documents and processing them for use. Young has spoken on women's issues and published articles in the *Annals of the American Academy of Political and Social Science, Journal of Politics,* and *Quarterly Journal of Accessions.* Her previously published books include *Thomas Carlyle and the Art of History,* and *Understanding Politics: A Practical Guide for Women.*

Recent Titles in
Contributions in American Studies